MANAGEMENT INFRASTRUCTURE FOR THE DEVELOPING WORLD

A Bibliographic Sourcebook

Kenneth L. Murrell
Robert H. Duffield

Kumarian Press

H.I.I.D.
HD
70
.D44
2995
x
1985

Copyright © 1985 Kumarian Press
630 Oakwood Ave., West Hartford, Connecticut 06110
All rights reserved under International and Pan-American Copyright Conventions. No part of this book may be reproduced or transmitted in any form or by any means, electronic or mechanical, including photocopy, recording or any information storage and retrieval system, without prior written permission of the publishers.

Printed in the United States of America

Cover design: Marilyn Penrod

Library of Congress Cataloging-in-Publication Data

Murrell, Kenneth L.
  Management infrastructure for the developing world.

  1. Management — Developing countries — Bibliography.
2. Organizational behavior — Bibliography. I. Duffield, Robert H. II.
II. Title.
Z7164.07M834 1985 016.658'009172'4 85-17225
[HD70.D44]
ISBN 0-931816-34-3

TABLE OF CONTENTS

FOREWORD

PREFACE

SECTION I.   OVERVIEW LITERATURE......................................1

SECTION II.   RESEARCH FOCUS LITERATURE............................29

SECTION III.   IMPLEMENTATION LITERATURE............................43

SECTION IV.   GEOGRAPHIC CASE STUDIES..............................81

SECTION V.   OTHER BIBLIOGRAPHIES AND SOURCEBOOKS.................115

APPENDIX I   CONTRIBUTING ORGANIZATIONS

ACKNOWLEDGEMENT

We deeply appreciate the support of the College of Business of the University of West Florida that made this volume a reality. We would also like to thank the host of authors, editors, and publishers who contributed the citations that appear in the book. Finally, we express our gratitude to the platoon of secretaries, staff, and librarians who deciphered our hieroglyphics to make this volume accessible to the professional community.

FOREWORD

For too long, the managerial dimension of development has been taken for granted. For too long, the direct transferability of management principles has been assumed across cultures. Only in the last few years has the managerial and organizational dimension of development emerged as worthy of serious consideration by both theoreticians and academicians, but the field is still a frontier. This book will help to generate new contributions, form new careers, and attract new professionals.

It is being published just when the professional interests of major international and bilateral agencies, following the lead of some of the major U.S. foundations, seem to be converging on the field. Also, it coincides with the realization by such agencies of the need to set up more institutions in developing countries, especially in Africa, that would deal with the national managerial realities, as do the Asian Management Institute in Manila, the Indian Institute of Management in Ahmedabad, the ESAN in Peru, and the Central American Management Institute.

All those working on such problems will find in this volume a valuable resource for information on past efforts, current trends, and new approaches, helping them to meet the management challenge of the developing world.

Francis Lethem
The World Bank

PREFACE

Management and related issues have been targeted as some of the crucial factors for economic development success in the decade to come. Little doubt remains that the neglect of these factors has been a cause of failure of many projects during the past two decades. This recognition has led to a flurry of thought and activity directed at the various aspects of the problem, including a striving toward a theory base, issues of transferability, strategies and plans, and methods of implementation, monitoring and evaluation. The literature has been mushrooming, and this fact has been a major impetus to compile this volume as a first attempt to organize this literature specifically as management, administration and organization in the developing world.

The framework for this volume is the concept of managerial infrastructure. For any national or cultural group, it is the collection of managerial skills and organizational structures that determine their ability to manage their own affairs. Post WWII Japan and Western Europe have this infrastructure, and so with the aid of capital, were able to rise quickly from the ashes. In cases where the managerial infrastructure is less developed, no amount of capital will create economic miracles, as has been evident in much of the Third World.

Implicit is the assumption that the managerial infrastructure can be strengthened. Beginning with an analysis of a current country situation, a process can be undertaken to build the infrastructure, to empower each nation toward the development of their rich human and physical resources.

With this need for information on management, administration and organization geared to the specific needs of developing nations before us, we set out to put together a sourcebook that would provide as broad a reference tool as possible. We scanned hundreds of existing bibliographies, indexes and catalogs, and canvased individuals and institutions throughout the developing world. We selected works for inclusion on the following bases: Timeliness -- the great majority of the listed publications are less than ten years old; Developing country focus -- the selections are directly concerned with management, administration or organization in the Third World, or their approaches are relatively free of Western cultural bias and therefore lend themselves to a Third World context; Overseas publications -- to assist readers to find locally available materials and to lend an international tone to the bibliography. Publications coming from Europe, Asia and Latin America are cited wherever possible.

We sincerely hope that the readers of this bibliograhic sourcebook will take whatever omissions they observe as an opportunity to participate in the improvement of the book. The volume can provide a valuable forum for the exchange of information at both global and interdisciplinary levels for practitioner, policy maker, academic and student. But to be truly effective, it must be updated from time to time. The groundwork has now been completed and we would most appreciate your participation in the ongoing search. Your response will be a contribution to a worldwide effort. Please send any information or suggestion you may have to:

Dr. Kenneth L. Murrell
Bibliography Project Director
Department of Management
The University of West Florida
Pensacola, Florida 32514-0103
USA

SECTION I
OVERVIEW LITERATURE

There are three major purposes to this annotated section. The first is to create a macro-level framework for management infrastructure development. Included are selected volumes addressing the theory and definition of economic development, modernization and cultural change. The multi-disciplinary nature of this task is emphasized by including volumes representative of business management, public administration, organizational development, economics, political science, anthropology, religion and psychology. There is a blend of classic and leading edge, practitioner and academic.

The second purpose is to provide a basis for reflection at the strategic and policy-making levels.

The final purpose is to acknowledge the work of many who made early and lasting contributions to the disciplines with which we are concerned. If any have been overlooked, please accept the editors' apologies.

A majority of the annotations have been prepared by the current editors. On occasion, however, an annotation has been used by permission, and is indicated by "(source)" placed immediately following.

Abraham, M. Francis. <u>Perspectives on Modernization: Toward a General Theory of Third World Development</u>. Washington, DC: Univ. Press of America, 1980.

    Provides a good overview of the contributions of the social scientists to the understanding of Third World development. Modernization is a process, not a goal. As defined by the author, it is "a comprehensive process of economic growth, social mobilization, and cultural expansion." The book attempts to describe the leading models of modernization and merge them toward a general theory.

Agarwala, Ramgopal. <u>Planning in Developing Countries: Lessons of Experience</u>. Staff Working Paper No. 576, Washington, DC: The World Bank, 1983.

    Reports that, in most developing countries, planning failed to live up to expectations. Outlines steps to remedy this situation. Recommends a general reorientation and emphasis on the most effective areas in the initial formulation of plans. Provides an in-depth review of the experience of planning in developing countries during the post-World War II period. Analyzes problems, successes, and failures, emerging trends, and lessons learned.

Argyris, C. <u>Intervention Theory & Method</u>. Reading: Addison-Wesley, 1970.

    The basic statement of the Argyrian approach to planned organization change. An excellent reference for those desiring to better understand the organic process model of change as opposed to the mechanistic (blueprint) models of change. The book serves as a guide as well as a theoretical grounding for what organization development is all about, complete with case examples and practical lessons on how to collect, analyze, and feed back data in order to facilitate organizational development.

Arndt, H. W. "Trickle Down Myth." <u>Economic Development and Cultural Change</u> 32 (Oct. 1983): 1-10.

    This article presents an overview of the failure of the 'Trickle Down' approach to development. A key lesson to be learned is that focus needs to be balanced between disparities among countries and disparities within a country.

Berger, Peter L. <u>Pyramids of Sacrifice: Political Ethics and Social Change</u>. New York: Basic Books, Inc., 1974.

    Focused on political ethics and Third World development, Berger has boldly developed an argument for a third way of development. His arguments against state controlled and free enterprise exploitation are preambles for the development of a humane development theory and practice. Both ideologies, he claims, need to be rejected and their myths of growth and revolution debunked. A new way is needed and he is willing to move toward that new thinking by questioning both prevailing super power world views.

Bhattacharya, Mohit. "Administrative and Organizational Issues in Rural Development." Indian Journal of Public Administration 24, No. 4,(1978): 1173-88.

The author writes from his experience with rural development within India. He cautions donor agencies against "indiscriminant organizational tampering," and places the responsibility on the field administration to improve the organizational effectiveness. It is of value both as a Third World voice and as a sound alternative in rural development strategy.

Birou, Alan, Paul Marc Henry, and John P. Schlegel, eds. Towards a Redefinition of Development. Oxford: Pergamon Press for OECD, 1977.

Noted experts from around the world are represented in this book as they respond to the crucial questions underlying Third World development. Part One examines the question of whether or not the term "development" is a misnomer and nine different views are offered in response to that question. Additionally, a critical analysis of the nature of development is presented with a conclusion offered the reader in the form of a diagnosis of advanced industrial societies. Part Two examines the conditions for another kind of world development as an attempt to develop alternative approaches and concludes with a discussion of "Development In A Global Perspective" and "Making the Earth a Fit Place to Live In." An assortment of views and perspectives about development is offered that definitely transcend the western model and explore alternative paradigms and assumptions.

Bowles, Chester. "Administration and Rural Development in Underdeveloped Countries." Community Development Review 8 (March 1963): 1-3.

The article provides a useful platform for reflection on past efforts. Advice is offered on the administrative structure appropriate for LDC's in order to get the most from foreign aid. The author calls for an integrated rural development approach as a key policy goal for U.S. foreign aid.

Brown, L. David. "Effective Change Strategies for Public Enterprises: Lessons from Turnaround Cases." *Vikalpa: The Journal for Decision Makers* 9, no. 2 (April-June 1984): 97-112.

A useful review of organization development and strategic management from the point of view of public enterprises in the developing countries. Through personal experience in the Third World, the author is able to present an up-to-date, culturally sensitive examination of change strategies. Case studies of Indian organization are included.

Brown, Lester R. *Seeds of Change: The Green Revolution and Development in the 1970's*. New York: Praeger, 1970.

Provides an excellent summary of a most significant event of international development effort--the green revolution. Special focus was given to the implications for the future (the 1970's). This book is still valuable as a foundation to understanding and for the lessons that can be learned from the past. In Eugene Black's optimistic foreward, a note of hope introduces an overview of accomplishments that is useful to reflect upon.

Bryant, Coralie, and Louise White. *Managing Development In the Third World*. Boulder: Westview Press, 1982.

Written as a basic text, the book is a comprehensive and timely overview of development administration and management. It summarizes organization theory and behavior in terms of how they affect development programs, and looks both at the theory and practice of development. From the first chapter where development is redefined as increasing choices and realizing human potential, to the last chapter on managing rural development, the book is a blend of new ideas and insights with practical wisdom in the field. A very valuable contribution for the new student as well as the more seasoned veteran in terms of development thought.

Caiden, Gerald E. *Administrative Reform*. Chicago: Aldine Publishing Co., 1969.

The author defines administrative reform as "the artificial inducement of administrative transformation against resistancy." He deals with the general questions of change within a society, as well as specific approaches and obstacles to administrative reform. He concludes that administrators must be reform conscious and must develop pro-active as well as re-active strategies.

Camps, Miriam, and Catherine Gwin. <u>Collective Management: The Reform of Global Economic Organizations.</u> New York: McGraw-Hill Book Co., 1981.

The authors present problem analysis and recommendations of macro level issues in development. Emphasis is given to inter-relations of global management levels--international, regional, country, and micro levels are discussed. This is a good basic text to consider the wider context of development and the management structure and environments that need to be appreciated, influenced, or controlled. It provides a useful environmental scan as well as an historical background report on current conditions in the fast changing world economic scene.

Chambers, Robert. <u>Rural Development: Putting the Last First.</u> London: Longman, 1983.

'The extremes of rural poverty in the Third World are an outrage.' Starting with this uncompromising statement, the author challenges preconceptions dominating rural development. The central theme of the book is that rural poverty is often unseen or misperceived by outsiders, since they themselves are not rural and poor. Dr. Chambers contends that researchers, scientists, administrators, and fieldworkers rarely appreciate the richness and validity of rural people's knowledge or the hidden nature of rural poverty. He argues for a new professionalism with fundamental reversals in outsiders' learning, values, and behavior, and proposes more realistic action for tackling rural poverty. (IDS Catalogue)

Chapel, Yves, ed. <u>Administrative Management for Development: A Reader.</u> International Institute of Administrative Sciences. Paris: UNESCO, 1977.

This reader assumes the vital need of advancement in administrative management for development. It is organized to include the institutional framework, the human factors, economic and financial aspects, and sectoral implementation of programs, as illustrated by public works. The reader is designed to stimulate discussion and extend knowledge rather than to present fundamentals. It is a comprehensive collection of 48 articles and short essays. A companion volume is published in French (UNESCO, 1974).

Cheema, G. Shabbir, and Dennis A. Rondinelli. <u>Decentralization and Development: Policy Implementation in Developing Countries.</u> Beverly Hills: Sage Pub., 1983.

Eight scholars discuss a crucial issue in the Third World: the degree to which central government can--or should--control development planning and administration. The authors explore the recent shift in emphasis toward smaller projects responsive to local as well as national concerns, focusing on decentralization experiments in Asia, Africa, and South

America. Their original essays highlight social, political, economic, and administrative factors that may determine whether a decentralized program is successful... and offer practical insights into when decentralized design and administration present a viable development alternative. In addition, they discuss various ways of organizing decentralized project administration. (Publisher).

Chenery, Hollis. *Structural Change and Development Policy*. New York: Oxford University Press for the World Bank, 1979.

This World Bank publication contains a comprehensive collection of articles on economic development in the Third World. The issues of policy framework, the internal structure of development including industrialization and economies of scale, the external structure with attention to the comparative advantage issues with case studies from Israel and Pakistan, and finally international development policy and foreign assistance are discussed. Though written primarily from an economist's perspective, the collection has value as a primer in development thought for the non-economist reader as well.

Chilcote, Ronald H. *Theories of Development and Underdevelopment*. Boulder: Westview Press, 1984.

Professor Chilcote offers a critical assessment and clarification of the diverse and often obscure literature and ideas on development and underdevelopment. New directions in development theory are identified, including theories of modes of production and the internationalization of capital. Also provided is a useful glossary of terms in the literature and a full bibliography of major contributions to theories of development and underdevelopment. (Publisher).

Cochrane, Glynn. *The Cultural Appraisal of Development Projects*. New York: Praeger Publishers, 1979.

This book originates from the 20 years experience of the author as an anthropologist and is based on the premise of needed improvement of the collaboration between project managers and social scientists, all of whom are concerned with the success of development efforts. A system for the cultural appraisal of development projects is presented. It seeks to increase the social scientists' ability to understand and communicate with the project manager and for the project manager to understand the implications of culture and to utilize the expertise of the social scientist. The book is an extension of an earlier project appraisal system the author developed for USAID in 1974, called the Social Soundness Analysis.

Cody, J., H. Hughes, and D. Wall, eds. <u>Policies for Industrial Progress in Developing Countries</u>. Washington, DC: Oxford University Press for the World Bank, 1980.

The book is a result of a study jointly sponsored by UNIDO and the World Bank and represents an overview of the industrialization of the Third World. It is written primarily for the practitioner concerned with the development of the manufacturing sector. It attempts to identify consistent and effective policies that reflect the realities of Third World environments. It provides analytical tools to assist in decision making and policy selection to improve the policy environment for industrialization in specific countries.

Conyers, Diana, and Peter Hills. <u>An Introduction to Development Planning in the Third World</u>. New York: John Wiley & Sons, 1984.

A comprehensive overview of planning in the Third World, giving a statement of the philosophy as well as the practical issues involved in planning. This is a timely effort to communicate to the reader what is going on, as well as normative suggestions about what should be going on, in relation to the issue.

Cook, W. D., and T. E. Kuhn. <u>Planning Processes in Developing Countries: Techniques and Achievements</u>. New York: North Holland Pub. Co., 1982.

This collection of articles is thought-provoking for the directions of development for the 1980's and 1990's. Some contributions call for drastic reorientations of development philosophy and policy direction. The authors gain from the use of micro level cases to support their ideas. Much of the book has a practical orientation on how to achieve better results based in the current situation.

Dresang, Dennis L. "Entrepreneurialism and Development Administration." <u>Administrative Science Quarterly</u> 18, no. 1 (March 1973): 76-85.

Administrative reform is often limited by a great many factors in the Third World. An alternative is the encouragement of entrepreneurism in a public bureaucracy. This phenomenon explains a variety of developmental successes despite the limited capacities of some bureaucracies. Evidence from Zambia is used to illustrate this conclusion.

Esman, Milton J. "Development Assistance in Public Administration: Requiem or Renewal," Public Administration Review, 40, No. 5 (Sept./Oct. 1980): 426-431.

The past three decades of development efforts have largely failed. However, the future holds promise if it is approached with an understanding of past mistakes, a concept of environmental plurality, and a spirit of innovation and multi-disciplinary cooperation. A good survey article to put the present in focus with the past and future.

Farmer, Richard N., and Barry M. Richman. Comparative Management & Economic Progress. Homewood: Richard D. Irwin, Inc., 1965.

A classic work still valuable in understanding the relationship of managerial effectiveness and economic development. A very comprehensive work.

Finkel, Jason L., and Richard W. Gable. Political Development & Social Change. 2nd ed. New York: John Wiley & Sons, 1971.

The editors state their unifying theme as the relationship of political development to social change. Included is consideration of economic and anthropologic factors, as well as power groups, social stratification, and ideology. This book provides some cohesiveness to the many factors which affect development efforts. A useful collection of articles for readers wanting to broaden their base of understanding in the primary disciplines of importance for development administration and social change.

Gable, Richard W. Development Administration: Background, Terms, concepts, Theories, and a New Approach, occasional papers, SICA series No. 7 Washington DC: American society for public administration, 1976.

This paper is an effort to lay out the field of development administration as a basic introduction for the novice, as well as training framework for the professional. It is a useful source of historical and definitional information.

Gamer, Robert E. The Developing Nations: A Comparative Perspective. Boston: Allyn & Bacon, Inc., 1976.

The author conceptualizes the process of development as a need to provide a "stable personal environment." His arguments are drawn from history and relate political structure, indigeneous social systems, and international trade. This is an alternative perspective on development, useful because of its differences.

Gant, George F. Development Administration: Concepts, Goals, Methods. Madison: University of Wisconsin Press, 1979.

The author, a former Tennessee Valley Authority official, deals with the concepts of development administration generally, as well as in major policy areas. Specific needs of management, organization, budgeting and training are discussed. Global pressures and the impact of foreign aid are also analyzed. This work is a comprehensive presentation grounded in the author's many years of field experience.

Ghosh, Pradip K., ed. Energy Policy and Third World Development. Westport: Greenwood Press, 1984.

This volume analyzes trends toward developing effective energy policies in the Third World. The social and economic impact of policies are examined. The work comprises an effective overview of energy developments which color all other aspects of development work.

Goh, Keng-Swee. "Public Administration and Economic Development in the LDC's." World Economy 6 (Sept. 1983): 229-243.

The author presents 19th century Japan as a model for the developing nations today. Only a slow and painful development of social and political institutions made the 20th century economic growth possible. A thought-provoking work on the strategies of international development.

Golembiewski, Robert, and W. Eddy, eds. Organization Development in Public Administration. 2 vols. New York: Marcel Dekker, 1978.

An organization development guidebook that spells out the basic concepts and uses a collection of excellent articles to supplement its main ideas of how organization development can work in public sector environments. Though not intended as international, it provides a needed perspective about organization development from a non-profit public administration point of view. This two volume set represents a valuable collection of organization development ideas and case studies that would aid the public administrator in identifying alternative ways of managing organizations.

Gorman, Robert F., ed. Private Voluntary Organizations as Agents of Development. Boulder: Westview Press, 1984.

Private voluntary organizations have an increasingly important role to play in the provision of development assistance, either as alternative forms of resource flow or as channels of aid that are systematically integrated into the official intergovernmental aid system. This book explores the practical and theoretical aspects of PVOs as fund-raisers in developed countries, as promoters of employment in the Third World, as facilitators of development programs, and as sources of administrative innovation. (Publisher).

Haire, M., E. E. Ghiselli, and L. W. Porter. <u>Managerial Thinking: An International Study</u>. New York: John Wiley and Sons, 1966.

As one of the classic works in comparative management research. It remains of value both for basic understanding of the concepts involved, as well as for recognizing specific managerial attitudes and values in the countries studied.

Harbison, F. H. <u>Human Resources As the Wealth of Nations</u>. New York: Oxford University Press, 1973.

In this book, Harbison provides an alternative to the GNP approach to development. He advocates the use of other indices (such as education, health and nutrition) to provide a more balanced appraisal than does the GNP approach. With the aid of cases, he analyzes the components of a key human resources problem, which is the underdevelopment and under-utilization of skills.

Harbison, F. H. and C. A. Meyers. <u>Education, Manpower and Economic Growth</u>. New York: McGraw-Hill, 1964.

This policy-oriented book discusses the problems and issues of human resource development. Attention is directed to the employment of a composite index, as well as to strategic choices and their consequences. There is some discussion of the integration of the human resource development of a country with its general development planning.

Harris, Philip R. <u>New World, New Ways, New Management</u>. New York: Amacom, 1983.

This book represents a timely reflection on the current state of management from an international perspective. Though written primarily for a western audience, Harris has done a good job of describing how current organizations, wherever in the world they exist, must be able to transform themselves into the forms necessary for success tomorrow. Reflecting current management concerns and issues, Harris has offered this book as a practical examination of the important changes occurring in management. He does this with sensitivity and awareness to the cultural dimension as well as a futures perspective, and this establishes his work as worthwhile reading for an international managerial audience.

Harris, Philip R. and Robert T. Moran. <u>Managing Cultural Differences</u>. Houston: Gulf Publishing Co., 1979.

A very thorough and comprehensive overview primarily from the viewpoint of the multi-national corporation but applicable more broadly. It stresses the need for all managers to develop inter-cultural skills in an increasingly global community. Both the impact of the manager and the impact on the manager are discussed. It is practitioner oriented with good appendices of other aids and readings included.

Harrison, Paul. <u>Inside the Third World: The Anatomy of Poverty</u>. New York: Pelican Original, 1981.

Based on five years of research and travel in eleven countries, the author offers a wide-ranging look at the problems--harsh climates, scarcity of land, overcrowded cities and exploding population, rising unemployment, malnutrition and disease, illiteracy--that make the poor nations of Asia, Africa, and Latin America so susceptible to economic turmoil and political upheaval.

Hauser, Philip M., ed. <u>World Population and Development: Challenges and Prospects</u>. Syracuse: Syracuse University Press, 1979.

A good overview of the situation of world population as it relates to development. It is a prerequisite in understanding for the formulation of overall development strategies and their implementation.

Heady, Ferrel. <u>Public Administration: A Comparative Perspective</u>. Englewood Cliffs: Prentice-Hall, 1966.

One of the first efforts at assessing comparative public administration, it sets a good foundation for understanding the early work and the growth of the field. Although somewhat dated, it is still useful for its description of various basic administrative systems in both the developing and the developed nations.

Hicks, Norman, and P. Streeten. "Indicators of Development: The Search for A Basic Needs Yardstick." <u>World Development</u> 7, no. 6 (1979): 567-580.

A good overview of the problem of the measurement of development. The consensus is that GNP is useful but inadequate. The most promising supplements are in social and human indicators centered around basic needs. No one measurement or index is yet agreed upon. The authors review many specific proposals for measurement.

Higgins, Benjamin, and Jean Downing Higgins. *Economic Development of A Small Planet*. New York: W. W. Norton and Co., 1979.

This book advocates attention to the interactions between the developed and underdeveloped nations of the world. The focus on economic growth alone is questioned and tempered with concerns about quality of life and ecology. Credit for these changes is given to the Third World itself, the failure of much past development effort, and the energy and food crisis of the past decade.

Hirschman, Albert O. *The Strategy of Economic Development*. New Haven: Yale University Press, 1958.

A classic work that had a great impact for many years. Good background reading for understanding the process and implications of economic development. In its time, the book represented a main critique of the balanced economic development theory and was a controversial contribution to the argument of how development takes place. Entrepreneurial and managerial capacity are included as essential elements of strategy.

Hofstede, Geert. *Culture's Consequences: International Differences in Work-Related Values*. Beverly Hills: Sage Publications, 1980.

A massive research effort to explore the differences across cultures in the following four areas: power distance, uncertainty avoidance, individualism, and masculinity. Forty different national groups were examined with a total of 116,000 questionnaires used in 1968 and 1972. The focus was on mental programs of respondents in general and the values and cultural issues in particular. The individual responses are combined to form collective tendencies in the populations which the author then uses for comparative as well as descriptive purposes in commenting on economic and managerial development among the different countries. The breadth of the survey is only limited in its focus on the employees of a large multinational firm, but even with that bias, the results are impressive. LDC's are described as having larger power distance, strong uncertainty avoidance, and a collectivist predisposition. The study is fast becoming a classic source of basic research on cross-cultural differences, and without a doubt, a reference work to use in examining management and organization issues in the developing countries.

Jantsch, E. _Design For Evolution: Self-Organization and Planning in the Life of Human Systems._ New York: G. Braziller, Inc., 1975.

One of a very limited number of books which are seen as breaking new ground. Jantsch's effort at relating the deeper philosophical issues of consciousness to the more pragmatic question of how human systems change can be of significant value to the reader interested in Third World development. The author presents a carefully laid out explanation of how design in human systems terms can be understood and appreciated from three levels: rational, mythological, and evolutionary. A rare work which is able to blend eastern and western philosophies to better comprehend the nature of change in order to design pragmatic approaches to managing change in human systems.

Jennings, A., and T. G. Weiss. _The Challenge of Development in the Eighties: Our Response._ New York: Pergamon Press, 1982.

Within the context of the U.N. Third Development Decade, this book presents a response to the Third World from a spectrum of interests in the developed countries. A good presentation of current thinking at the macro level to fit specific development efforts into the larger picture. A diverse range of opinion is represented but all agree on the danger of refusing to come to grips with the problems of world poverty facing us.

Jones, Garth N., and Aslam Niaz. "Strategies and Tactics of Planned Organizational Change: A Scheme of Working Concepts," _Philippine Journal of Public Administration_ 7 (Oct. 1963), 275-85.

By the technique of content analysis, this article identifies and classifies fourteen strategies which have been derived from case studies on planned organizational change. In addition, eight types of tactics were noted. The strategies have been classified according to their essential characteristics into three categories: normative, coercive, and utilitarian.

Kettering, Merlyn H. _Toward a "Performance Approach": A Distinct Strategy Shift for Management Development Efforts_ (draft). Washington, DC: Development Project Management Center, Office of Cooperation and Development, U.S. Dept. of Agriculture, 1981.

A re-examination of the strategic goals of management development, with attention given to the contributions from the LDC systems management development activity and specific project management. The process emphasis must shift away from 'capacity building,' i.e.: imparting knowledge about management, to a 'performance strategy,' the accomplishment of the work of management. The author attempts to isolate specifics which can be integrated into current efforts.

Kiggundu, Moses N., Jan J. Jorgensen, and Taieb Hafsi. "Administrative Theory and Practice in Developing Countries: A Synthesis." <u>Administrative Science Quarterly</u> 28 (Mar. 83): 66-84.

This article is an attempt at synthesis of 94 articles on organizations in developing countries. The conclusion emphasizes that managers can best transfer theory and techniques that deal with the 'technical core' of the organization. The more the environment is involved, the more one must precede utilization by 'a situational analysis' to identify the relevant contingencies and their interrelationships.

Killick, Tony, ed. <u>The IMF and Stabilization: Developing Country Experiences</u>. New York: St. Martins Press, 1984.

This volume is prepared through the support of the Overseas Development Institute. The issues are timely and of a critical nature to those in development work, with a focus on the stabilization policies of the IMF against the general economic management context of the LDC's. The purpose of the book is to help reconcile the differences between the groups. A case study format is used covering Latin America, Indonesia, Jamaica, and Kenya.

Korten, David C., and Felipe Alfonso, eds. <u>Bureaucracy and the Poor: Closing the Gap</u>. West Hartford: Kumarian Press, 1983.

In this book management specialists have taken on a new task; that of studying the management problems of the culture of poverty and of developing a new management technology for it. They draw on experiences from Asia, Latin America and Africa. This book will be of interest to development professionals, to researchers and students concerned with the design and change of large organizations and to the self-informed public.

Korten, David C., and Rudi Klauss, eds. <u>People Centered Development: Contributions Toward Theory and Planning Frameworks</u>. West Hartford: Kumarian Press, 1984.

People-Centered Development is a collection of thirty essays which have been carefully selected by the editors to provide an integrated theoretical and pragmatic perspective on a development approach which, though for some time a key element in many development projects, has only recently begun to receive scholarly attention. "Although development economics may be in the doldrums, scholars and practitioners from disciplines beyond economics have been engaged in a spirited debate that is laying the foundation for a bold alternative strategy of development. No one interested in development can ignore the evidence in this volume, People-Centered Development--a new framework, based on social learning processes and the empowerment of people and communities, is emerging with critical relevance both to the developing countries and the industrialized states of the West." (Laurence D. Stifel, Vice President, Rockefeller Foundation)

Kubr, Milan, and John Wallace. *Successes and Failures in Meeting the Management Challenge: Strategies and Their Implementation*. Staff working paper, no. 585. Washington, DC: World Bank, 1984.

The authors examine the original nature of key management problems faced by developing countries and outlines proven strategies for improving management competence and performance. They present approaches to management development recently introduced by enterprises and institutions such as business clinics and self-development programs for management, as well as tailored and action-oriented programs.

Kumar, Krishna. *Transnational Enterprises: Their Impact on Third World Societies and Cultures*. Boulder: Westview Press, 1980.

The focus is on impacts of MNC's which have received considerable attention over the past several years. Especially relevant are the implications for, and effects on the development of entrepreneurs in the Third World. Both positive and negative factors are noted in the socio-cultural realm as well as the economic.

Lammers, Cornelis J., and David J. Hickson, eds. *Organizations Alike and Unlike: International Studies in the Sociology of Organizations*. London: Routledge & Kegan Paul, 1979.

A valuable collection of original papers put together over several years. The development of a comparative sociology of organization is an apparent goal of this collection and for the reader this is a useful single reference to this large and growing field and a guide to the current thinking of cross-national organizational sociologists.

Landell-Mills, P. "Management: A Limiting Factor in Development." *Finance and Development* 20, no. 3 (1983): 11-17.

This short article offers an insightful discussion of the role of local government in improving the managerial infrastructure in a developing country context. Instead of focusing on the criticism of Third World bureaucracies, the author spells out a number of areas in which they could make significant positive impact. In the words of the author, the process, to be successful, must be "pursued with vision, tenacity and strong political backing."

LaPalombara, Joseph. "Alternative Strategies for Developing Administrative Capabilities in Emerging Nations." In <u>Frontiers in Development Administration</u>, edited by Fred W. Riggs. Durham: Duke University Press, 1970.

An older work by a highly respected author, which has current value for the positive and negative lessons related to attempts to improve development administration in the sixties.

LaPalombara, Joseph, ed. <u>Bureaucracy and Political Development</u>. Princeton: Princeton University Press, 1967.

A fundamental collection of works evaluating the impact of bureaucracy on the transformation process in developing countries. Special attention is given to bureaucratic organization as it relates to political and economic development. Bureaucracy is presented as a critical variable that "both affects and is conditioned by the process itself," (quoted from the author). A selected bibliography of administration and political development is also included in this second edition.

Lawrence, P., and J. W. Lorsch. <u>Organization and Environment: Managing Differentiation and Integration</u>. Homewood: Irwin, 1969.

A work dealing with industrial organization as it relates to economic and technological environments. Though based on U.S. research, it has application especially for the internal structure of organizations in the Third World. It is good background reading and a recognized classic in the field of organization design and theory.

Long, Norman. <u>An Introduction to the Sociology of Rural Development</u>. Boulder: Westview Press, 1977.

The author identifies and evaluates theoretical and conceptual approaches to rural development, as presented by sociologists and anthropologists. Modernization theory as well as Marxist dependency theory is discussed. Particularly useful are the inclusions of empirical examples to test the various theories. As the title suggests, it is an excellent introduction and is rich in its citations of actual cases--particularly in the planned social change area.

Marini, Frank. <u>Toward a New Public Administration: The Minnowbrook Perspective</u>. Scranton: Chandler Publishing Co., 1971.

A piece of ground breaking literature in the field of public administration. The reports from this 1968 conference set the tone and tenor of much of the pubic administration thought over the last 15 years. Chapter 8, which discusses the history of the comparative administration group (CAG), is particularly worth attention.

McClelland, David. The Achieving Society. 2nd ed. New York: Irvington Publishers, 1976.

One of the foundation books in the field of both the behavioral sciences and comparative administration. The book presents the formulation of McClelland's motivation theory as it was developed from economic as well as psychological theories applied to individual achievement and national development.

Mead, Margaret, ed. Cultural Patterns and Technical Change. New York: Mentor Books for UNESCO, 1955. (A manual prepared by the World Federation for Mental Health).

A classic work focusing on the cultural stress, evidenced in the individual, that is inherent in technical change. The emphasis is on facilitating change to lessen stress and promote mental health. The basic principles are a guide, not a blueprint. Specific attention is given to the aspects of technical change still at the forefront of current development effort. A bibliography is included on the literature available in the fifties.

Meyer, Marshall W. Change in Public Bureaucracies. Cambridge: Cambridge University Press, 1979.

A very comprehensive volume bringing out the implications of organizational theory and research. Although discussion centers around the developed nations, the broad base provides for timely perspectives of analysis for Third World situations.

Migdal, Joel S. Peasants, Politics and Revolution: Pressures Toward Political and Social Change in the Third World. Princeton: Princeton University Press, 1974.

This author does not glorify peasants, but rather deals with their changing role within a society and the forces that bring about changes. The results are considered in terms of their organizational and political out-working, as well as economic and social complications.

Mintzberg, Henry. The Nature of Managerial Work. New York: Harper & Row, 1973.

The modern classic that closely examines the real nature of managerial work. New perspectives on what managers do open up new questions about what must be taught and what skills must be acquired in order for managers to manage. Useful to a Third World audience because it questions or rejects as myths much of what has been assumed to be truth about what managers do. The research methods also present useful alternatives for studying management cultures other than one's own.

Montgomery, John D. "Administering to the Poor (or If We Can't Help Rich Dictators, What Can We Do For the Poor?)" Public Administration Review 40 (1980): 421-425.

Discusses various special problems of human resource development in developing countries, as well as the core of the solutions. Implementation necessitates difficult trade-offs for both donors and host governments. The U.S. is critiqued as no longer able to provide a model as "donor" and is in fact retrenching in foreign aid. Momentum has swung to the international agencies.

Montgomery, John, and William J. Siffin. Approaches to Development: Politics, Administration, and Change. New York: McGraw-Hill Book Company, 1966.

The first in a series of studies undertaken by the Comparative Administration Group to utilize the recent advances in the social sciences in the study of comparative administration. This volume examines the relationship between administrative concepts and their socio-political context as part of a larger concern with administration as an instrument of development in non-Western settings.

Moris, J. Managing Induced Rural Development. Bloomington: International Development Institute, Indiana University, 1981.

This book presents a comprehensive overview of integrated rural development but does not rest with fundamentals. It is diagnostic, demonstrating how most fundamental problems are ones of organization and management. It is practical, thought-provoking, prescriptive, and on the leading edge of the IRD concept. It contains excellent field material as well as a 1000 plus citation bibliography.

Munoz, Heraldo, ed. From Dependency to Development: Strategies to Overcome Underdevelopment and Inequality. Boulder: Westview Press, 1981.

An excellent, up-to-date analysis of dependency theory with the emphasis on what can be employed to overcome dependency. The book presents the viewpoints of many well-known authors, researchers, and practitioners. It is a useful work for anyone who must deal with dependency theory at the professional level. The viewpoints expressed are balanced in that they reject both the conventional capitalistic development theories as well as the totalitarian socialist doctrine. The majority express faith and hope for a participative democratic solution to underdevelopment and a way out of the dependency conditions experienced by many Third World nations.

Murrell, Kenneth L. "OD in the Third World." OD Journal (Summer 1984): 16-20.

A practical approach is presented for the Organization Development consultant operating in the Third World. The author's position is that the organization development profession must be active in the Third World, although limited expectations of success are realistic. The approach presented is useful for all development personnel to review in terms of how it reflects on their own approach.

Murrell, Kenneth L. "Management Infrastructure Development in the Third World." International Organization Development Journal, (forthcoming).

The author develops the basic core concepts of management as they relate to Third World development. He calls for a more systematic program of development focusing on the managerial capacity, or infrastructure, in his terms and taking into consideration the full range of cultural conditions that affect the act of managing. The article lays out seven steps for beginning a process of infrastructure development for Third World management.

Nash, Manning. Unfinished Agenda: The Dynamics of Modernization in Developing Nations. Boulder: Westview Press, 1984.

Based on in-depth anthropological field work and uniting ethnographic material with broader generalizations about the processes of modernization, this book presents an analysis of social change since decolonization in Latin America, the Middle East, and particularly in Southeast Asia. The book offers an orderly theoretical platform for the understanding of modernization, providing a basis for future cross-cultural comparison. It supplies, as well, a macro-structural perspective often missing in social scientific modernization studies. (Publisher).

Negandhi, A. R. "Advanced Management Know-How in Underdeveloped Countries." California Management Review 10 No. 3, (1968): 53-60.

The author deals with the question, 'Can advanced management techniques be transferred to underdeveloped countries?' This article is one of the earliest on the issue of management development in the Third World. Though coming from an optimistic era based on industrial development, it is still of value as background and analysis.

Nelson, Nici. "Mobilizing Village Women: Some Organizational and Management Considerations." Journal of Development Studies 17 (Apr. 1981): 47-58.

A helpful article for those seeking to understand the practical issues of the increased involvement of women in the development process. Two case studies are included by way of illustration.

Nobe, Kenneth, and Rajan K. Sampath. Issues in Third World Development. Boulder: Westview Press, 1984.

A recent work dealing with current issues that concern development planners and practitioners. Methodological and strategic aspects are discussed, along with specific material on land and water resource management. Included is an article on the management factor in the developing nations that focuses on management as the missing link in development progress.

Ozgediz, Selcuk. Managing the Public Service in Developing Countries: Issues and Prospects. Staff working paper, no. 583, Washington, DC: The World Bank, 1983.

Better ways to manage human resources are identified to meet escalating demand for improved public services in developing countries, where public service employment is growing four times faster than in developed countries. Resultant problems in personnel management, public service training programs, and the applicability of western management practices in developing country settings are considered. A section is also included examining the cultural dynamics of management and a discussion of some failures in the transfer of management technology.

Paul, Samuel. Strategic Management of Development Programs: Guidelines for Action. Geneva: International Labour Office, 1983.

Strategic management is missing in many development programs and is a leading cause of failure. Strategic management includes the program environment, strategy, organization structure, and organization process. These cannot be taken for granted. The book is very practical and draws heavily from program experiences as well as private sector management. It suggests principals and guidelines rather than a blueprint approach.

Paul, Samuel. Training for Public Administration and Management in Developing Countries: A Review. Staff working paper, No. 584. Management and Development Series, No. 11. Washington, DC: The World Bank, 1983.

This is a report of survey results on the trends, development, and problems in public administration and training in developing countries.

Examination is made of growth of management training, the status of training institutes, evaluation procedures and design of training and recent developments. The paper concludes with a policy analysis critical of the elite orientation, an absence of LDC policies, institutional development problems and inadequate investment in development of training faculty, curriculum, materials and methods by the developing countries.

Perrett, Heli, and Francis Lethem. *Human Factors in Project Work*. Staff Working Paper, No. 397. Washington, DC: World Bank, 1983.

The authors address the need to re-examine the assumptions about human behavior as it relates to development efforts. They have designed an operational framework to deal with human behavioral issues on the levels of strategy formulation and implementation. The framework is well grounded in the experiences of the authors.

Perroux, Francois. *A New Concept of Development*. New York: UNESCO, 1983.

The concept of development brings out the major paradox of our era: the desire for progress and the mistrust of its consequences. Francois Perroux, a leading political economist whose innovative thinking has made a major contribution to development studies, aims in this work to analyze the ideas and theories propounded by an economic approach to development, and to clarify the meaning and direction of current research.

Prebisch, Raul. "The Dynamics of Peripheral Capitalism." In *Democracy and Development in Latin America*, edited by Louis Lefeber and Lisa L. North. Toronto: LARU, 1980.

Studies on the political economy, society, and culture of Latin America and the Caribbean. A recently written perspective on development from the noted Latin American economist.

Ranis, Gustav, Robert L. West, Cynthia Taft Morris, and Mark Leiserson. *Comparative Development Perspectives*. Boulder: Westview Press, 1983.

Included are the writings of 20 American and Canadian economists on the comparative perspectives of the general problems of development. Focusing on the 1980's the collection is highly economic in its outlook, but very timely and of interest to a reader wanting to see how current economic thought applies to the questions of development.

"Religion and Development Survey." Development 22, No. 1 (1980): 25-52.

   A collection of nine short essays compiled by the editors of the Journal. The focus is on the role of religion in development as both an institutional and "inner" force. It is a good overview emphasizing current examples and implications for the future. Useful at both the macro level strategy and planning as well as micro level management process. Summaries are included in French and Spanish.

Riggs, Fred W. Administration in Developing Countries: The Theory of Prismatic Society. Boston: Houghton Mifflin Co., 1964.

   A classic work in the understanding of administration in developing countries. The author presents a theoretical framework for analysis that differs from frameworks patterned after developed countries. Emphasis is placed on transitional societies in totality and then the administrative and political aspects which emerge.

Riggs, Fred W. "The Ecology and Context of Public Administration: A Comparative Paper." Public Administration Review 40, No. 2, (1980): 107-115.

   The improvement of administration can only come as the global environmental framework is considered i.e., global problems and tension. As well, one must consider the context of interdependency among bureaucratic systems in an increasingly interdependent world. Conventional approaches are now impossible.

Riggs, Fred W., ed. Frontiers of Development Administration. Durham: Duke University Press, 1971.

   This collection of papers remains a classic in its field. It deals with strategy, functional approach, structural analysis, and frameworks for reform in terms of development administration. Sponsored by the Comparative Administration Group, the edited volume represents a fundamental reader for anyone wanting a stronger background in development administration practice and theory.

Roberts, Hayden. Community Development: Learning and Action. Toronto: The University of Toronto Press, 1979.

   Hayden Roberts rethinks the traditional concept of "community development" and presents it as a viable force for development today. The analysis emphasizes the political nature of this process, as well as the central role of adult education. Various theories and models from diverse disciplines are integrated into a comprehensive theory with a practical approach. The author draws heavily on his experience in Africa and Canada. Also included is a chapter on organization development and socio-technical systems useful to the community development audience as well as to the manager.

Rostow, Walt W. The Stages of Economic Growth: A Non-Communist Manifesto. Cambridge: Cambridge University Press, 1960.

The traditional view of economic development from a fundamentally capitalistic view.

Roxborough, Ian. Theories of Underdevelopment. Atlantic Highlands: Humanities Press, Inc., 1979.

The book is designed as an attempt to explore the theoretical as well as methodological issues in the study of Third World social change. It contains a critical review of other development theories from both the position that the others are overly generalized, and that they are historical in nature. Its position is that change in the Third World is determined more from exogenous variables, and that all endogenous change paradigms are suspect. The author's experience base is primarily Latin American, but contrary to his criticisms of over-generalizing, he feels he has something to offer for all developing country contexts. The book offers the reader a well written critical essay on development theory.

Roy, Robert H. The Cultures of Management. Baltimore: Johns Hopkins University Press, 1977.

Though the cultures referred to are not specifically Third World, the book still offers useful insight into the philosophical and practical problems associated with formal organizations and their technologies as they relate to culture.

Schumacher, E. F. Small Is Beautiful. New York: Harper & Row, 1973.

A classic work that has strongly influenced change in development strategy over the past decade. It presents a call to return economics to a people focus and away from a mathematical preciseness that is based on faulty assumptions, and to deal with the scale of an organization as an independent and primary problem. An essential reading for anyone involved in development efforts, or wanting a contemporary understanding of the writings which are changing the way the world is viewed.

Seligson, Mitchell A., ed. *The Gap Between Rich and Poor: Contending Perspectives on the Political Economy of Development.* Boulder: Westview Press, 1984.

This book focuses on the debate as to whether the gap between rich and poor countries is widening or narrowing. Both sides are presented objectively, with explanations supported by empirical studies and case studies. A very helpful, rigorous overview.

Sharkansky, Ira. *The United States: A Study of a Developing Country.* New York: McKay & Co., Inc., 1975.

A valuable study of the internal dynamics of the U.S. as concerns the developing country nature of both its poorer states and its large urban slums. An insightful look at development problems in the U.S. with comparisons to African and Asian situations. A book that forces the reader, particularly if he or she is from the U.S., to reexamine the assumptions about economic wealth and development.

Siffin, W. J. "Two Decades of Public Administration in Developing Countries." In *Education and Training for Public Sector Management in Developing Countries*, edited by Lawrence D. Stifel, James S. Coleman, and Joseph E. Black. New York: Rockefeller Foundation, 1977. Also published in *Public Administration Review* 36 (Jan-Feb 1976): 61-71.

An historic overview of the efforts of the past two decades. The author concisely presents key lessons from these past attempts, as well as prime needs for the future. A final lesson is given, which is that the West stands in need of the "developing" countries. In the author's words, "there is much that we can learn together, that we can truly share instead of peddle."

Simon, Herbert A. *Administrative Behavior*, 3rd ed. New York: The Free Press, 1976.

The classic 1945 publication with six new chapters added. This is the basic book on decision making and choice as the key variable in understanding organizations. It is the foundation work for those involved in organization design or analysis. Though not culturally sensitive, the process allows for cross-cultural application.

Smith, William E., Francis Lethem, and Ben A. Thoolen. The Design of
    Organizations for Rural Development Projects: A Progress Report.
    Staff Working Paper, No. 375. Washington, DC: The World Bank, 1980.

This report goes into detail in explaining the critical design features
associated with rural development project work. Building on the work of
leading systems thinkers, the authors have taken the concept of the
appreciated, influenced, and controlled environmental factors and have
applied them to the challenge of assessing power and commitment factors in
order to aid in organization design. A framework is developed and the
explanation of its application is provided for the reader interested in
improving the management and organization of rural development work. A
very useful and valuable work, giving considerable effort to relate the
theoretical idea of design to the real problems of managing rural
development.

Stahl, O. Glenn. "Managerial Effectiveness in Developing Countries."
    International Review of Administration Sciences 45, no 1 (1979): 1-5.

The author expresses the viewpoint that if developing countries "want to
succeed in management and stimulation of an efficient, effective
bureaucracy to guide the state toward higher productivity and material
wealth... they will very likely have to accept fundamental changes in
culture." He develops the argument based not on inherent
superior/inferior cultures, but the "if" of the above statement.

Stockwell, Edward G., and Karen Lordlow. Third World Development: Problems
    and Prospects. Chicago: Nelson Hall, Inc., 1981.

A useful overview of the development process from a general framework of
western values, but it is minimally ideological in discourse. Three
factors are given primary attention--the economics, demographics, and
sociocultural dimension.

Swerdlow, Irving, ed. The Public Administration of Economic Development. New
    York: Praeger Publishers, 1975.

An examination of how the LDC governments go about achieving economic
development with the primary attention being on the public administration
component. The "what governments do" to foster economic development is
the central focus, and the author uses economic concepts as well as
administrative behavior to examine this subject. It is a sizable volume
combining economics and administration in a way well suited to a
comprehensive review of the subject of development.

Swerdlow, Irving, ed. <u>Development Administration: Concepts & Problems</u>.
Syracuse: Syracuse University Press, 1963.

This work stems from the early discussions of development administration as distinct from public administration generally. The contributing authors deal with specific aspects of administration in the developing countries. It remains a fundamental and useful collection of writing. Particularly valuable articles by Waterston on planning, and Bharati on cultural hurdles in development (India) make this 1963 publication useful as a historical review.

Tachau, Frank, ed. <u>The Developing Nations: What Path to Modernization?</u>
Toronto: Dodd, Mead, and Co., 1972.

An anthology on the basis and factors of modernization, as well as First, Second, and Third World paths to modernization. It is a useful, fundamental overview for a reader who wants to better understand the modernization concepts.

Tendler, Judith. <u>Inside Foreign Aid</u>. Baltimore: Johns Hopkins University Press, 1975.

A very useful book concerning Western development assistance from inside the agencies and institutions responsible. Why projects and programs occur as they do is explained in terms of the agencies' internal dynamics and external pressures. Included are analyses of communication, organization, and design issues that effect the way assistance is administered. These factors in turn often affect the host country's managerial behavior as well, and are often the models that are emulated.

Terpstra, Vern. <u>The Cultural Environment of International Business</u>.
Cincinnati: Southwestern, 1978.

Though the examination is broadly business focused from the perspective of a Westerner, the environmental analysis concerned with the basic cultural impacts on management is very useful. Language, religion, values and attitudes, social organization, education, technology, and the political/legal factors are examined as to how they impact on organizations and management.

Thompson, V. A. "Administrative Objectives for Development Administation." <u>Administrative Science Quarterly</u> 1 (June 1964), 91.

The focal question is what contribution the discipline of public administration can make to economic development. Adaptive administrative principles can be derived from the research and theories of the behavioral sciences. Discussion centers on the administrative conditions necessary for the most effective development administration: an innovative atmosphere, combination of planning and action, operational and shared planning goals, a cosmopolitan atmosphere, the diffusion of influence, the tolerance of independence, avoidance of bureaupathology, centralization and decentralization, communication and feedback, and participation in planning.

Waterston, Albert. *Development Planning: Lessons of Experience*. Baltimore: The Johns Hopkins University Press, 1969.

A comparative analysis of development planning in over one hundred countries in Asia, Africa, Europe, and the Americas. Part I of the study describes and analyzes the planning process in the countries under review, with special emphasis on the problems associated with implementation of development plans, and lays the substantive foundation for the organizational and administrative discussion in Part II.

Weinshall, T. D., ed. *Culture and Management*. New York: Penguin, 1977.

A broad collection of essays and previously published articles from the comparative management field. Culture is examined as a major factor of importance in understanding management and the articles included examine the issues from the perspective of what was known in the 60's and 70's about culture's impact on management. This edited version includes the classics in the field and would serve well as a primer on the subject.

The World Bank. *Employment and Development of Small Enterprises*. Sector Policy Paper. Washington, DC: The World Bank, 1970.

The focus of this monograph is the employment of urban unskilled labor. The conclusions suggest the benefits of small-scale enterprise because it is usually less capital-intensive and more labor-intensive. The relation of small-scale enterprise to other development activity is discussed. Other chapters consider the financial and technical support necessary from within a country and from outside agencies with reference to bank policies and technical assistance.

The World Bank. *World Development Report*. New York: Oxford University Press, 1978-84.

An annual publication focusing on critical issues of Third World development. The 1983 issue focused in part on the management factor in development.

SECTION II

RESEARCH FOCUS LITERATURE

Comparative studies in management, administration, and organization have emerged over the past two decades as recognized disciplines of study and research. No consensus of theory yet exists, nor does any strong theory base. However, the literature bears many indications that efforts to establish such a base are being intensified.

As the field moves towards emergent theory, the fact remains that much of the empirical work is already a valuable tool that can be utilized by the practitioner. The practitioner too is contributing to emergent theory by becoming more rigorous in the approach to assessing the management infrastructure of a nation while in the field.

The literature covers several major themes. Methodology of research is discussed, as are various aspects of theory and conceptualization. Beyond this are the field studies which asssess a particular infrastructure component of a country or region, and a few ambitious works which attempt to group together or compare a variety of countries. Some studies are empirical and some descriptive. Attention is also given to research into the issue of the transferability of managerial infrastructure components between nations.

One limiting factor of this section is the unavailability of much research data in the literature. Much seems to remain unpublished. It is the hope of the editors that in the near future more of the data can be made available, as it is indeed valuable to the task ahead.

Abdulrahman Al-Jafary, and A.T. Hollingsworth, "An Exploratory Study of Managerial Practices in the Arabian Gulf Region." Journal of International Business Studies 14, no. 2 (Fall 1983): 143-152.

Adedeji, Adebayo, and C. Baker, eds. Education and Research in Public Administration in Africa. London: Hutchinson, 1980.

Adedeji, Adebarjo, and Goran Hyden. Developing Research on African Administration: Some Methodological Issues, Management and Administration Series No. 4. Ife, Nigeria: University of Ife Press, 1974.

Adler, Leonore Loeb, ed. Cross Cultural Research at Issue. NY: Academic Press, 1982.

Adler, Nancy J. "Understanding the Ways of Understanding: Cross-Cultural Management Methodology Reviewed." In Advances in International Comparative Management edited by R. N. Farmer. Greenwich: JAI Press, 1984.

Adler, Nancy J. "A Typology of Management Studies Involving Culture." Journal of International Business Studies 14, no. 2 (Fall 1983): 29-47.

Ahanotu, A.C. The Relationship Between Perceived Effectiveness and Education/Training of Nigerian Managers. Ann Arbor: University Microfilms International, 1983.

Ahmed, Sheikh. The Muslim Concept of Administration. Karachi, Pakistan: Institute of Arts and Design, 1975.

Ajiferuke, M., and J. Boddewyn. "Culture and Other Explanatory Variables in Comparative Management Studies." Academy of Management Journal 13 (1970):153-163.

Albert, Ethel M. "Socio-Political Organization and Receptivity to Change: Some Differences Between Ruanda and Urundi." Southwestern Journal of Anthropology 16 (Spring 1960):46-74.

Altimus, C., Jr., et. al. "Cross-Cultural Perspectives on Need Deficiencies of Blue-Collar Workers." Quarterly Journal of Management Development 2 (June 1971): 91-103.

Armenakis, A.A.; A.G. Bedeian, and S.B. Pond, III. "Research Issues in OD Evaluation Past, Present and Future." Academy of Management Review 8 (Apr. 1983): 230-238.

Badaway, M.K. "Styles of Middle East Managers." California Management Review 22 (Spring 1980): 51-58.

Badaway, M.K. "Role Orientations of Middle Eastern Executives: A Cross-Cultural Analysis." Human Organization 39 (1980): 271-275.

Baldridge, J. Victor, and Robert A. Burnham. "Organizational Innovation: Individual, Organizational and Environmental Impacts." Administrative Science Quarterly 20 (1975): 165-176.

Balogun, M.J. "Decentralization under Civilian and Military Regimes: The Pattern in Western Nigeria, 1953-73." Studies in Comparative Local Government 8 (1974): 50-58.

Barlett, Peggy, ed. Agricultural Decision-Making: Anthropological Contributions to Rural Development. New York:Academic Press, 1980.

Barrett, B.W., and B.M. Bass. "Cross Cultural Issues in Industrial and Organizational Psychology." In Handbook of Industrial and Organizational Psychology, edited by M.D. Dunnette. Chicago:Rand McNally Publishing Company, 1976.

Bass, Bernard M. "Combining Management Training and Research." Training and Development Journal 21 (1967): 2-7.

Bass, Bernard M. "Utility of Managerial Self-planning on a Simulated Production Task with Replications in Twelve Countries." Journal of Applied Psychology 62 (1977): 506-509.

Bass, Bernard M., and Philip C. Burger. Assessment of Managers: An International Comparison. New York: The Free Press, 1979.

Bennett, Mick. "Testing Managment Theories Cross-culturally." Journal of Applied Psychology 62 (Oct 1977): 578-581.

Bennett, R. Management Research: Guide for Institutions and Professionals Geneva: International Labour Office, 1983.

Benzi, E.J. "Managers Abroad - They Are Different." Advanced Management Journal 33 (1968): 31-36.

Berry, Albert K., and William R. Cline. Agrarian Structure and Production in Developing Countries. Baltimore: The Johns Hopkins University Press, 1979.

Berry, J.W. "Research in Multicultural Societies: Implications for Cross-Cultral Methods." Journal of Cross-Cultural Psychology 10, no. 4 (1979): 415-434.

Bhagat, S. Rabi, and Sara J. McQuaid. "Role of Subjective Culture in Organizations: A Review and Directions for Future Research." Journal of Applied Psychology 67 (Oct. 1982): 653-685.

Blimes, Jacob Maury. "Interaction and Decision-Making in a Northern Thai Village." Unpublished Ph.D. Dissertation, Stanford University, 1974.

Blunt, Peter. "Cultural and Situational Determinants of Job Satisfaction Amongst Management in South Africa - A Research Note." Journal of Management Studies 10 (1973): 133-140.

Boyd, Tom. "Value Orientations Influencing Decision Making in Rural Communities: An Exploratory Study." Development and Change 2, no. 2 (1971/72): 41-58.

Braibanti, Ralph, ed. Asian Bureaucratic Systems. Durham: Duke University Press, 1966.

Brislin, Richard W. "Cross-Cultural Research Methods." In Human Behavior and Environment edited by Irwin Altman, Amos Rapoport, and Joachim F. Wohlinwill. New York: Plenum Publishing Co, 1980.

Britain, Gerald M., and R. Cohen, eds. Hierarchy and Society. Anthropological Perspectives on Bureaucracy. Philadelphia: I.S.H.I Publications, 1980.

Britto, A.J. "Cultural Variables and Managerial Effectiveness: Is Western Know-how Transferable?" Social Action 23 (1973): 1-11.

Brokensha, David; D.M. Warren, and Oswald Werner. Indigenous Knowledge Systems and Development. Washington D.C.: University Press of America, 1980.

Brossard, M., and M. Maurice. "Is There a Universal Model of Organizational Structure?" International Studies of Management and Organization 6 (Fall 1976).

Butterfield, D.A., and G.F. Farris. "The Likert Organizational Profile: Methodological Analysis and Test of System 4 Theory in Brazil." Journal of Applied Psychology 59 (Feb. 1974): 15-23).

Cancian, Frank. "Can Anthropology Help Agricultural Development?" Culture and Agriculture 2 (1977).

Carlson, J.A., and C.M. Davis. "Cultural Values and the Risky Shift. A Cross Cultural Test in Uganda and the U.S." Journal of Personality and Social Psychology 20 (1971): 392.

Casley, D.J., and D.A. Lury. Data Collection in Developing Countries. New York: Oxford University Press, 1981.

Cavusgil, S.T. "Transfer of Management Know-how to Developing Countries: An Empirical Investigation." Journal of Business Research 12 (Mar 1984): 35-45.

Chenery, Hollis B. "Interaction Between Theory and Observation in Development." World Development 11 (Oct. 1983): 853-861.

Child, John. "Culture, Contingency and Capitalism in the Cross-National Study of Organizations." In Research in Organizational Behavior 3, edited by L.L. Cummings and B.M. Staw. Greenwich: JAI Press, 1981.

Child, John and Monir Tayeb. "Theoretical Perspective in Cross-national Organizational Research." International Studies of Management and Organization 12 (Winter 1982-83): 23-70.

Cleave, John H. "Decision making on the African Farm." IAAE Occasional Paper. No.1 (1977): 157-79. Issued in World Bank Reprint Series, no. 92.

Copur, Halil. Local Organization Dimensions of Rural Development in Turkey: Socio-Economic Stratification Orientations Toward Participation, and Attitudinal Modernity. n.p.: 1980.

Coward, E. Walter, Jr. and G. Levine. The Analysis of Local Social Organization for Irrigation Project Preparation Studies: An Exploration of Possibilities. Paper prepared for World Bank Sociological Workshop. 1978.

Cruzier, M. "The Cultural Determinants of Organizational Behavior." In Anant Environmental Settings in Organizational Functioning. edited by R. Negandhi. Kent: Comparative Administration Research Institute, Kent State University, 1973.

Das, G.S. "Organizational Determinants of Anxiety Based Managerial Stress." Vikalpa 7 (July 1982): 217-223.

Das, T.H. "Qualitative Research in Organizational Behavior." Journal of Management Studies 20 (July 1983): 301-314.

de la Torre, Jose, and Brian Toyne. "Cross-National Managerial Integration: A Conceptual Model." *Academy of Management Review* 3 (July 1978): 462-474.

DeNisi, A., M. Watson, A. Al-jafary, and A. Hollingsworth. "Management in Transition: A Study of Management Styles in Saudi Arabia." Accepted: Academy of Management Meeting. Dallas, 1983.

Desai, K. G. "A Comparative Study of Blue Collar and White Collar Workers." *Indian Journal of Social Work* 28 (1968): 379-387.

Dhingra, O. P., and V. K. Pathak. "Organizational Culture and Managers." *Indian Journal of Industrial Relations* 8, no. 3 (January 1973): 387-405.

Dlugos, G., and K. Wierermain, eds. *Management Under Differing Value Systems*. Berlin: de Gruyter, 1981.

Doktor, Robert. "A Cognitive Approach to Culturally Appropropriate HRD Programs. *Training and Development Journal* 36 (Oct. 1982): 32-36.

England, G. W. *The Manager and His Values: An International Perspective from the United States, Japan, Korea, India and Australia*. Cambridge: Ballinger Publishing Company, 1976.

England, G. W., and I. Harpaz. "Some Methodological and Analytic Considerations in Cross-National Comparative Research." *Journal of International Business Studies* 14, no. 2 (Fall 1983): 49-59.

England, G. W., and R. Lee. "The Relationship Between Managerial Values and Managerial Success in the U.S., Japan, India, and Australia." *Journal of Applied Psychology* 59, no. 4 (1974): 411-419.

England, G. W.; A. R. Negandhi, and B. Wilpert, eds. *Organizational Functioning in a Cross Cultural Perspective*. Kent State: Comparative Administration Research Institute, Kent State University, 1979.

Evans, William. "Measuring the Impact of Culture on Organizations." *International Studies of Management and Organization* 5, no. 1 (1975): 91-113.

Evans, William. "Organizational Research: Cross National and Cross Cultural" *International Studies of Management and Organization.* 5 (1975).

Everett, James E.; B. W. Stening, and P. A. Longton. "Some Evidence for An International Managerial Culture." *Journal of Management Studies* 19 (1982): 153-162.

Farmer, Richard N. "Organizational Transfer and Class Structure." *Academy of Management Journal* 9 (Sept 1966): 204-216.

Farmer, Richard N., ed. *Advances in International Comparative Management*. Greenwich: JAI Press, 1984.

Farmer, Richard N., and Barry M. Richman. "A Model for Research in Comparative Management." *California Management Review* 7 (Winter 1964): 55-68.

Farris, George F., and Anthony D. Butterfield. "Control Theory in Brazilian Organization." *Administrative Science Quarterly* 17 (1972): 574-585.

Faucheux, Claude, and Jacques Rojot. "Social Psychology & Industrial Relations: A Cross Cultural Perspective." Chapter 2 in *Industrial Relations: A Social Psychological Approach*. edited by G.M. Stephenson and C.J. Brotherton. New York: John Wiley & Sons, 1979.

Fiedler, F.; G.E. O'Brien, and D. R. Llgen. "The Effect of Leadership Style Upon the Performance and Adjustment of Volunteer Teams Operating in Stressful Foreign Environment." *Human Relations* 22 (1969): 503-514.

Fiedler, F. "The Effect of Leadership and Cultural Heterogeneity on Group Performance: A Test of the Contingency Model." *Journal of Experimental Social Psychology* 2 (1966): 237-264.

Fernea, Robert A. *Shaykh and Effendi: Changing Patterns of Authority among the El Shabana of Southern Iraq*. Cambridge: Harvard University Press, 1970.

Fliegel, Frederick C. "A Comparative Analysis of the Impact of Industrialism on Traditional Values." *Rural Sociology* 41, no. 1 (1976): 431-451.

Foa, U. G., and M. M. Chemers. "The Significance of Role Behavior Differentiation for Cross-cultrual Interaction Training." *International Journal of Psychology* 2, no. 1 (1967): 45-57.

Form, W. H., and A.A. Blum. *Industrial Relations and Social Change in Latin America*. Gainesville: University of Florida Press, 1965.

Freeman, H. E. et al. "Guatemalan and U.S. Concepts of Success and Failures." Human Organization 40 (Summer 1981): 140-145.

Friedmann, J., and G. Abonyi. "Social Learning: A Model for Policy Research." Environment and Planning Annual 8 (1976): 927-940.

Fromm, E., and M. Maccoby. Social Character in a Mexican Village. Englewood Cliffs: Prentice-Hall, 1970.

Fyans, L. J. Jr., et al. "Cross Cultural Explorations into the Meaning of Achievement." Journal of Personal and Social Psychology 44 (May 1983): 1000-13.

Ganesh, S. R., and P. Joshi. "Exploration of Relationships Between Leadership Behavior, Institution Building Processes and Institutional Performance: Preliminary Work with Reference to Dr. Vickram Sarabhai." Based on the General Processual Model of Institutional Building. Indian Inst. Of Management, Ahmedabad, 1979.

Gibb, C. "Summary report: International Conference on Social Psychological Research in Developing Countries: Ibadan, Nigeria, 29 December 1966--5 January 1967." Australian Psychologist 2, no. 1 (1967): 40-45.

Glaser, W. "Cross National Comparisons of Organizations." In Organizational Theory edited by M. Landau. Chapel Hill: Duke University Press, 1972.

Goodman, Paul and B. Moore. "Critical Issues of Cross-Cultural Management Research." Human Organization 31, no. 1 (1972): 39-45.

Goodstein, Leonard. "Commentary: Do American Theories Apply Abroad?" Organizational Dynamics 10 (Summer 1981): 49-54.

Graham, W. K., and K. H. Roberts. Comparative Studies in Organizational Behavior. New York: Holt, 1972.

Graves, D. "Cultural Determinism and Management Behavior." Organizational Dynamics 1 (1972):46-59.

Graves, D. Management Research - A Cross-Cultural Perspective. London: Elsevier Scientific Pub. Co., 1973.

Gregory, K.L. "Native View Paradigms: Multiple Culture Conflicts in Organizations." Administrative Science Quarterly 28 (Sept. 1983): 359-376.

Gudykunst, William B. Intercultural Communication Theory Beverly Hills: Sage Publications, 1983.

Gudykunst, William B., and Young Yun Kim. Methods for Intercultural Communication Research. Beverly Hills: Sage Publications, 1984.

Habibullah, M. "Managerial Motivation." Management Development (Bangledesh) 6 (1975):19-32.

Haire; M., E. E. Ghiselli, and L. W. Porter. "Cultural Patterns in the Role of the Manager." Industrial Relations 2 (1963): 95-117.

Hall, Budd L. "Participatory Research: Expanding the Base of Analysis." International Development Review (Focus) 19, no. 4 (1977): 23-26.

Halpern, Joel J. "Culture Change in Laos and Serbia: Possible Tendencies toward Universal Organizational Patterns." Human Organization 20 (Spring 1961):11-14.

Halpern, Manfred. The Politics of Social Change in the Middle East and North Africa. Princeton: Princeton University Press, 1969.

Harris, D. G. "How National Cultures Shape Management Styles." Management Review 71 (July 1982): 58-61.

Harrison, R. Work and Motivation: A Study of Village-Level Agricultural Extension Workers in the Western State of Nigeria. Ibadan: Nigerian Institute of Social and Economic Research, 1969.

Heller, F. A.; R. Mays, and B. Wilpert. Methodology for Multinational Study of Managerial Behaviour: The Use of Contingency Theory. Presented at the 3rd Congress of Cross-Cultural Psychology, Tilburg, Netherlands, 1976.

Helmich, D. L., and A. J. Papageorge. "Cross-cultural Aspects of Executive Leadership Styles." Akron Business and Economic Review 7 (1976): 28-33.

Herskovits, Melville J. "Motivational and Culture-Patterns in Technological Change" in UNESCO, Social Change and Economic Development (1963): 41-52.

Hesseling, Pjotr. Effective Organization Research for Development. New York: Pergamon Press,1982.

Hesseling, Pjotr. "Studies in Cross-Cultural Organization." Columbia Journal of World Business (Dec. 1973): 120-134.

Hickson, D.J., C.J. McMillan, K. Azumi, and D. Horvath. "Grounds for Comparative Organization Theory: Quicksands or Hardcore?" In *Organizations Alike and Unlike*. edited by Cornelius J. Lammers and David J. Hickson. London: Routhledge and Kegan Paul, 1979.

Hofstede, Geert. "The Cultural Relativity of Organizational Practices and Theories." *Journal of International Business Studies* 14 (Fall 1983): 75-89.

Hofstede, Geert. "The Cultural Relativity of the Quality of Life Concept." *The Academy of Mangement Review* 9, no. 3 (1984): 389-398.

Hofstede, Geert. "Culture and Organizations." *International Studies of Management and Organization* 10 (1981):15-41.

Hofstede, Geert. "Do American Theories Apply Abroad?: A Reply to Goodstein and Hunt." *Organizational Dynamics* 10 (Summer 1981):63-68.

Hofstede, Geert. "Hierarchical Power Distance in Forty Countries." In *Organizations Alike and Unlike: International and Inter-Institutional Studies in the Sociology of Organizations*, edited by C. J. Lammers and D. J. Hickson. London: Routledge and Kegan Paul, 1979.

Hofstede, Geert. "Motivation, Leadership and Organization: Do American Theories Apply Abroad?" *Organizational Dynamics* 9 (Summer 1980): 42-63.

Hofstede, Geert. "National Cultures in Four Dimensions: A Researsch Based Theory of Cultural Differences Among Nations." *International Studies of Management and Organization* 13 (1983): 46-74.

Hong, B.S. *A Study of Management Related Perceptions of Workers with Confucian Cultural Background*. Ann Arbor: University Microfilms International, 1983.

Hopkins, Nicholas S. "Leadership and Consensus in Two Malian Cooperatives." In *The Anthropology of Development in Sub-Saharan Africa*, edited by D. Brokensha and Marian Pearsall. Lexington: Society for Applied Anthropology, 1969.

Horton, S. *Labor Productivity: Un Tour D'Horizon*. World Bank Staff Working Paper No. 497. Washington, DC: The World Bank, October 1981.

Horvath, D., C. J. McMillan; K. Azumi, and D.J. Hickson. "The Cultural Contest of Organizational Control: An International Comparison." In *Organization and Nation*, (The Aston Programme IV) edited by P.J. Hickson and C.J. McMillan. Fainborough, Hampshire: Gower Pub., 1981.

Hunt, John W. "Applying American Behavior Science: Some Cross Cultural Problems." *Organizational Dynamics* 10 (Summer 1981):55-62.

Inzerilli, Giorgio. "Preface: Some Conceptual Issues in the Study of the Relationships Between Organizations and Societies." *International Studies of Management and Organization* 10 (Winter 1980-1981):3-14.

Inzerilli, Giorgio. "Some Hypotheses on the Nature of Managerial Roles in Developing Countries." *Proceedings of the Academy of Management*, edited by J. C. Susbanet. San Francisco: Academy of Management, 1978.

Jaeger, Alfred M. "The Transfer of Organizational Culture Overseas: An Approach to Control in the Multinational Corporation." *Journal of International Business Studies* 14, no. 2 (Fall 1983): 91-113.

Jamieson, Ian N. "The Concept of Culture and its Relevance for an Analysis of Business Enterprise in Different Societies." *International Studies of Management and Organization* 12(Winter 1982-83):71-105.

Johnson, Allen W. "Security and Risk-Taking Among Poor Peasants: A Brazilian Case." In *Studies in Economic Anthropology* edited by George Dalton. Washington, DC: American Anthropological Association, 1971.

Kakar, Sudhir. "Authority Patterns and Subordinates' Behavior in Indian Organizations." *Administrative Science Quarterly* 16, no. 1 (Sept. 1971): 298-307.

Kakar, Sudhir. "Authority Relations in Indian Organizations." *Management International Review* 12 (1972): 51-56.

Kanungo, R. N. "Work Alienation and the Quality of Work Life: A cross-cultural Perspective." Paper presented at the 20th International Congress of Applied Psychology, Edinburgh, Scotland, 1982.

Kanungo, R.N., and Richard W. Wright. "A Cross-Cultural Comparative Study of Managerial Job Attitudes." *Journal of International Business Studies* 14 (Fall 1983): 115-129.

Kaplan, B. ed. *Studying Personality Cross-Culturally*. New York: Harper, 1961.

Kapp, W. K. *Hindu Culture: Economic Development and Economic Planning In India*. New York: Asia Publishing House, 1963.

Kearl, Bryant, ed. *Field Data Collection in the Social Sciences: Experiences in Africa and the Middle East*. New York: Agricultural Development Council, 1976.

Khandwalla, P.N. "Validating an Instrument for Measuring Pioneering Motivation." *Indian Inst. of Management Ahmedabad*, n.d.

Kiggundu, M. "The Quality of Working Life in developing countries: Beyond the sociotechnical model." Paper presented at the 20th International Congress of Applied Psychology, Edinburgh, Scotland, 1982.

Klauss, R., and B. M. Bass. "Group Influence on Individual Behavior Across Cultures." *Journal of Cross-Cultural Psychology* 5 (1974): 236-46.

Koontz, Harold. "The Management Theory Jungle." *Academy of Management Journal* 4, no. 3 (Dec. 1961): 174-188.

Koontz, Harold. "The Management Theory Jungle Revisited." *Academy of Mangement Journal* 23, no. 2 (1980).

Koontz, Harold. "Model for Analyzing the University and Transferability of Management." *Academy of Management Journal* 12, no. 12 (1969): 415-430.

Koppel, B., and C. Schlegel. "Sociological Perspectives on Energy and Rural Development: A Review of Major Frameworks for Research on Developing Countries." *Rural Sociology* 46 (Summer 1981): 215-219.

Korten, D. C. "Situational Determinants of Leadership Structure." *The Journal of Conflict Resolution* 6, no. 3 (Sept. 1962): 222-235.

Kraut, Allen I. "Some Recent Advances in Cross-National Management Research." *Academy of Management Journal* 18 (Sept. 1975): 538-547.

Kyi, Khin Maung, and R.S. Wickramasuriya. "Educational Profiles of Singapore Managers." *Singapore Management Review* 6, no. 2 (July 1984): 53-70.

Langenderfer, Harold Q. "The Egyptian Executive: A Study in Conflict." *Human Organization* 24, no. 1 (Spring 1965):89-95.

Lasswell, Harold D., Daniel Lerner, and John D. Montgomery. *Values and Development: Appraising Asian Experience*. Cambridge: MIT Press, 1977.

Laurent, A. *Cultural Dimensions of Managerial Ideologies: National vs. Multinational Cultures*. Paper presented at the 5th Annual Meeting of the European International Business Association, London Business School, England, 1979.

Laurent, Andre. "The Cultural Diversity of Management Conceptions." *International Studies of Management and Organization* 13 (Spring 1983)

Laurent, Andre. "Matrix Organizations and Latin Cultures: A Note on the Use of Comparative Research." *International Studies of Management and Organization* 10 (Winter 1980-1981): 101-114.

Lee, J.A. "The Social Science Bias in Management Research (Values of Managers vs. Behavioral Scientists)." *Business Horizons* 26 (May-June 83): 42-50, Discussion 25 (N-D 82): 21-31.

Lee, Y. *A Comparative Study of Managers' Perceptions in Korea and the U.S. on Selected Socio-cultural Dimensions*. Ann Arbor: University Microfilms International, 1982.

Lewis-Beck, Michael S. "Influence Equality of Organizational Innovation in a Third World Nation: An Additive - Non-Additive Model." *American Journal of Political Science* 21 (1977): 1-11.

Lincoln, J.R.; J. Olson, and M. Hanada. "Cultural Effects on Organizational Structure: The Case of Japanese Firms in the United States." *American Sociological Review* 43 (1978): 829-847.

Lincoln, J.R.; M. Hanada, and J. Olson. "Cultural Orientations and Individual Reactions to Organizations: A Study of Employees of Japanese Owned Firms." *Administrative Science Quarterly* 26 (Mar. 1981): 93-115.

Lindzey G., and E. Aronson. eds. *The Handbook of Social Psychology*. (2nd ed.) Reading: Addison-Wesley, 1968-1969.

Louis, Meryl R. "A Cultural Perpsective on Organizations: The Need for and Consequences of Viewing Organizations as Culture-Bearing Milieux." Paper presented at the National Academy of Management Meeting. Detroit: August 1980.

Machungwa, P. D. and N. Schmitt. "Work Motivation in a Developing Country." *Journal of Applied Psycology* 68 (Feb. 1983): 31-42.

Macrae, J. "Underdevelopment and the Economics of Corruption: A Game Theory Approach." *World Development* 10 (Aug. 1982): 677-87.

McCann, E. "An Aspect of Management Philosophy in the U.S. and Latin America." In *Management in International Perspective* edited by S.B. Prasad. New York: Appleton-Century-Croft, 1967.

McCann, E. "Anglo American and Mexican Management Philosophies." MSU Business Topics, Summer 1970: 28-37.

McClelland, David C.; and David G. Winter. *Motivating Economic Achievement*, New York: The Free Press, 1969.

McCollom, I. "Industrial Psychology Around the World: Part II." Eastern Europe, Africa, Asia, and Australia *International Review of Applied Psychology* 17 (1968): 137-152.

Macy, Joanna. *Dharma and Development: Religion as a Resource in the Sarvodaya Movement*. West Hartford: Kumarian Press, 1985.

Mangin, William. "Thoughts on Twenty-Four Years of Work in Peru: The Vicos Project and Me." *Long-Term Field Research in Social Anthropology*. New York: Academic Press, 1979.

Maule, H. G. "The Application of Industrial Psychology to Developing Countries. *International Labour Review* 92, no. 4 (1965): 284-297.

Maurice, Marc. "Introduction: Theoretical and Ideological Aspects of the Universalistic Approach to the Study of Organizations." *International Studies of Management and Organizations* 6 (1976): 3-10.

Mazur, A., and E. Rosa. "Empirical Test of McClelland's Achieving Society Theory." *Social Forces* 55 (March 1977): 769-774.

Meade, R.D., and J.O. Whittaker. "A Cross-Cultural Study of Authoritarianism." *Journal of Social Psychology* 72 (1967): 3-7.

Mencher, Joan P. "The Caste System Upside Down, or the Not-So-Mysterious East." *Current Anthropology* 15, no. 4 (1974): 469-494.

Mendonsa, Eugene L. "Elders, Office-Holders and Ancestors Among the Sisala of Norther Ghana." *Africa* 46, no. 1 (1976): 57-65.

Meltzer, H., and Walter Nord. "The Present Status of Industrial and Organizational Psychology." *Personnel Psychology* 26 (1973): 11-29.

Meyer, Alan. "How Ideologies Supplant Formal Structures and Shape Responses to Environments." *Journal of Management Studies* 19 (1981): 45-61.

Miller, Norman N. "The Political Survival of Traditional Leadership." *Journal of Modern African Studies* 6, no. 2 (1968): 183-198.

Miller, Stephen W., and Jack L. Simonetti. "Culture and Management: Some Conceptual Considerations." *Management International Review* 11, no. 6 (1974): 87-100.

Milne, R. S. "Mechanistic and Organic Models of Public Administration in Developing Countries." *Administrative Science Quarterly* 15 (1970): 57-67.

Montgomery, J. "Allocation of Authority in Land Reform Programmes: A Comparative Study of Administrative Process and Outputs." *Administrative Science Quarterly* 17, no. 1 (1972): 62-75.

Moore, R. "The Cross Cultural Study of Organizational Behavior." *Human Organization* 33 (1974): 37-45.

Moscardi, Edgardo, and Alain deJanury. "Attitudes Toward Risk Among Peasants: An Econometric Approach." *American Journal of Agricultural Economics* 59, no. 4 (1977): 710-716.

Moulik, T.K. "On Entrepreneurial Achievements in an Industrially Progressive Rural Setting." *Administration for Rural Development* (1981): 163-178.

MOW International Research Team. "The Meaning of Working." In *Management Under Differing Value Systems: Political, Social and Economical Perspectives in a Changing World*. edited by G. Dlugos and K. Weiermair. Berlin-New York: Walter De Gruyter & Co., 1981.

Mulford, Charles L. and Mary A. Mulford. "Commitment and Interorganizational Perspectives on Cooperation and Conflict." *Rural Sociology* 42, no. 4 (1977): 569-590.

Murrell, K.L. "A Cultural Analysis of the Egyptian Management Environment." In *Innovation in Global Consultation.* edited by Philip R. Harris and Garld H. Malin. Washington, DC: ICF (1979).

Nath, R. "A Methodological Review of Cross-Cultural Management Research." *International Social Science Journal* 20 (Jan. 1968): 35-61.

Nebeker, Delert M. "Situational Favorability and Perceived Environmental Uncertainty: An Integrative Approach." *Administrative Science Quarterly* 20 (1975): 281-294.

Negandhi, Anant. "Comparative Management and an Open System Theory." *Academy of Management Proceedings.* (1973): 150-155a.

Negandhi, Anant. "American Management Abroad: A Comparative Study of Management Practices of American Subsidiaries and Local Firms in Developing Countries." *Management International Review* 11 (1971): 97-107.

Negandhi, Anant. "Comparative Management and Organization Theory A Marriage Needed." *Academy of Management Journal* 18, no. 2 (June 1975): 334-344.

Negandhi, Anant "Cross-cultural Management Research: Trends and Future Directions." *Journal of International Business Studies* 14 (Fall 1983): 17-28.

Negandhi, Anant. "Cross-Cultural Management Studies -- Too Many Conclusions, Not Enough Conceptualization." *Management International Review* 14 (1974): 59-67.

Negandhi, Anant. "Management in the Third World (comparison of American Subsidiaries with comparable local firms in six developing countries). In *Advances in International Comparative Management.* edited by R.N. Farmer. Greenwich: JAI Press, 1984.

Negandhi, Anant. *Organization Theory in an Open System: A Study of Transferring Advanced Management Practices to Developing Nations.* New York:Dunellen Publishing Co., 1975.

Negandhi, Anant, and B.D. Estafen. "A Model for Analyzing Organizations in Cross-Cultural Settings: A Conceptual Scheme and Some Research Findings." *Comparative Administration and Research Conference.* Kent: Kent University, 1969.

Negandhi, Anant, and B.D. Estafen. "A Research Model to Determine the Applicability of American Management Know-How in Different Cultures and/or Environments." *Academy of Management Journal* 8 (1965):309-318.

Negandhi, Anant, and B. Raimann. "A Contingency Theory on Organization Re-examined in the Context of a Developing Country." *Academy of Management Journal* 2 (1972): 137-146.

Negandhi, Anant and D. Robey. "Understanding Organizational Behavior in Multinational and Multicultural Settings." *Human Resource Management* 16, no. 1 (Spring 1977): 16-239.

Oberg, W. "Cross-cultural Perspectives on Management Principles." *Academy of Management Journal* 6 (1963):129-143.

Onibokun, Adepoju. "Directions for Social Research on Self-Help Projects and Programmes in Nigeria." *Community Development Journal* 11 (1976): 60-69.

Orpen, C. "Risk Taking Attitudes Among Indian, U.S. and Japanese Managers." *Journal of Social Psychology* 120 (Aug. 1983): 283-84.

Ostor, Akos. *Culture and Power.* Beverly Hills: Sage Publications, 1984.

Palmer, D., J. Veiga, and J. Vora. "Managerial Value Profiles Decisions in a Cross Cultural Setting." *Academy of Management Proceedings,* (1979):133-37.

Pareek, U. and Khanduralla and Anuthai. "Indigenous Styles of Management." *Indian Institute of Management* Ahmedabad: n.d.

Pennings J. "The Relevance of the Structural Contingency Model for Organizational Effectiveness." *Administrative Science Quarterly* 20 (1975):393-410.

Perrow, C. *Organizational Analysis: A Sociological View.* Beont: Wadsworth,1970.

Pestonjee, D.M., and U.B. Singh. *An Intervention on Job Satisfaction as a Function of Role Stress, Locus of Control, Participation and Organizational Climate in an Electricity Supply Company.* P.S.G. Mono No. 47, Ahmedabad: Public Systems Group, Indian Institute of Management, 1982.

Pestonjee, D.M., A.P. Singh, and Y.K. Singh. "Productivity in Relation to Alienation and Anxiety." *Indian Journal of Industrial Relations* 18, (1982): 71-76.

Peterson, Richard B. "A Cross Cultural Perspective of Supervisory Values." *Academy of Management Journal* 15 (Mar. 1972): 106-117.

Pfeiffer, J. "Management as Symbolic Action: The Creation and Maintenance of Orgaizational Paradigms." In *Research in Organizational Behavior*. edited by Larry L. Cummings and Barry M. Staw. Greenwich: JAI Press, 1981.

Pizam, Abraham, and Arie Reichel. "Cultural Determinants of Managerial Behavior." *Management International Review* 17 (1977): 65-72.

Prasad, S. B., ed. *Management In International Perspective*. New York: Appleton-Century, 1967.

Pratap, Reddy, K. "Impact of Culture on Organizational Design." *Vikalpa* 9, no. 2 (1984): 143-154.

Rao, T. V., and R. Vijagashree. *Psychological Maturity and Motivational Profile of Management Students*. Ahmedabad, India: PSG Group, Indian Institute of Management, 1983.

Ray, J. J. "Achievement Motivation and Authoritarianism in Manila and some Anglo-Saxon Cities." *Journal of Social Psychology* 115 (Oct. 1981): 3-8.

Raza, M. Ali. "Management Ideologies and Resources in Pakistan." *Journal of Industrial Relations* (Mar 1965): 50-73.

Reading, S. G., and T. A. Martyn-Johns. "Paradigm Differences and Their Relation to Management, with Reference to South-East Asia." In *Organizational Functioning in a Cross-cultural Perspective*. edited by G.W. England, A.R. Negandhi and B. Wilpert. Kent: Comparative Administration Research Institute, 1979.

Redding, S. G. "Cognition as an Aspect of Culture and its Relations to Management Processes: An Exploratory View of the Chinese Case. *Journal of Management Studies* 17 (May 1980): 27-48.

Reddy, K. Pratap. "Impact of Culture on Organizational Design." *Vikalpa* 9 (April-June 1984): 143-154.

Rhinesmith, Steven H. *Cultural Organizational Analysis - The Interrelationships of Value Orientations and Managerial Behavior*. Cambridge: McBer and Co., 1968

Richman, Barry. "Significance of Cultural Variables." *Academy of Management Journal* 8 (Dec 1965): 292-303.

Riggs, F. W. "The Ecology and Context of Public Administration: A Comparative Perspective." *Public Administration Review* 40 (1980): 107-115.

Roberts, K. H. "On Looking at an Elephant: An Evaluation of Cross-Cultural Research Related to Organizations." *Psychological Bulletin* 4 (Nov. 1970): 327-350.

Roberts, R.H., and C. Snow, eds. "A Symposium: Cross National Organizational Research." *Industrial Relations* 14 (May 1975): 137-249.

Rogers, Everett, and Rekha Agarwhla Rogers. *Communication in Organizations*. New York: The Free Press,1976.

Rokkan, S. Comparative Cross-national Research. II bibliography. *International Social Science Bulletin* 1 (1955): 622-641.

Roling, Niels. "Adaptions in Development: A Conceptual Guide for the Study of Noninnovative Responses of Peasant Farmers." *Economic Development and Cultural Change* 19 (1979): 71-85.

Rosen, Bernard C. *The Industrial Connection. Achievement and the Family in Developing Societies*. New York: Aldine Publishers, 1982.

Rossi, I., and E. O'Higgins. *The Development of Theories of Culture*. New York:Praeger, 1980.

Rubin, Herbert J. "Will and Awe: Illustrations of Thai Villager Dependency upon Officials." *Journal of Asian Studies* 32, no. 3 (1973): 425-444.

Rubin, Herbert J., and Irene S. Rubin. "Effects of Institutional Change upon a Dependency Culture: The Commune Council 275 in Rural Thailand." *Asian Survey* 13, no. 3 (1973): 270-287.

Ruhl, Mark J., and Everett Egginton. "The Influence of Agrarian Reform Participation on Peasant Attitudes: The Case of Colombia." *Inter-American Economic Affairs* 28, no. 3 (1974): 27-43.

Ryterband, E.C., and G.V. Barrett. "Manager's Values and Their Relationships to the Management of Tasks: A Cross-Cultural Comparison." In *Managing for Accomplishment* edited by B.M. Bass, R.C. Cooper, J.A. Haas, Lexington: Heath Lexington, 1970.

Sallery, R.D., and H.C. Lindgren. "Arab Attitudes Toward Authority: A Cross-Cultural Study." *Journal of Social Psychology* 69 (1966): 27-31.

Saiyadain, M. S. Personal Characteristics and Job Satisfaction: India-Nigeria Comparison." Working Paper No. 455. Ahmedabad: Indian Institute of Management, 1985.

Salili, F. "Determinants of Achievement Motivation for Women in Developing Countries." Journal of Vocational Behavior 14, no. 3 (1979): 297-305.

Sarien, R.G., ed. Managerial Styles in India. Agra: Ram Prasad, 1973.

Savadogo, B. Management Theory and Socio-Economic Development: An Exploratory Framework for the Study of Development from a Macro Managerial Perspective. Ann Arbor: University Microfilms International, 1983.

Schatzman, Leonard Strouss. Field Research: Stategies for a Natural Sociology. Englewood Cliffs: Prentice Hall, 1973.

Schauup, Dietrich L. A Cross-cultural Study of a Multinational Company. New York: Praeger Publishers, 1978.

Schollhammer, H. "The Comparative Management Theory Jungle." Academy of Mangement Journal 12 (1969): 81-97.

Seibel, H.D., and A. Massing. Traditional Organizations and Economic Development Studies of Indigenous Cooperatives in Liberia. New York: Praeger Publishers, 1974.

Sekaran, U. "Methodological and Theoretical Issues and Advancements in Cross-cultural Research." Journal of International Business Studies 14, no. 2 (Fall 1983): 61-73.

Sekaran, U. "Are U.S. Organizational Concepts and Measures Transferable to Another Culture? An Empirical Investigation." Academy of Management Journal 24 (June 1981): 409-417.

Sekaran, U. "The Dynamics of Job Involvement." Unpublished Ph.D. Dissertation, UCLA, 1977.

Sekaran, U. "Highlights of Some Current and Contemplated Comparative Management and International Research Projects." International Management Division of the Academy of Management, 1982.

Sekaran, U. "Nomological Networks and the Understanding of Organizations in Different Cultures." Proceedings of the Academy of Management. (1982): 54-58.

Sfeir-Younis, Alfredo, and Daniel W. Bromley. Decision Making in Developing Countries: Multiobjective Formulation and Evaluation Methods. New York: Praeger Publishers, 1977.

Sigelman, Lee. "In Search of Comparative Administration." Public Administration Review 36 (1976): 625.

Sirota, D., and J.M. Greenwood. "Understand Your Overseas Work Force." Harvard Business Review 49, no. 1 (1971): 53-60.

Slocum, John W. "A Comparative Study of the Satisfaction of American and Mexican Operatives." Academy of Management Journal 14 (1971): 89-97.

Slocum, John W., and Paul M. Topichak. "Do Cultural Differences Effect Job Satisfaction?" Journal of Applied Psychology 56, no. 2 (1972): 177-178.

Smircich, K. "The Concept of Culture and Organizational Analysis." Paper presented at the ICA/SCA Conference on Interpretive Approaches to Organizational Communication. Alta: (July 1981).

Smircich, L. "Organizations as shared meanings." In Organizational Sympolism edited by Louis R. Pondy, Peter Frost, Gareth Morgan, and Thomas Dandridge. Greenwich: JAI Press, 1983.

Smircich, L. "Studying Organizations as Cultures." In Beyond Method: Social Research Strategies edited by Gareth Morgan. Beverly Hills: Sage, 1983.

Sorge, Arndt. "Cultured Organization." International Studies of Management and Organization 12 (Winter 1982-83): 106-138.

Springer, J. F. "Empirical Theory and Development Administration: Prologue and Promise." Public Administration Review 36 (1976): 636-641.

Springer, J.F., and R.W. Gable. "Impact of Informal Relations on Organizational Rewards: Comparing Bureaucracies in S.E. Asia." Comparative Politics 12 (Jan. 1980): 191-210.

Stephens, D.B. "Cultural Variation in Leadership Style: A Methodological Experiment in Comparing Managers in the U.S. and Peruvian Textile Industries." Management International Review 21, no. 3 (1981): 47-55.

Tapia-Videla, Jorge. "Understanding Organizations and Environments: A Comparative Perspective." Public Administration Review 36, no. 6 (1976): 631-636.

Takezawa, S., and A.M. Whitehall, Jr. "Human Values in Industrial Management." *Cross Cultural Social Psychological Newsletter* 4 (May-June, 1967).

Thiagarajan, K.M. "A Cross-cultural Study of Relationships Between Personal Values and Managerial Behavior." Technical Report No. 23 University of Rochester Management Research Center, 1968.

Thiagerajan, K.M., and S.D. Deep. "A Cross-Cultural Study of Preferences for Participative Decision-Making by Supervisors and Subordinates." Technical Report No. 33 Office of Naval Research, (Sept. 1969).

Thiagarajan, K.M., and W.S. Whittaker. "Realistic Goal Setting as a Key Indicator of Entrepreneurship: A Cross-Cultural Comparison." Technical Report No. 30 Office of Naval Research, Sept. 1969.

Toyne, B. "Host Country Managers of Multinational Firms - Evaluation of Variables Affecting Their Managerial Thinking Patterns." *Journal of International Business Studies* 7 (1976): 39-55.

Triandis, H.C. "Dimensions of Cultural Variation as Parameters of Organization Theories." *International Studies of Management and Organization* 12 (Winter 1982-83): 139-169.

Triandis, H.C. "Interpersonal Relations in International Organizations." *Organizational Behavior and Human Performance* 2 (1967): 26-55.

Triandis, H.C. "Review of Culture Consequences: International Differences in Work Related Values." *Human Organization* 41 (Spring 1982): 86-90.

Trice, Harrison M., and Janice M. Beyer. "The Ceremonial Effect: Manifest Function or Latent Dysfunction in the Dynamic Organization." Paper presented at the Conference on Myths, Symbols, and Folklore: Expanding the Analysis of Organizations. University of California at Los Angeles, 1983.

Tummula, Krishna. *The Ambiguity of Ideology and Administrative Reform.* Bombay:Allied Publishers Private, Ltd., 1979.

Turner, B.A. "The Use of Grounded Theory for the Qualitative Analysis of Organizational Behavior." *Journal of Management Studies* 20 (July 1983): 333-348.

Tyree A. et. al. "Gaps and Glisandes: Inequality, Economic Development and Social Mobility in 24 Countries." *American Sociological Review* 44(Jan 1979):410-424.

UNESCO. *International Social Science Journal* 20, no. 3 (1968). An issue devoted to motivational patterns for moderni- zation.

Van Maanen, J. "The Fact of Fiction in Organizational Ethnography." *Administrative Science Quarterly* 24 (1979): 539-550.

Van Maanen, J. and Stephen R. Barley. *Occupational Communities: Culture and Control in Organizations.* TR-10, Cambridge: Sloan School of Management, MIT (1982).

Waldo, Dwight, Symposium Editor. "Symposium: Comparative and Development Administration, Retrospect and Prospect." *Public Administration Review* 36 (1976): 615-654.

Webber, Ross. *Culture and Management: Text and Readings in Comparative Management.* Homewood: R.D. Irwin, 1969.

Whitely, W.T., and G.W. England. "Variability in Common Dimensions of Managers Values Due to Value Orientation and Country." *Personnel Psychology* 33 (1980): 77-90.

Whorton, Joseph W., and John A. Worthley. "A Perspective on the Challenge of Public Management: Environmental Paradox and Organizational Culture." *Academy of Management Review* 6 (1981): 357-363.

Whyte, W.F. *Organizational Behavior: Theory and Application.* Homewood: Irwin-Dorsey, 1969.

Wilbert, Bernard, A. Kudat, and Y. Ozkan, eds. *Workers Participation in an Internationalized Economy.* Kent: Kent State Univ. Press, 1978.

Wilkins, A. L., and W. G. Ouchi. "Efficient Cultures: Exploring the Relationship Between Culture and Organizational Performance." *Administrative Science Quarterly* 28 (Sept. 83): 468-481.

Williams, L.K., W.F. Whyte, and C.S. Green. "Do Cultural Differences Affect Workers' Attitudes?" *Industrial Relations* 5, no. 3 (May 1966) 105-117.

Wright, G. "Cultural and Task Influence on Decision Making Under Uncertainty." *Current Anthropology* 22 (June 1981): 290-1.

Zurcher, L.A. "Value Orientation, Role Conflict, and Alienation from Work: A Cross-Cultural Study." *Dissertation Abstracts* 26, no. 8 (1966): 48-58.

SECTION III

IMPLEMENTATION LITERATURE

This section is concerned with recent efforts to actually build the managerial infrastructure of nations, and so the authors and editors are most often practitioners. The word "implementation" is not limited to the stricter sense of project implementation, but rather encompasses the complete range of activities from planning through evaluation. It includes those projects carried out both with and without the assistance of international development agencies. The full range of topics are listed and coded for easier reference on the following page.

The body of literature that could have been included in this section is immense, especially if one digresses too far into specific sector development such as integrated rural development and community development. Whole bibliographies have been devoted to these, and as much of this literature goes beyond our narrower scope, it has been largely omitted.

The focus is on the timely issues facing the development of management infrastructure. Emphasis is placed on methodology. Citations more than ten years old have been largely omitted because of space limitations. There is also a limited number of general works on management, administration or organization. The ones included are less western culture bound and are therefore more readily transferable.

Finally, the editors have included a broad representation of literature originating in the developing nations. This is an extremely important feature of this bibliography, and we are indebted to our global network for making it a reality.

Subject Codes

Overall Focus

(M) Management Development Centered (skill building/training)

- focus on the individual manager/administrator
- formal programs as well as those integrated into actual task or work performance

(O) Organizational Development, institution building, administrative system design and reform

- focus on overall organization and includes environmental interface areas

General Settings: Sector Development

(1) IRD - integrated rural development
    - agriculture, fisheries, forestry,

(2) Public Service Sector

- health, traffic, transport, population, education

(3) Industrial, business, entrepreneurship

(4) Community Development

- participation
- programs to build skills and voice of community

Specific Skills Process

(PO) policy formulation, strategy, planning, guidelines, organization and design

(PI) project implementation and management

(EM) evaluation, monitoring and control

(DM) decision making and analysis

(IS) MIS, communications and use of information

(HR) HRD, personnel, gender issues

(FB) finance, accounting and budgeting

(TA) technical assistance, cooperation and consulting

Abramson, Robert. An Integrated Approach To Organization Development and Performance Improvement Planning. West Hartford: Kumarian Press, 1978.
O-PO.

Abramson, R., and W. Halset. "Planning for Improved Enterprise Performance: A Guide for Managers and Consultants. Management Development Series No. 15 Geneva: I.L.O., 1979.

Adams, J.R., and M.S. Kirchof. "Developing Project Managers: Adapting Training to an Organization's Needs." In Project Management Tools and Visions. Copenhagen: Report of the 7th World Congress on Project Management, 1982.
M-PI

Adedeji, Adebayo, ed. Problems and Techniques of Administrative Training in Africa. Ife, Nigeria: University of Ife Press, 1969.
M-

Adler, John M. "The Economic Development Institute of the World Bank." International Development Review 5 (Mar. 1963): 7-13.
M-EM

Adler, Nancy J. "Cultural Synergy: The Management of Cross-cultural Organizations." In Trends and Issues in O.D.: Current Theory and Practice edited by W. Warner Burke and Leonard D. Goodstein. San Diego: University Associates, 1980.
MO

Adler, Nancy J., and Moses N. Kiggundu. "Awareness at the Crossroad: Designing Translator Based Training Programs." In Handbook of Intercultural Training: Issues In Training Methodology edited by D. Landis and R. Brislin. New York: Pergamon Press, 1983.
M-TA

Agricultural Information Development Bulletin. "Consultative Meeting on Alternative Strategies for Development with Focus on Local Level Planning and Development." Agricultural Information Development Bulletin 2 (n.d.): 19-21.
1-PS

Ahmad, Y.R. "Administration of Integrated Rural Development Programmes: A Note on Methodology." International Labor Review 3 (Feb. 1975): 119-142.
1-PI

Ajuogu, M.O. "Technology Dynamics in Lifelong Education and Development of Managers in Developing Economies." International Review of Administrative Sciences 47 (1981): 71-76.
M-HR

Aldrich, Howard. "Resource Dependence and Interorganizational Relations: Local Employment Service Offices and Social Services Sector Organizations." Administration and Society 7, no. 4 (1976): 419-453.
O-2-PO

Aldrich, Howard. "Visionaries and Villains: The Politics of Designing Interorganizational Relations." In Organization Design: Theoretical Perspectives and Empirical Findings edited by Elmer Burack and A.R. Negandhi. Kent: Kent State Univ. Press, 1977.
O-PO

Alldred, Neil. "Some Contradictions in Community Development: The Need for a Stronger Community Approach." Community Development Journal 11 (1976): 134-140.
-4-

Al-Salem, Faisal S.A. The Ecological Dimensions of Development Administration. New Delhi: New Delhi Associated Publishing House, 1977.
O-

Alvi, S. "An Overview of Research for Management Training." Pakistan Management Review (Second Quarter 1980): 83-90.
M-HR

Anderson, Dennis. "Small Industry in Developing Countries: A Discussion of Issues." World Development 10 (Nov. 1982): 913-948.
-3-

Anderson, Dennis. Small Industry in Developing Countries: Small Issues. Working Paper 518. Washington, DC: World Bank, 1982.
M-TA

Anderson, L.R. "Management of the Mixed Cultural Work Group." Organizational Behavior and Human Performance 31 (June 1983): 303-330.
M-HR

An Introductory Course in Teaching and Training Methods for Management Development. Seventh impression. Geneva: International Labour Office, 1981.
M-TA

Appleby, Paul H. Public Administration for a Welfare State. New Delhi: IMH Press Private, Ltd., 1961.
O-2-PI

Arensberg, C.M. and Arthur H. Niehoff. Introducing Social Change. A Manual for Community Development 2nd ed., Chicago: Aldine-Atherton, 1971.
-4-TA

Argyris, Chris. *Integrating the Individual and the Organization.* New York: John Wiley and Sons, 1964.
O-

Armor T., G. Honadle, C. Olson, and P. Weisel. "Organizing and Supporting Integrated Rural Development Projects: A Two-fold Approach to Administrative Development." *Journal of Administration Overseas* 18, no. 4 (1979): 276-286.
MO-1-PO

Arnold, Steven H. *Implementing Development Assistance: European Approaches to Basic Needs.* Boulder: Westview Press, 1982.
-PI,TA

Arora, Ramesh, and Jagdish C. Kukar, eds. *Training and Administrative Development.* Jaipur, India: HCM State Institute of Public Administration, 1979.
M-HR

Ashmawg, Saad, and R.W. Revans. *The Nile Project, an Experiment in Educational Autotherapy.* London: ALP International Publications, 1967.
MO-HR

Asian Productivity Organization. *Approaches to Rural Industrialization, Some Experiences.* Tokyo: APO, 1983.

Asian Productivity Organization. *Farm Water Management for Rice Cultivation.* Tokyo: APO, 1971.
M-I

Avriel, D. "Scientists as Consultants to Industry in a Developing Country: An Analysis of Their Roles and Economic Effectiveness." *Research Policy* (July 1981): 244-259.
-3-TA

Axinn, G.H. "Development Cycle: New Strategies from an Ancient Concept." *International Development Review* 19 (1977): 9-15.
-PO,PI

Axinn, G. H. *New Strategies for Rural Development.* East Lansing: Rural Life Associates, 1978.
-1-PO

Baetz, Reuben C. *Development and Participation: Operational Implications for Social Welfare.* New York: Columbia Univ. Press, 1975.
-2-DM,PI

Bainbridge J., and S. Sapire. *Health Project Management: A Manual of Procedures for Formulating and Implementing Health Projects.* Geneva: United Nations World Health Organization, 1974.
-2-PO,PI

Balassa, Bela. "Reforming the System of Incentives in Developing Countries." Staff Working Paper IBRD-203. Washington, DC: The World Bank, n.d.
O-HR

Baldwin, Gene. "The Diffusion of Management Development and Knowledge and Techniques Among Domestic Institutions in Taiwan." Presentation to the Annual Meeting of the Academy of International Business, Montreal, Quebec, 1981.
M-HR

Barnett, Stanley A., and Nat Engel. *Effective Institution Building: A Guide for Project Designers and Project Managers Based on Lessons Learned from the AID Portfolio.* AID Program Evaluation Discussion Paper No. 11, Office of Evaluation, Bureau for Program and Policy Coordination. Washington, DC: USAID, 1982.
O-PO,PI,EM

Barriga, C. *Management in Cooperative Farming: Its Importance For Agricultural Development, With A Comparative Study.* Ann Arbor: University Microfilms International, 1973.
-1-PO,EM

Baum, Warren C. "The Project Cycle." *Finance and Development* 7, no. 2 (June 1970): 2-13.
-PO,TA,PI

Baumgartel, H. "The Penetration of Modern Management Technology and Organizational Practices in Indian Business Organizations." *Indian Administrative and Management Review* 3 (1971): 1-13.
MO-3

Beer, Michael, and Edgar Huse. "A Systems Approach to Organizational Devlopment." *Journal of Applied Behavioral Science* 8, no. 1 (Jan./Feb. 1972): 79-101.
O

Belshaw, D.G.R., and R. Chambers. *A Management Systems Approach To Rural Development.* Nairobi, Kenya: Institute for Development Studies, University of Nairobi, 1973.
M-1-PI,EM

Belshaw, D.G.R., and R. Chambers. *PIM: A Practical Management System for Implementing Rural Development Programmes and Projects.* Nairobi, Kenya: Institute of Development Studies, University of Nairobi, 1973.
M-1-PI,PO

Bennis, Warren G., Kenneth D. Benne, and Robert Chin, eds. *The Planning of Change.* New York: Holt, Rinehart and Winston, 1976.
O

Bennett, Nicholas. *Barriers and Bridges for Rural Development.* Bangkok: Krung Siam Press, 1978.
-1-PI

Benor, D., and J.Q. Harrison. *Agricultural Extension: The Training and Visit System.* Washington, DC: The World Bank, 1977.
-1-HR,EM

Benveniste, Guy, and Warren F. Ilchman. *Agents of Change: Professionals in Developing Countries.* New York: Praeger Publishers Co., 1969.
MO-TA

Berger, Peter L., and Richard J. Neuhaus. *To Empower People: The Role of Mediating Structures in Public Policy.* Washington, DC: American Enterprise Institute for Public Policy Research, 1977.
O-4-PO

Berger, W. "Local Initiative and the Planning Process in Developing Countries." *Sociologia Ruralis* 10, no. 1 (1970): 57-73.
-4-PO

Bertrand, O., J. Timar, and F. Achio. "The Planning of Training in the Third World." *International Labour Review* 120, no. 5 (1981): 531-544.
-HR,PO

Bharati, Agehananda. "Cultural Hurdles in Development Administration." In *Development Administration: Concepts and Problems.* edited by Irving Swerdlow. Syracuse: Syracuse University Press, 1963.
MO-TA

Biddle, W. "Deflating the Community Developer." *Community Development Journal* 3, no. 4 (1968): 191-194.
-4-HR

Bjur, Wesley. "The International Manager and the Third Sector." Public Administration Review 35 (1975) 453-467
M-3

Black, Joseph E., Laurence D. Stifel, and James S. Coleman, eds. *Education and Training for Public Sector Management.* New York: Rockefeller Foundation, 1977.
M-2-HR

Blue, Richard. "Institution Building and the Foreign Aid Relationship." In *Rural Development: The Interplay of Analysis and Action* edited by Amy G. Monn and Jan Mirocle. PASITAM, Bloomington: International Development Research Center, Indiana University, 1975.
O-1-TA

Boon, G.K. "Dualism and Technological Harmony for Balanced Development." *Industry and Development* 9 (1983): 51-73
O-3-PO

Boserup, Ester, and Christina Liljencrantz. "Integration of Women in Development: Why, When, How." New York: United Nations Development Programme: 1975.
-HR

Bottral, A.F. *Comparative Study of the Management and Organization of Irrigation Projects.* Staff Working Paper no. 458. Washington, DC: The World Bank, 1981.
MO-1-PI

Bottral, A.F. "Technology of Management in Irrigated Agriculture." *Overseas Development Institute Review* 2 (1978): 22-50.
M-1-PI

Bourgeois, L.J. III, and M. Boltvinik. "OD in Cross Cultural Settings: Latin America." *California Management Review* 23, no. 3 (Spring 1981): 75-81.
O-TA

Boyatzis, Richard E. *The Competent Manager: A Model For Effective Performance.* New York: Wiley Interscience, 1982.
M-HR,EM

Boydell, Tom. *Management Self Development.* Management Development Series No. 21. Geneva: I.L.O., in preparation.
M-

Braibanti, Ralph. "Administrative Reform in the Context of Political Growth." In *Frontiers of Development Administration.* edited by Fred W. Riggs, Chpt. 6. Durham: Duke Univ. Press, 1970.
O-PO

Braun, H.G. "Concepts and Problems of Decentralized Industrialization in Developing Countries." *Economics* 24 (1981): 68-86.
MO-3-PO

Branch, Kristi, Douglas A. Hooper, James Thompson, and James Creighton. *Guide to Social Assessment: A Framework for Assessing Social Change.* Boulder: Westview Press, 1984.
-EM

Braun, H.G. "Concepts and Problems of Decentralized Industrialization in Developing Countries." *Economics* 24 (1981): 68-86.
MO-3-PO

Brian, J. "Contingency Approach to Management Development: Some Perspectives and A Diagnostic Model." Management International Review 19, no. 1 (1979): 123-128.
M-DM,EM

Brinkerhoff, D. "Inside Public Bureaucracy: Empowering Managers to Empower Clients." Rural Development Participation Review 1, no. 1 (1979): 7-9.
M-1-HR

Brinkerhoff, D. "Linking Accountability, Client Participation and Quality of Life in the Public Sector: A Structural Framework." Review of Public Administration 3, no. 1 (Fall 1982): 67-76.
M-4-EM

Bromley, Daniel W., D. Taylor, and D. Parker. "Water Reform and Economic Development: Institutional Aspects of Water Management in the Developing Countries." Economic Development and Cultural Change 28, no. 2 (1980): 365-387.
O-1-PI

Brown, Anthony. "Technical Assistance to Rural Communities: Stopgap or Capacity Building." Public Administration Review 40, no. 1 (1980): 18-23.
1-TA,PO,HR

Brown, L. David. "Effective Change Strategies for Public Enterprises." Vikalpa 9 (Apr.-June 1984): 97-112.
O-2-PO,HR

Brown-West, O.G. Transportation System Management in Developing Countries: A Review of Programs and A Framework for Effectiveness Evaluation. Ann Arbor: Univ. Microfilms Int'l, 1983.
M-2-EM

Bryant, Coralie. "Organizational Impediments to Making Participation A Reality: 'Swimming Upstream in AID.'" Rural Development Participation Review 1 (1980): 8-10.
MO-TA

Bryant, Coralie and Louise G. White. Managing Rural Development: Peasant Participation in Rural Development. West Hartford: Kumarian Press, 1980.
M-1,4-PO,PI

Bryant, Coralie and Louise G. White. Managing Rural Development With Small Farmer Participation. West Hartford: Kumarian Press, 1984.
M-1-PO,PI

Butterfield, Samuel H. "Rural Development: Why It Is Hard for Development Country Leadership to Get Started." International Development Review 19 (1977): 8-12.
O-1-PO

Caiden, Gerald. "Administrative Reform: A Prospectus." International Review of Administrative Sciences 44 (1978): 106-120.
MO

Caiden, Naomi, and A. Wildavsky. Planning and Budgeting in Poor Countries. New York: John Wiley and Sons, 1974.
-PO,FB

Caire, Guy. "Participation by Employers' and Workers' Organizations in Planning." International Labour Review 96, no. 6 (1967): 557-580.
O-4-DM,PO

Cancian, Frank. "Can Anthropology Help Agricultural Development?" Culture and Agriculture 2 (1977).
-1-po,DM

Canonici, A., J.R. Hopper, and R.J. Levin. "Management Training Overseas: (1) In Developed Nations; (2) In Developing Nations." Personnel 45, no. 5 (1968): 22-35.
M-HR

Carley, Michael J., and Eduardo Bustelo. Social Impact Assessment and Monitoring: A Cross-Disciplinary Guide to the Literature. Boulder: Westview Press, 1984.
-EM

Carpenter, N.R. "Small Farmer Development: The Problems and the Programme From A Farm Management Perspective." Farm Management Notes for Asia and the Far East. 1 (July 1975).
M-1-PO,PI

Casley, Dennis J., and Denis A. Lury. Monitoring and Evaluation of Agriculture and Rural Development Projects. Washington, DC: The World Bank, 1982.
M-1-EM

Casse, Pierre. Training for the Cross Cultural Mind: A Handbook for Cross Cultural Trainers and Consultants. Washington, DC: SIETAR, 1980.
M-HR

Casse, Pierre. Training for the Multicultural Manager. Washington, DC: SIETAR, 1982.
M-HR

Central American Institute of Public Administration. Diseno Administrative para la ejecucion de Proyectos. Washington, DC: Interamerican Development Bank, 1980.
MO-PO,PI

Central American Institute of Public Administration. Modelos y Technicas de Sistemas Aplicados a la Administracion de Proyectos. Washington, DC: Interamerican Development Bank, 1979.
M-PI,PO,IS

Cernea, Michael M., and Benjamin J. Tepping. A System for Monitoring and Evaluating Agricultural Extension Projects. Staff Working Paper 272, Washington, DC: The World Bank, 1977.
M-1-PO,EM

Chabala, H.H.A., D.H. Kiru, S.W. Mukuna, and D.K. Leonard. An Evaluation of the Programming and Implementation Management (PIM) System. Nairobi, Kenya: Institute of Development Studies, University of Nairobi, 1973.
MO-EM,PO

Chambers, Robert. "Administrators: A Neglected Factor in Pastoral Development in East Africa." Journal of Administration Overseas 18, no. 2 (1979): 84-94.
M-1-PO,HR

Chambers, Robert. Rural Poverty Unperceived: Problems and Remedies. Staff Working Paper 400. Washington, DC: The World Bank, 1980.
MO-IRD-TA

Chandavarkar, A.G.. "Technical Cooperation Within the Third World." Finance and Development 9, no. 4 (Dec 1972): 17-22.
-TA

Charlton, Sue Ellen M. Women in Third World Development. Boulder: Westview Press, 1984.
-HR

Chatterjee, P.K. "Social Work and Community Development: A Case Study in Community Organization." International Review of Community Development 35-36 (1976): 167-188.
O-2,4-EM

Chattopadhyay, Somnath, and Udair Parcek. Organization Development in a Voluntary Organization. Ahmedabad, India: PSG Group, The Indian Institute of Management, 1983.
O-2-HR

Cline, William R. "Can The East Asian Model Of Development Be Generalized?" World Development 10 (1982): 81-90.
IM

Cochrane, Glynn. "Cultural Dimensions of Project Implementation." In International Development Administration. Implementation Analysis for Development Projects edited by G. Honadle and R. Klauss. New York: Praeger Publishers, 1979.
-PI,EM

Cochrane, Glynn. Policies for Strengthening Local Government in Developing Countries. Management and Development Series No. 9. Staff Working Paper 582. Washington, DC: The World Bank, 1982.
O-2-PO

Cochrane, Glynn and Raymond Noronha. A Report with Recommendations on the Use of Anthropology in Project Operations of the World Bank Group. Washington DC: The World Bank, March 1973.
-PO,PI,EM

Cody, John. "Industrialization and Development: A Stocktaking." Industry and Development 2 (1979)
-3-EM

Cohen, John M. The Administration of Economic Development Programs: Baselines for Discussion. Development Discussion Paper 79. Cambridge: Harvard Institute for International Development, 1979.
MO-PI

Cohen, John M., and Norman T. Uphoff. Rural Development Participation: Concepts and Measures for Project Design, Implementation and Evaluation. Rural Development Mimeograph No. 2. Ithaca: Cornell Univ., Center for International Studies, Rural Development Committee, 1977.
1-PO,PI,EM

Colle, R. Paraprofessionals in Rural Development. Ithaca: Cornell Univ., Rural Development Committee, 1979.
1-PO

Collinson, Michael. Farm Management in Peasant Agriculture. Boulder: Westview Press, 1983.
M-1-PI

Commonwealth Secretariat. Effective Use of Training Methodologies, Report and Recommendations of an Expert Group. London: Commonwealth Secretariat, 1979.
M-2-PO

Commonwealth Secretariat. National Policies and Programmes for Public Enterprise Management Training (Report of a Meeting of Senior Officials, 5-7 November 1979). London: Commonwealth Secretariat, 1980.
MO-3-PO

Connor, J.J., and W.M. Carson. *Manpower Planning and Development: The Developing World*. Boston: International Human Resources Development Corporation, 1982.
M-HR,PO

Cooper, Lauren. *The Twinning of Institutions: Its Use As A Technical Assistance Delivery System*. Technical Paper 23. Washington, DC: The World Bank, 1984.
O-TA

Coukis, Basil. *Labor-Based Construction Programs: A Practical Guide for Planning and Management*. New Delhi: Oxford Univ. Press, 1984.
-3-DM,PO

Coward, Walter E., Jr. "Indigenous Organization, Bureaucracy, and Development: The Case of Irrigation." *The Journal of Development Studies* 13, no. 1 (1976): 92-104.
O-1-PO

Coward, Walter E., Jr. "Irrigation Management Alternatives: Themes from Indigenous Irrigation Systems." *Agricultural Administration* 4, no. 3 (1977): 223-237.
M-1-PI

Coward, Walter E., Jr. "Principles of Social Organization in an Indigenous Irrigation System." *Human Organization* 38, no. 1 (1979): 29-36.
1-PO

Craig, Rober L., ed. *Training and Development Handbook*, 2nd ed. New York: McGraw-Hill, 1976.
M-PO,HR,PI

Crosby, J. "Personnel Management in a Developing Country." *Personnel Management* 8 (1976): 19-23.
M-HR

Cullinan, T. "Latin American Management, Education and Recruitment: An Environmental Perspective." *California Management Review* 12 (1970): 35-43.
M-PO

Currie, Laughlin. "The Role of Economic Advisers in Developing Countries." Westport: Greenwood Press, 1981.
O-TA,EM

Daniels, John. "The Non-American Manager. Especially as a Third Country National in U.S. Multinationals. A Separate But Equal Doctrine?" *Journal of International Business Studies* 5, no. 2 (1974): 25-40.
M-3

Davis, Louis E., and Albert B. Cherno. *The Quality of Working Life - Vol. I: Problems, Prospects and the State of the Art. Vol. II: Cases and Commentary*. New York: Free Press, 1975.
MO-HR,PI

Delamotte, Yves, and Takezawa Shin-ichi. *Quality of Working Life in International Perspective*. Geneva: ILO, in preparation.
IM-3-HR

Department of Administrative Studies. *Public Administration Training Methodology*. Manchester: University of Manchester, 1974.
M-HR

Derman, William, and Scott Whitefand, eds. *Social Impact Analysis and Development Planning in the Third World*. Boulder: Westview Press, 1984.
MO-2-PO,EM

Desai, D.K. *Management in Rural Development*. Mono. No. 101. Ahmedabad: The Center for Management in Agriculture, The Indian Institute of Management, n.d.
M-I

Desai, D.K., P.S. George, V.K. Gupta, S. Kakkar, K.B. Kothari, S.M. Patel, A.V.S. Narayanan, and Michael Halse. *Studies in Block Development and Co-operative Organization*. Mono. No. 1. Ahmedabad, India: Center of Management in Agriculture, The Indian Institute of Management, n.d.
O-4-EM,PI

Deva, Satya. "Western Conceptualization Of Administrative Development." *International Review of Administrative Sciences* 45 (1979): 59-63.
MO-2-TA

Development Project Management Center. Inter-American Institute for Cooperation on Agriculture/Costa Rica and International Development Management Center. *Guidance System Improvement: An Emergency Approach for Managing Agricultural and Rural Development*. Working paper. College Park: 1983.
IM-M-EM

Dholakia, B.H. "Improving Public Enterprise Performance Through Management Development." In *Management Development and Training in Public Enterprises* edited by R.K. Mishra and S. Ravishankar. New Delhi: Ajanta Publications, 1983.
MO-HR

Dholakia, B.H. "Performance Evaluation of Public Enterprises: Some Issues Relating to Evaluation Criteria and Information Needs." In Public Enterprises in India edited by Sankar, Mishra and Ravishankar. Bombay: Himalaya Publishing House, 1983.
MO-2-EM,IS

Dholakia, N., R. Khurana, L. Bhandari, and M.N. Vora. "On Normative Policy Models in Developing Countries." Omega 7, no. 4 (1979): 359-360.
M-2-DM,PO

Dickens, Roy S. Jr., and Carole E. Hill, eds. Cultural Resources: Planning and Management. Boulder: Westview Press, 1979.
M-PO

Diehl, L.W. "The Environmental Constraint On Certain Management Practices." Akron Business and Economic Review 12 (Winter 1981): 12-16.
M-3-TA

Dorner, Peter. "Institutional Reform: The Conflict Between Equity and Productivity." American Journal of Agricultural Economics 52, no. 5 (1970): 716-718.
O-1-PO

Dotlich, D.L. "International and Intracultural Management Development." Training and Development Journal 36 (Oct. 1982): 26-28.
M-TA

Doughton, Morgan J. "People Power: An Alternative to Runaway Bureaucracy." The Futurist 14 (Apr 1980): 13-22.
MO-4-HR

Douglas, Johnson E., ed. Successful Seed Programs: A Planning and Management Guide. Boulder: Westview Press, 1980.
M-1-PO,DM

Duncan, R.B. "The Ambidextrous Organization: Designing Dual Structure for Innovation." In The Management of Organization Design edited by R. Kilmann, L. Pondy, and D. Slevin. New York: North-Holland, 1976.
O-PO

Duncan, Richard. Institution Building: Incidents, Ideas and Applications. Washington, DC: USAID, 1975.
O-PO,EM

Du Sautoy, Peter. "Some Administrative Aspects of Community Development." Journal of Local Administration Overseas 1 (Jan. 1962): 39-46.
M-4-PO

Eaton, Joseph W., ed. Institution Building and Development: From Concepts to Application. Beverly Hills: Sage Publications, 1972.
IM

Economic Development Institute. Available Training Materials. Washington, DC: The World Bank, Economic Development Institute, 1980.
M-HR,PO

Economic Development Institute. Readings for Training Trainers 3rd ed. Washington, DC: Economic Development Institute, 1980.
M-HR,PO

Eldin, H.K., and S. Sadig. "Suggested Criteria for Selecting Foreign Management Consultants in Developing Countries." Management International Review 4, no. 5 (1971): 123-132.
M-TA

Ellsworth, David F. Maximizing Individual and Project Performance in Technical Assistance-Institutional Building Projects. Lafayette: Purdue University, 1968.
MO-PI,TA

Esman, M.J. The Politics of Development Administration. Chicago: Comparative Administrative Group of American Society for Public Administration, 1963.
O-PO,PI

Esman, M.J. Paraprofessionals in Rural Development: Issues in Field-level Staffing for Agriculture Projects. Staff Working Paper No. 573, Washington, DC: The World Bank, 1983.
-1-HR

Esman, M.J., and J. Montgomery. "Development Administration and Constituency Organization." Public Administration Review 38, no. 2 (Mar./Apr. 1978): 166-172.
O-PO

Esman, M.J., and J. Montgomery. "Systems Approaches to Technical Cooperation: The Role of Developmental Administration. Public Administration Review 29 (1969): 507-539.
O-TA

Esman, M.J., and J. Montgomery. The Administration of Human Resource Development. Staff Working Paper No. 403. Washington, DC: The World Bank, 1980.
M-HR

Esman, M.J. and N.T. Uphoff. Local Organization and Rural Development. Ithaca: Cornell Rural Development Committee, 1982.
O-1-4-

Espinasse, S. "Formation des cadres moyens de developpement du secteur rural. Quelques principles pour guider l'action." *Developement et Civilisations* 52-53 (1973): 147-152.
M-1-PO

Etienne, G. "Some Guiding Points in Teaching on Problems of Development." In *Organization for Economic Development, Training Programs in Economic Developments*. Belgium: Organization for Economic Development, 1963.
-HR,PO

Ettinger, Karl G. *Management Primer*. Tokyo: Asian Productivity Organization, 1973.
M-PO

Etzioni, Amitai. "Beyond Integration Toward Guidability." In *World Population and Development: Challenges and Prospects* edited by Phlip M. Hansen, Syracuse: Syracuse University Press, 1979.
O-2-PO

Ewing, Claude H. "Skilled Manpower Training to Support Industrial Growth in a Developing Nation." In *U.S. Government, Science Technology and Development of Human Resources*, Washington: U.S. Government Printing Office, 1962
M-3-HR

FAO. "Farm Management Research for Small Farmer Development." New York: FAO 1980.
M-1-

FAO. *Improving the Organization and Administration of Agricultural Development in the Near East*. Rome: FAO. 1981
MO-1

FAO. *Network Analysis for FAO Project Managers and Project Personnel*. Document #WA/C2153 Rome: FAO (n.d.)
-DM,PO,EM

Fernandez, Raul. "Third World Industrialization: A New Panacea?" *Monthly Review* 32 (1981): 10-18.
-3-

Fernando, Eustace P. "Use of Interdependency Matrix for Expediting Implementation of an Integrated Development Programme in a Developing Country." In *Project Planning by Network Analysis*, H.J.M. Lombaers. Amsterdam: North Holland Publishing Co., 1969.
-1-PI,PO

Fiedler, F.E., T. Mitchell, and H.C. Triandis. "The Culture Assimilator: An Approach to Cross-Cultural Training." *Journal of Applied Psychology* 55 (1971): 95-102.
M-TA,HR

Fischer J., and W.W. Shaner. "Problems in Planning Integrated Rural Development." *Integrated Rural Development Review* 1, no. 1 (1975): 36-43.
-1-PO

Fondo Nacional de Preinversion. *Seleccion de Articulos para Cursos de Administracion de Proyecto de Desarrollo*. 4 vols. Washington, DC: Interamerican Development Bank, 1977.
MO-PI

Fraser, Colin. "Involving the People in Development Projects." *Cooperation Canada* (May/June 1974): 14-19.
-4-PO

Fukuda, K.J. "Transfer of Management: Japanese Practices for the Orientals?" *Management Decision* 21, no. 4 (1983): 17-26.
M-TA,PI

Gable, R., and J.F. Springer. *Administering Agricultural Development in Asia: A Comparative Analysis of Four National Programmes*. Boulder: Westview Press, 1976.
M-1-EM

Gable, R., and J.F. Springer. "Evaluating Development Programs: Administrative Self-Assessment in Four Asian Nations." *Studies in Comparative International Development* 14 (Fall/Winter 1979): 63-83.
M-EM

Gagnon, Gabriel. "Cooperatives, Participation and Development: Three Failures." In *Popular Participation in Social Changes*, edited by June Nash. The Hague: Mouton Publishers, 1976.
O-4-EM

Gaikwad, V.R. "*Local Participation in Economic Development and Organizing the Rural Poor*" National Seminar on Rural Development Administration held at Bangalore, Nov. 4-5, 1982.
-4-PO

Gaikwad, V.R., and D.S. Parmar. *Rural Development Administration Under Democratic Decentralization: Expenditure Patterns and Organizational Realities* Mono #78. Ahmedabad: The Center for Management in Agriculture, The Indian Institute of Management, n.d.
O-1-PO,DM

Gaitskell, A. Problems of Policy in Planning Agricultural Development in Africa South of the Sahara, in Economic Development of Tropical Agriculture. Gainesville: Univ. of Florida Press, 1968.
1-PO,EM

Galbraith, J., and D.A. Nathason. Strategy Implementation: The Role of Structure and Process. St. Paul: West Publishing Co., 1978.
O-PO,PI

Galjart, B. "A Model of Local Systems for Understanding Development Processes in the Third World." Rural Sociology 40 (1975): 344-352.
O-4-EM -2-PI

Ganesh, S.R. "From Thin Air to Firm Ground: Empirical Guidelines for a General Processual Model of Institution Building." Human Relations 32 (1979): 751-779.
O-PO

Ganesh, S.R., P. Murari, and Neera Shethi. Experiences of MBO Implementation in a State Government, 1974-82. Ahmedabad, India: The PSG Group, The Indian Institute of Management, 1983.

Gant, M., and George F. "A Note on Applications of Development Administration." Public Policy 15 (1966): 199-211.
MO-PO,PI

Garcia-Zamor, Jean-Claude (ed.) Public Participation in Development Planning. Boulder: Westview Press, 1984.
3-PO,PI

Gasson, R. "Farmers' Participation in Co-operative Activities." Sociologia Ruralis 27, no. 1/2 (1977): 102-123.
1,PO

Gaur, I.N.R. "Community Development Training: The Indian Point of View." Community Development Journal 33-34 (1975): 235-243.
M-4-HR

Gendzier, Irene L. Managing Political Change: Social Scientist and The Third World. Boulder: Westview Press, 1984.
MO

George, P.S., and U.K. Srivastava. Planning and Implementation of Rural Development Projects by a Banking Organization. Mono #55. Ahmedabad: The Center for Management in Agriculture, The Indian Institute of Management, n.d.
-1-PO,PI

Ghosh, Pradip K., ed. Economic Policy and Planning in Third World Development. Westport: Greenwood Press, 1984.
MO-PO

Ghosh, Pradip K., ed. Industrialization and Development: A Third World Perspective. Westport: Greenwood Press, 1984.
no code

Gilbert, N., and H. Specht. Co-ordinating Social Services: An Analysis of Community, Organizational and Staff Characteristics. New York: Praeger Publishers, 1977.
O-3-DM

Gitelson, Susan A. "UNDP Technical Assistance: The Promotion of Self Reliance in Africa?" Journal of World Trade Law 5, no. 5 (1971): 553-566.
4-TA

Gittell, Marilyn. "A Typology of Power for Measuring Social Change." The American Behavioral Scientist 9 (Apr. 1966): 23-28.
MO-DM,EM

Glen, Thaddeus M., and Charles F. James, Jr. "Difficulties in Implementing Management Science Techniques in a Third World Setting." Interfaces 10 (1980): 39-44.

Gomez, Henry, and Ramon Pinango. "Shaping Management Strategies for Latin American." In Management Development in Population Progress edited by Sagar Jain. Chapel Hill: Dept. of Health Administration, University of North Carolina, 1983.
M-PO

Goodman, Louis J., and R.N. Love. Project Planning and Management: An Integrated Approach. New York: Pergamon Press, 1980.
M-PO,PI

Goonatilake, P.C.L. "Production Management - The Forgotten Factor in the Industrialization Policy in Developing Countries." World Development 11 (Sept. 1983): 845-850.
M-3-PI

Gordon, David L. Development Finance Companies, State and Privately Owned: A Review Working Paper 578 Washington, DC: The World Bank, 1983.
O-FB,PO

Gordon, David L. Employment and Development of Small Enterprises. Washington, DC: The World Bank, 1978.
O-3-TA,HR

Gorvine, Albert. "Socio-Cultural Factors in the Administration of Technical Assistace Programs." *International Review of Administrative Sciences* 28, no. 3 (1962): 282-290.
M-TA,EM

Gosavi, M.S. *Management Gap in a Developing Economy.* Bombay: Progressive, 1971.
M-PO

Gould, David J., and Jose A. Amaro-Reyes. *The Effects of Corruption on Adminstrative Performance: Illustrations from Developing Countries.* Working Paper 580. Washington, DC: World Bank, n.d.
M-PI,EM

Gow, David D. *An Information System for Rural Area Development -- Rapati Zone Project.* Washington, DC: Development Alternatives, Inc., 1980.
-1-IS

Gow, D.D., and J. Vansant. "Beyond the Rhetoric of Rural Development Participation; How Can It Be Done?" *World Development* 11 (May 1983): 427-446.
-1,4-PI

Gow, David D., ed. *Local Organizations and Rural Development: A Comparative Reappraisal* 2 vols. Washington, DC: Development Alternatives, 1979.
O-1-EM

Grindle, Merilee S. "Anticipating Failure: The Implementation of Rural Development Programs." *Public Policy* 29 (Winter 1981): 51-74.
MO-PI

Grindle, M.S., ed. *Politics and Policy Implementation In The Third World.* Princeton: Princeton Univ. Press, 1980.
O-PO,PI

Gross, Bertram. "The Administration of Economic Development Planning. Principles and Fallacies." *Public Administration Review* 27 (Mar. 1967): 51-56.
O-PO

Gross, Bertram. "Management Strategy for Economic and Social Development: Part 1." *Policy Sciences* 2 (Dec 1971): 339-372.
M-PO

Gross, Bertram. "Management Strategy for Economic and Social Development: Part 2." *Policy Sciences* 3 (March 1972): 1-26.
M-PO

Grover, Brian. *Water Supply and Sanitation Project Preparation Handbook, 3 vols.* World Bank Technical Papers 12-14. Washington, DC: The World Bank, 1983.
MO-2-PO

Gudykunst, William B., Lea P. Stewart, and Stella Ting-Toomey. *Communication, Culture, and Organizational Processes.* Beverly Hills: Sage Publications, 1985.
O-IS

Gupta, A.K. "Barriers to Innovations in Lower Bureaucracy." *Vikalpa* 7, no. 4 (Oct./Dec. 1982): 267-271.
O-2-PI

Gupta, Ranjit. *Building The Indian Institute of Forest Management: Task Process and Approaches.* Ahmedabad: The Center for Management in Agriculture. The Indian Institute of Management, n.d.
O-1-PO,PI

Gurder, Singh, and Krishna Kumar. *Management of Captial Flows on Farms.* Ahmedabad: The Center for Management in Agriculture, The Indian Institute of Management, n.d.
MO-1-FB

Guthrie, Colin. *Planning and Implementing Management Improvement Programs in the Distribution Sector.* Geneva: International Labor Office, Management Development Branch, 1979.
M-PO,PI

Hall, Budd L., and J. Roby Kidd. *Adult Learning for Development.* New York: Pergamon Press, 1978.
-HR

Halse, Michael, V.K. Gupta, A.V.S. Narayanan, and A.G.K. Murty. *Planning and Implementation in Agriculture Studies in Intensive Cattle Development Programme.* Ahmedabad: Center for Management in Agriculture, The Indian Institute of Management, n.d.
-1-PO,PI

Halstead, John M., Robert A. Chase, Steve H. Murdock, and Larry F. Leistritz, eds. *Socioeconomic Impact Management.* Boulder: Westview Press, 1984.
M-2-EM,PO

Hamer, John H. "Prerequisites and Limitations in the Development of Voluntary Self-Help Associations." *Anthropological Quarterly* 49, no. 2 (1976): 107-134.
O-4-PI

Hancock, Alan, ed. *Technology Transfer and Communications* New York: UNESCO, 1985.
IS-TA

Haque, W., N. Mehta, A. Rahman and P. Wignaraja. "Micro-Level Development: Design and Evaluation of Rural Development Projects." *Development Dialogue* 2 (1977): 71-137.
1-PO,EM

Haque, W., N. Mehta, A. Rahman, and P. Wignaraja. "Towards a Theory of Rural Development." *Development Dialogue* Special Issue (1977).
MO-1-PO

Harberger, Arnold C. *Project Evaluation: Collected Papers*. London: Macmillan, 1972.
-EM,FB

Harbison, F. "The African University and Human Resource Development." *Journal of Modern African Studies* 3, no. 1 (1965): 53-62.
M-HR

Harbison, F. and C. Myers. "Logic of Management Development." In *Management in International Perspective*, edited by S.B. Prasad. New York: Appleton-Century, 1967.
M-

Harbison, F., and C.A. Myers. *Manpower and Education: Country Studies in Economic Development*. New York: McGraw-Hill, 1965.
M-HR,EM

Harper, J. *The Systematic Development of Management, A Case Study*. Cairo: The American University in Cairo, 1979.
M-2,3-PO

Hart, Stuart L., Gordon A. Enk, and William F. Hornick, eds. *Improving Impact Assessment*. Boulder: Westview Press, 1984.
M-EM,DM

Harris, P.R. "Cross-cultural Consulting Effectiveness." *Consultation* 1, no. 2 (1982): 4-10.
MO-TA

Harris, P. R., and Garald H. Malin. *Innovation in Global Consultation*. Washington, DC: International Consultants Foundation, 1980.
M-PI,TA

Harris, P.R., and R.T. Moran. *Managing Cultural Differences*. Houston: Gulf Publishing, 1979.
M-HRD

Harrison, F.L. *Advanced Project Management*. New York: John Wiley and Sons, 1981.
M-PI,PO

Harwood, Richard R. *Small Farm Development: Understanding and Improving Farming Systems in the Humid Tropics*. Boulder: Westview Press, 1979.
-1-PI,DM

Harvey, Charles, Jake Jacobs, Geoff Lamb, and Bernard Schaffer. *Rural Employment and Administration in The Third World: Development Methods and Alternative Strategies*. Farnborough, England: Saxon House, 1979.
MO-1-TA

Havens, A. Eugene, and William Flinn. "Green Revolution Technology and Community Development: The Limits of Action Programs." *Economic Development and Cultural Change* 23, no. 3 (1975): 469-481.
-1,4-PI

Hayes, S.P. *Evaluating Development Projects*. Paris: UNESCO, 1966.
-PO,OM

Hayward, B. "The Participatory Planning Process for Education." In *Participation Planning in Education*. Paris: OECD, 1974.
-2,4-HR

Heaver, Richard. *Adapting the Training and Visit System for Family Planning, Health and Nutrition Programs*. Working Staff Paper No. 662. Washington, DC: The World Bank, 1984.
-2-PI

Heaver, Richard. *Bureaucratic Politics and Incentives in the Management of Rural Development*. Staff Working Paper No. 537 Washington, DC: The World Bank, 1983.
M-1-EM,PI

Heenan, David A., and Calvin Reynolds. "RPO's - A Step Toward Global Human Resources Management." *California Management Review* 18, no. 1 (Fall 1975): 5-9.
M-HR

Hegde, M. "Western and Indian Models of Turnaround Management." *Vikalpa* 7 (Oct 1982): 289-304.
M-PO,DM-EM

Heller, F.A. "The Role of Business Management in Relation to Economic Development." *International Journal of Comparative Sociology* 10 (1969): 292-298.
MO-3-TA

Herbert, Adam W. "Management Under Conditions of Decentralization and Citizen Participation." *Public Administration Review* 32 (Oct 1972): 631-632.
M-4-PI

Heseltine, Nigel. "Administrative Structures and the Implementation of Development Plans." *Journal of Administration Overseas* 6 (April 1967): 75-84.
O-PI,PO

Hildebrand, Peter. *Comments About Multi-Disciplinary Team Efforts.* Paper presented to the Conference on Rapid Rural Appraisal held at the Institute of Development Studies, University of Sussex, Dec 4-7, 1979.
M-TA

Hill, R.E. "Managing Interpersonal Conflict in Project Teams." *Sloan Management Review* 18, no. 2 (1977): 45-61.
M-PI,TA

Hirschman, Albert O. *Development Projects Observed.* Washington, DC: The Brookings Institution, 1967.
MO-PI

Hoetjes, B.J.S. "Politics and Government - Background to Corruption in Public Administration in Developing Countries." *Netherlands Journal of Sociology* 12, no. 1 (1976): 47-77.
O-EM

Hofstede, Geert. *Cultural Dimensions for Project Management.* Published proceedings of the 7th World Congress on Project Managment. Copenhagen, Denmark, Sept. 12-17, 1982.
M-PI

Holdcroft, Lane E. *The Rise and Fall of Community Development in Developing Countries 1950-65: A Critical Analysis and An Annotated Bibliography.* MSO Rural Development Papers. East Lansing: Michigan State University, 1977.
-4-DM,EM

Holmquist, Frank W. "Toward a Political Theory of Rural Self-Help Development in Africa." *Rural Africana* 18 (1972): 60-79.
-1,4-PO

Hollnsteiner, Mary. "Mobilizing the Rural Poor Through Community Organization." *Philippine Studies* 27 (1979): 387-416.
O-4

Honadle, George. "Anticipating Roadblocks in Organizational Terrain: Lessons from a Case Study of How Organization Design Makes a Difference." In *International Development Administration. Implementation Analysis for Development Projects* edited by George Honadle and Rudi Klauss. New York: Praeger Publishers, 1979.
O-PO

Honadle, George. *Fishing for Sustainability: The Role of Capacity Building in Development Administration.* IRD Working Paper No. 8, Washington, DC: Development Alternatives, Inc., 1981.
O-

Honadle, George. *Rapid Reconnaissance Approaches to Organizational Analysis for Development Administration.* Washington, DC: Development Alternatives, Inc., 1979.
O-1

Honadle, George. "Supervising Agricultural Extension: Practices and Procedures for Improving Field Performance." *Agricultural Administration* 9 (1982): 29.
M-1-PI

Honadle, George and David Gow. *Putting the Cart Behind the Horse: Participation, Decentralization, and Capacity Building for Rural Development.* Washington, DC: Development Alternatives, Inc., n.d.
MO-4-TA

Honadle, George, and John P. Hannah. "Management Performance for Rural Development Packaged Training on Capacity Building." *Public Administration and Development* 2 (1982): 295-307.
MO-1-PI

Honadle, George, and Marcus Ingle. *Project Management for Rural Equality.* Washington, DC: USAID, 1976.
-1-PI

Honadle, George, and Rudi Klauss. *International Development Administration. Implementation Analysis for Development Projects.* New York: Praeger Publishers, 1979.
O-PI,EM

Honadle, George, and Gerry Van Sant. *Implementation and Sustainability: Lessons from Integrated Rural Development.* West Hartford: Kumarian Press, (in press).
M-1-PO,PI

Honadle, George, Elliot Morss, Jerry VanSant, and David Gow. *Integrated Rural Development: Making It Work?* Washington, DC: Development Alternatives, Inc., 1980.
1-PO,PI

Honey, John C. *Toward Strategies of Public Administration Development in Latin America.* Syracuse: Syracuse University Press, 1968.
O-PO

Hope, Kempe R., and Aubrey Armstrong. "Toward the Development of Administrative and Management Capability in Developing Countries." *International Review of Administrative Sciences* 46, no. 4 (1980): 315-321.
M-PO,PI

Howe, Charles W., ed. *Managing Renewable Natural Resources in Developing Countries*. Boulder: Westview Press, 1982.
-1-PI

Howell, John. "Training Managers for Agricultural Development Projects." *Agricultural Administration Network Papers* (May 28 - June 8), 1979.
M-1

Howell, John. "What's Wrong with Managers?" *Overseas Development Institute Review* 1 (1978): 53-69.
M-EM

Huizer, Gerrit. "The Role of Community Development and Peasant Organization in Social Structural Change." *International Review of Community Development* 17-18 (1967): 293-304.
O-4-

Humes, Samuel. "The Role of Local Government in Economic Development in Africa." *Journal of Administration Overseas* 12, no. 1 (1973): 21-27.
O-PO

Hunt, Robert C., and Eva Hunt. "Canal Irrigation and Local Social Organization." *Current Anthropology* 17, 3 (1976): 389-411.
-1-PO

Hunter, G. "The Implementation of Agricultural Development: Towards Criteria for the Choice of Tools." *Agricultural Administration* 1, no. 1 (1974): 51-72.
1-PI,EM

Hurtubise, Rolland. *Managing Information Systems: Concepts and Tools*. West Hartford: Kumarian Press, 1983.
M-IS

Hutton, John. "Management Education for a Changing International Environment." *Singapore Management Review* 6, no. 2 (July 1984): 71-82.
IM-M-HR

Ickis, John C. "Rural Development Management: Strategy, Structure, and Managerial Roles." In *Population and Social Development Management* D. Korten. Caracas: IESA, 1979.
M-1-PO

Iglesias, G., ed. *Implementation: The Problem of Achieving Results*. Manila: Eastern Regional Organization for Public Administration, 1976.
-PI

Ikonicoff, M. "On the Steps of Industrialization in the Third-World." *Trimestre Econimico* 50, no. 200 (1983): 2153-2172.
-3-PI

Ingle, M.D. *Implementing Development Prgrammes: A State-of-the-Art Review*. Washington, DC: United States Agency for International Development, 1979.
M-PI

Ingle, M.D., Noel Berge, and Marcia Hamilton. *Microcomputers in Development: A Manager's Guide*. West Hartford: Kumarian Press, 1983.
M-IS

Ingle, M.D., Noel Berge, and Marcia Teisan. *Acquiring and Using Microcomputers in Agricultural Development: A Manager's Guide*. College Park: International Development Management Center and Development Project Management Center, 1983.
IM-M-O,1-IS

Ingle, M.D., and Irving Swerdlow. *Public Administration Training for the Less Developed Countries*. Syracuse: Maxwell Graduate School of Citizenship and Public Affairs, 1974.
M-HR

Interamerican Development Bank and Interamerican School of Public Administration. *Proyectos de desarrolo: Planificacion, Implementacion y Control* 4 vols. Mexico City: Editorial Limusa, 1979.
M-1,3-PI

Interamerican Institute of Agricultural Sciences. *Guia de Menejo de Proyectos*. 8 vols. San Jose, Costa Rica: Organization of American Status, Interamerican Institute of Agricultural Sciences, 1978.
MO-TA,PI

International Labour Office. *An Introductory Course in Teaching and Training Methods for Management Development*. Geneva: International Labour Office, 1981.
M-PI

International Labour Office. *Co-operation Among Management Development Institutions - Oppoortunities and Priorities for Co-operation*. Geneva: International Labour Office, Management Development Branch, 1981.
MO-TA

International Labour Office. Job Evaluation. Geneva: International Labour Office n.d.
M-EM

International Labour Office. Management of Larger Agricultural Co-operatives. An In-service Programme. Geneva: International Labour Office, 1983.
M-1-PI

International Labor Office. Management and Population Questions. Geneva: ILO, 1985.
MO-2

International Labour Office. Meeting Basic Needs: Strategies for Eradicating Mass Poverty and Unemployment. Geneva: International Labour Office, 1977.
MO-PO

International Labour Office. Project Preparation and Appraisal: Material for Management Training in Agricultural Co-operatives. Geneva: International Labour Office, 1983.
M-PI -PO

International Labor Office. Results-oriented Maintenance Management Programmes: A Preliminary Report Geneva: International Labour Office, 1982.
MO-PI,PO

International Labour Office. Staff Management. Material for Management Training in Agricultural Co-operatives. Geneva: International Labour Office, 1983.
M-1-HR,PI,TA

International Labour Office. Storage Management. Material for Management Training in Agricultural Co-operatives. Geneva: International Labour Office, 1983.
M-1-PI

International Labour Office. Technical Co-operation Among African Countries in Management Development. Geneva: International Labour Office, 1982.
M-TA

International Labor Office. Transport Management. Geneva: ILO, 1984.
MO-2

International Labour Office. Transport Management. Material for Management Training in Agricultural Co-operatives. Geneva: International Labour Office, 1983.
M-1-PI

International Labour Office. Women in Rural Development: Critical Issues. Geneva: International Labour Office, 1980.
-HR

International Labour Review. "Social and Cultural Factors in Management Development: Extracts from the Conclusions of a Meeting of Experts." International Labour Review 94, no. 2 (1966): 175-185.
M-PI

International Program Development Office and International Development Management Center. International Development Program and Project Implementation: A Management Perspective. Pullman: Washington State University, 1984.
IM-M-PI

International Social Science Journal 20 no. 1 (1968). Special issue: "Theory, Training and Practice in Management."
M

International Social Science Journal 21, no.1 (1969). Special issue: "Innovation in Public Administration."
MO-2-PO

Isely, Raymond B. "Problems Encountered in Providing Consulting Services to Governments of Sub Saharan African Countries." Consultation 2, no. 3 (Summer 1983): 10-14.
MO-TA

Islam, M.S. "Management and Organizational Development." Management Development 9 (1980): 81-95.
MO-PO,HR

Islam, M.S. "Management Development." Management Development 7 (1978): 29-48.
M-HR

Israel, Arturo. "Management and Institutional Development." Finance and Development 20 (Sept. 1983): 15-18.
MO-

Israel, Arturo. "Towards Better Project Implementation." Finance and Development 15, no. 1 (Mar. 1978): 27-30.
-PI

Iversen, Robert W. "Personnel for Implementation: A Contextual Perspective." In International Development Administration. Implementation Analysis for Development Projects edited by George Honadle and Rudi Klauss. New York: Praeger Publishers, 1979.
MO-PI,HR

Jain, S.C., eds. Management Development in Population Programmes. Durham: North Carolina School of Public Health, 1981.
M-2-

Jain, S.C., F. Joubert, and J.K. Satia. "Management of National Population Programs." In World Population and Development: Challenges and Prospects edited by Philip M. Hauser. Syracuse: Syracuse University Press, 1979.
M-2

Jedlicka, A. Organization for Rural Development: Risk Taking and Appropriate Technology. New York: Praeger Publishers, 1977.
O-1-PI,PO

Johnston, Bruce F. Rural Development Strategies: A Survey of Policy Options and the Concepts of Integration and Basic Needs. Final report submitted to AID/DS/RAD, Washington, D.C.: USAID, 1979.
O-1-PO

Johnston, Bruce F., and William C. Clark. Redesigning Rural Development, A Strategic Perspective. Baltimore: John Hopkins Univ. Press, 1982.
O-1-PO

Jones, Garth N. "Change Catalyst in Managed Organizational Change." Indian Journal of Public Administration 22 (Oct./Dec. 1966): 717-42.
MO-PO,PI

Jones, Garth N. "Failure of Technical Assistance in Public Administration Abroad: A Personal Note." The Journal of Comparative Administration 2, no. 1 (May 1970): 3-51.
M-TA

Jones, Garth N. "Managing Changes in Organizations." NIPA Journal 5 (June 1966): 111-131.
MO-PI,PO

Jones, Garth N. "Pacemaker in Managed Organizational Change." NIPA Reporter 5 (March 1966): 23-27.
MO-PI

Jones, Garth N. Planned Organizational Change: A Set of Working Documents. Los Angeles: Center for Research in Public Organization, School of Public Administration, Univ. of Southern California, 1964.
O-EM

Jones, Garth N. Planned Organizational Change: A Study in Change Dynamics. New York: Frederick A. Praeger Co., and London: Rutledge and Kegan Paul, 1969.
O-PI,EM

Jones, Garth N. Planned Organizational Change: Operational Focus for the Administrator. Djakarta: Lembaga Administratrol Negara, 1963.
O-PI

Jones, Garth N. "Preventive Medicine at Work: A Hypothetical Case on Planned Organizational Change." Philippine Journal of Public Administration 9 (July 1965): 241-255.
O-PI

Jones, Garth N. "Strategies and Tactics of Planned Organizational Change: Case Examples in the Modernization Process of Traditional Societies." Human Organization 24 (Fall 1965): 192-200.
O-PO,PI

Journal of Public Administration 15 (1980). Issue devoted to the SAIPA conference on "Administrative Innovation" held in Pretoria Sept. 8, 1980.
O-PO

Joy, Leonard. Report on Responses to a Workbook on Social Development Management. Washington, DC: NASPAA, 1983.
M-2-

Kalshoven, Geert. "Irrigation Systems: Some Organizational Considerations." Sociologia Ruralis 16 (1976): 238-57.
O-1

Kanawaty, George, and Einar Thorsrud. "Field Experiences with NEw Forms of Work Organization." International Labor Review 120 (May/June 1981): 263-77.
MO-PO

Kanawaty, George, ed. Managing and Developing New Forms of Work Organization. Management Development Series #16. Geneva: International Labor Office, 1981.
MO-PO

Kanazawa, Natsuki. "Roles of Government and Farmers in Irrigation Water and Management." In Farm Water Management for Rice Cultivation, Tokyo: Asian Productivity Organization, 1977.
O-1-

Kaplan, Paul F. "The Impact of Planned Change and the Testing of a New Framework for Community Development." Journal of Developing Areas 8, no. 3 (1974): 363-374.
O-4-PI,EM

Karim, M.N. "Management Development and the Developing Countries." Management Development. 5 (1974): 43-55.
M-HR

Karras, E.J. "Training -- A Link to Organizational Change." Training and Development Journal 5 (1973): 12.
MO-PI

Katz, Saul M. A System Approach to Development Administration: A Framework for Analyzing Capability of Action for National Development. Chicago: Comparative Administration Group of the American Society for Public Administration, 1965.
O-EM,PI

Keatinge, Elsie B. "Latin American Peasant Corporate Communities: Potentials for Mobilizing and Political Integration." Journal of Anthropological Research 29, no. 1 (1973): 37-58.
O-4-

Kelly, J.B. "The Selection of Projects in Community Development." Community Development Journal 3, no. 3 (1968): 128-133.
-4-DM

Khan, Akhter Hameed, and A.K.M. Mohsen. "Mobilizing Village Leadership." International Development Review 4, no. 3 (1962): 4-9.
M-1-PI

Khan, Akter Hameedd. Planning Evaluation and Strengthening of the Rural Works Programme. Geneva: International Labour Office, 1978.
-1-EM,PO,PI

Khandwalla, P.N. "The Architecture of Indian Top Management." Indian Management 22, no. 4 (April 1983): 11-17.
M-

Khandwalla, P.N. The Design of Organizations. New York: Harcourt-Bruce, 1977.
O-PO

Khandwalla, P.N. "Mass Output Orientation of Operations Technology and Organization Structure." Administrative Science Quarterly 19 (1974): 74-97.
O-PO

Khandwalla, P.N. "Some Lessons for the Management of Public Enterprises." Vikalpa 7, no. 4 (Oct-Dec 1982): 311-326.
M-EM

Khandwalla, N. "Strategy for Turning Around Complex Sick Organizations." Vikalpa 6 (July-Oct 1981): 143-165.
O-PO,PI

Kieloch, Edward A. "Innovation in Administration and Economic Development." Indian Journal of Public Administration 12 (July-Sept. 1966): 599-611.
O-PI

Kilby, Peter, ed. Entrepreneurship and Economic Development. New York: The Free Press, 1971.
MO-3-

Kim, L. "Organizational Innovation and Structure." Journal of Business Research 8, no. 2 (1980): 225-245.
O-PO

Kim, L. "Stages of Development of Industrial Technology in a Developing Country: A Model." Research Policy 9, no. 3 (1980): 154-177.
-3-PI

King, Ambrose, and Davy Leung. The Chinese Touch in Small Industrial Organizations. Hong Kong: Social Research Center, Chinese Univ. of Hong Kong, 1975.
-2-PI

Kirkhart, L., and N. Gardner. "Organization Development." Public Administration Review 34 (1974): 97-140.
O-

Kizibash, A.H. New Perspectives on Training Managers for Developing Countries. American Marketing Association Combined Proceeding, 36 (1974): 647-656.
M-HR

Klatzman, Joseph, ed. The Role of Group Action in the Industrialization of Rural Areas. New York: Praeger Publishers, 1971.
MO-3-

Klauss, Rudi. "Interorganizational Relationships for Project Implementation." In International Development Administration Implementation Analysis for Development Projects edited by George Honadle and Rudi Klauss. New York: Praeger Publishers Ltd., 1979.
O-PI

Klitgaard, Robert. "Managing the Fight Against Corruption: A Case Study (of an Unnamed Developing Country)." Public Administration and Development 4 (Jan./Mar. 84): 77-98.
M-PI

Knight, K. ed. Matrix Management: A Cross-functional Approach to Management. Farnborough: Gower Press, 1977.
M-PO

Knight, P.T., ed. Implementing Programmes of Human Development Staff Working Paper No. 403. Washington, DC: The World Bank, 1980.
M-HR

Korten, D.C. "A Learning Process Approach to Working with the Rural Poor." Innotech Journal 4, no. 1 (Jan.-June 1980): 11-23.
-1-PI

Korten, D.C. "Beyond Accustomed Territory." The Journal of Applied Behavioral Science 10, no. 1 (Jan.-Mar. 1974): 53-60.
MO-TA

Korten, D.C. "The Bureaucrats Can't Do It Alone." Development Forum (March 1984): 16.
M-3-PI

Korten, D.C.: "Community Organization and Rural Development: A Learning Process Approach." Public Administration Review 40, no. 5 (Sept./Oct. 1980): 480-511.
O-1,4-

Korten, D.C. "INCAE: Success Story in Central America." Harvard Business School Bulletin 49, no. 3 (May-June 1973).
O-PI

Korten, D.C. Learning From The USAID Field Experience. Institutional Development and the Dynamics of the Project Process. Working Paper No. 7, Washington, DC: NASPAA June 1983.
O-TA

Korten, D.C. "Management for Social Development: Experience from the Field of Population." In Education and Training for Public Sector Management for Developing Nations edited by Lawrence D. Stifel, James S. Coleman, and Joseph E. Black. New York: Rockefeller Foundation, 1977. Also appears in Philippine Journal of Public Administration 20, no. 3 (July 1976): 262-283.
M-2-PI,PO

Korten, D.C. "The Management of Social Transformation." Public Administration Review 41, no. 6 (Nov./Dec. 1981): 609-18.
M-2-PI

Korten, D.C. "New Issues, New Options: A Management Perspective on Population and Family Planning." Studies in Family Planning 10, no. 1 (January 1979): 3-14.
M-2-PO,PI

Korten, D.C. "Planning Frameworks for People-Centered Development." In People-Centered Development edited by D.C. Korten and R. Klauss. West Hartford: Kumarian Press, 1984.
O-4-PO

Korten, D.C., ed. Population and Social Development Management: A Challenge for Management Schools. Caracas: Instituto de Estudios Superiores de Administracion, 1979.
M-2-PO,PI

Korten, D.C. "Population Programs 1985: A Growing Management Challenge." Studies in Family Planning 6, no. 7 (July 1975): 178-187.
MO-Z

Korten, D.C. "Strategic Management for People-Centered Development." Public Administration Review (July-Aug. 1984): n.p.
M-PO,PI

Korten, D.C. "Toward a Technology for Managing Social Development." In Population and Social Development Mangement edited by D.C. Korten. Caracas: IESA, 1979. Excerpted in Development Digest 19, no. 1 (Jan. 1981).
M-2-PI

Korten, D.C., and Frances F. Korten. "Strategy, Leadership and Context in Family Planning: A Three Country Comparison." In Patterns of Policy: Comparative and Longitudinal Studies of Population Events edited by John D. Montgomery, Harold D. Lasswell and Joel Migdal. New Brunswick: Transaction Books, 1979.
M-2-PO

Korten, D.C., and Norman Uphoff. "Bureaucratic Reorientation for Participatory Rural Development." NASPAA Working Paper No. 1. Washington, DC: NASPAA, 1981.
O-1,4-PO,PI

Korten, D.C., Norman Uphoff, and William F. Whyte. "Bureaucratic Reorientation for Agricultural Research and Development." In Higher Yielding Human Systems for Agriculture William F. Whyte, and Damon Boynton. Ithaca: Cornell Univ. Press, 1983.
O-1-PO

Krefetz, J. "Participation for What or for Whom? Some Considerations for Research." Journal of Comparative Administration 5, no. 3 (1973): 367-380.
-4-PI

Kubr, M., ed. Managing a Management Development Institution. Geneva: International Labour Office, 1982.
MO-PO,PI

Kubr, M., ed. Management Consulting, A Guide to the Profession. Geneva: International Labour Office, 1982.
M-TA

Kulp, Earl M. Designing and Managing Basic Agricultural Programs. Bloomington: Indiana University International Development Institute, 1977.
M-PO,PI

Kumar, Krishna, and Maxwell G. McLeod. Multinationals from Developing Countries. Lexington: Lexington Books, 1981.
O-3-PO

LaPorte, Robert. Public Administration and Public Corporations in the Less Developed Countries: Training the Corporate Managers. Paper presented at Maxwell School of Development Administration Conference, Syracuse University, NY, April 18-19, 1974.
MO-3-HR

Lauter, Geza Peter. "Sociological-Cultural and Legal Factors Impeding Decentralization of Authority in Developing Countries." Academy of Management Journal 12 (Sept. 1969): 367-378.
M-PO,PI

Lazaro, Rogelio C., and Thomas H. Wickham. "Improvements of Irrigation Systems' Facilities: Technical and Management Concepts." In Implementing Public Irrigation Programs edited by William Staub. Honolulu: East-West Center Food Institute, 1977.
M-1-PI

Lazaro, Rogelio C., Donald C. Taylor, and Thomas H. Wickham. "Irrigation Systems in Southeast Asia: Policy and Management Issues." Teaching and Research Forum. Singapore: The Agricultural Development Council, Inc., 1977.
M-1-PO

Lee, Hahn-Been. "An Application of Innovation Theory to the Strategy of Administrative Reform in Developing Countries." Policy Sciences 1 (Summer 1970): 177-190.
O-PO

Lee, J.A. "Developing Managers in Developing Countries." Harvard Business Review 46, no. 6 (1968): 55-65.
M-PO,PI,HR

Lehmann, David, ed. Peasants, Landlords and Governments: Agrarian Reform in the Third World. New York: Holmes and Meier Publishers, Inc., 1974.
O-1-PO

Lele, Uma. "Co-operative and the Poor: A Comparative Perspective." World Development 9 (Jan 1981): 55-72.
M-TA

Lele, Uma. The Design of Rural Development: Lessons from Africa. Washington, DC: The World Bank, 1975.
O-1-PO

Lele, Uma. "Designing Rural Development Programs: Lessons from Past Experience in Africa." Economic Development and Cultural Change 24, no. 2 (1976): 287-308.
O-1-PO,PI

Leonard, D.K., and D.R. Marshall, eds. Institutions of Rural Development for the Poor: Decentralization and Organizational Linkages. Berkeley: University of California, 1982.
O-1-PO

Lethem, F., and L. Cooper. Managing Project-related Technical Assistance. Staff Working Papers, 586. Management and Development Series No. 13. Washington, DC: The World Bank, 1983.
M-TA

Lethem, Francis, and Vincent Riley. "The World Bank's Technical Assistance: A Review of the Bank's Activities and the Lessons of its Experiences." Finance and Development (Dec 1982): 16-21.
-TA-EM

Leupolt, Manfred. "Integrated Rural Development: Key Elements of an Integrated Rural Development Strategy." Sociolgia Ruralis 17, no. 1/2 (1977): 7-28.
-1-PO

Levine, C.H. et al. "Organizational Design: A Post Minnowbrook Perspective for the New Public Administration." Public Administration Review 35 (1975): 425-435.
O-

Levi, Yair. "Institution Building Through Self-Help in Rural Developing Areas: An Integrated Approach." International Review of Community Development 31-32 (1974): 261-291.
O-1,4-PI

Lindenberg, Marc, and Ben Crosby. Managing Development: The Political Dimension. West Hartford: Kumarian Press, 1981.
M-PI

Lippitt, Gordon S. Organizational Renewal; A Wholistic Approach to Organization Development. Englewood Cliffs: Prentice-Hall, 1982.
O

Lippitt, Gordon S., and Warren H. Schmidt. "Crisis in a Developing Organization." Harvard Business Review (Nov.-Dec. 1967): 102-112.
O-PI

Littrell, W.B. "Bureaucracy in the Eighties: Introduction." Journal of Applied Behavioral Science 16 (July-Sept. 1980): 263-277.
O-2-PO

Livingston, I. "On the Concept of Integrated Rural Development Planning in Less Developed Countries." Journal of Agricultural Economics 30, no. 1 (1979): 49-53.
-1-PI

London, Paul A. "A Role for Merchants in Development." International Development Review 18, no. 3 (1976): 11-13.
-3-

Lynton, R.P., and U. Pareek. Training for Development. West Hartford: Kumarian Press, 1978.
M-PI,PO

McCallum, J. Douglas. "Reflections on Foreign Planning Consultancy (Organization and Execution of a Foreign Project, Typically, Planning All or Part of a Growing City in a Developing Country)." Planner 60 (Nov. 1974): 883-888.
-PI,TA

McInerney, John P. The Technology of Rural Development. Staff Working Paper No. 295, Washington, DC: World Bank, 1978.
-1-PO,PI

McNulty, Nancy G. The International Directory of Executive Education. Elmsford: Pergamon Press, 1985.
IM-M-HR

McNulty, Nancy G. Training Managers: The International Guide. New York: Harper and Row, 1969.
M-PI

Maihotra, Ram C. "Monitoring and Evaluation of Rural Development Project and Programmes." PRASHASAN, The Nepalese Journal of Public Administration 41 (Nov. 1984).
MO-1-EM

Mailick, Sidney, ed. The Making of the Manager: A World View. Garden City: Anchor Press/Doubleday, 1974.
M-PO,PI

Malek, T. Abdel. "Some Problems of Technical Assistance Administration in Developing Countries." International Review of Administrative Sciences 34 (1968): 315-323.
M-TA,PI

Manik, M.W. "Towards a Definition of Public Administration Training." Management Development 13 (1984): 24-36.
M-HR

Mann, Amy G., and Jan Miracle, eds. Rural Development: The Interplay of Analysis and Action. PASITAM, Bloomington: International Development Research Center, Indiana University, 1975.
-1-PI,PO

Markwell, D.S., and T.J. Roberts. Organization of Management Development Programmes. London: Gower Press, 1969.
MO-PI,PO

Marston, R.C. "Management Expertise: Its Application in Developing Countries." The Personnel Administrator 23, no. 8 (1978): 54-56.
M-HR

Matlon, P., ed. Coming Full Circle, Farmer's Participation in the Development of Technology. Washington, D.C. IDRC, 1984.

Matheson, Ross. People Development in Developing Countries. New York: John Wiley, 1978.
M-HR,PI

Mathur, B.C., K. Diesh, and C. Chandra Sekharan, eds. Management in Government (Selected Readings). New Delhi: Publication Division Ministry of Information and Broadcasting, Government of India, 1979.
MO-EM

Matthai, Ravi J., Vdair Pareek, and T.V. Rao. Institution Building in Education and Research from Stagnation to Self Renewal. New Delhi: All India Management Association, 1976.
O-2-EM,PI

Mauck, Elwyn A. Public Administration Training in African Universities Problems of Course Evaluation and Teaching Methods. Ife, Nigeria: Nigerian Institute of Administration, University of Ife, 1970.
M-HR,EM

Mawhood, Philips. "Decentralization for Development: A Lost Cause?" In Local Politics, Development and Participation F.C. Bruhns. Pittsburg: University of Pittsburg, Center for International Studies, 1974.
O-4-PO

Mayo-Smith, Ian. Managing People. Three International Case Studies. West Hartford: Kumarian Press, 1981.
M-HR

Mayo-Smith, Ian. Planning A Performance Improvement Project: A Practical Guide. West Hartford: Kumarian Press, 1981.
MO-PO,PI

Meadows, Paul, "Motivation for Change and Development Administration." In Development Administration Concepts and Problems edited by Irving Swerdlow. Syracuse: Syracuse University Press, 1964.
M-PI,PO

Meehan, Eugene. In Partnership with People: An Alternative Development Strategy. Washington, DC: Inter-American Foundation, 1978.
M-4-HR

Mehta, S.R. Rural Development Policies and Programmes. Beverly Hills: Sage Pub., 1984.
O-1-

Mehta, Prayag. "Participation of Rural Poor in Rural Development." IFDA Dossier 9 (July 1979): n.p.
O-1,4-PI,PO

Meier, Gerald M. Pricing Policy for Development Management. Washington, DC: World Bank, 1983.
-FB,PI,PO

Meier, Peter M. Energy Planning in Developing Countries. Boulder: Westview Press, 1984.
-PO,DM

Mendoza, Gabine A. "The Transferability of Western Management Concepts and Programs, An Asian Perspective." In Education and Training for Public Sector Management in Developing Countries edited by Lawrence D. Stifel, James S. Coleman, and Joseph G. Black. New York: The Rockefeller Foundation, 1977.
M-4

Meulmeester, J., and M. Levin, eds. Traditional Cooperation and Modern Co-operatives. Amsterdam: Royal Tropical Institute, 1983.
O-PO,PI

Mial, H. Curtis, and Dorothy Mial. "The Development Training and Use of Leadership Resources in Community Development Programs." Community Development Review 7, no. 1 (1962): 21-28.
M-4-

Michael, Donald N. On Learning to Plan and Planning to Learn: The Social Psychology of Changing Toward Future - Responsive Societal Learning. San Francisco: Jossey-Bass Publishers, 1973.
M-4

Mickelwait, Donald R. "Information Strategies for Implementing Rural Development." In International Development Administration, Implementation Analysis for Development Projects edited by George Honadle and Rudi Klauss. New York: Praeger Publishers, 1979.
M-1-IS,PI

Mickelwait, Donald R., Charles F. Sweet, and Elliott R. Morss. New Directions in Development: A Study of U.S. Aid. Boulder: Westview Press, 1979.
-TA

Mickelwait, Donald R., et al. Information for Decision-making in Rural Development, 2 vols. Washington, DC: Development Alternatives, Inc., 1978.
M-1-IS,DM

Mickelwait, Donald R., Donald R. Jackson, Craig V. Olson, Alan Roth, Charles F. Sweet, and Peter F. Weisel. Personnel Requirements for Project Development in East and Southern Africa. A report prepared for the Regional Economic Development Services Office (REDSO) for East and Southern Africa, 1977, by Development Alternatives, Inc.
-HR

Miller, David W. Management Assistance to LCADP Transportation Logistics: Observations and Recommendations. IRD Project Field Report. Prepared for the United States Agency for International Development. Washington, DC: Development Alternatives, Inc., 1979.
M-2-TA

Miller, Eric J. "A Negotiating Model in Integrated Rural Development Projects." In Exploring Individual and Organizational Boundries edited by W. Gorden Lawrence. Chichester: John Wiley and Sons, 1979.
MO-TA

Miller, V.A. The Guidebook for International Trainers in Business and Industry. Madison: American Society for Training and Development, 1979.
M-3-PI,PO,HR

Ministry of Overseas Development. Project Data Handbook. London: Ministry of Overseas Development, 1979.
-PO,PI

Moddie, A.D. "The Making of the Indian Executive." Indian Management 9, no. 8 (Aug 1970): 43-49.
M-PI

Mohanan, N., and P. Purushotham. "Have Third World Cooperatives Failed?" Business Standard (Feb 17 1983): 5.
O-EM

Mohanty, R.P. "Hierarchical Analysis For Complex Systems: Application to an Irrigation System." *Vikalpa* 6 (July - Oct. 1981): 189-199.
O-2-DM

Monappa, A. *Designing Personnel Policies to Meet Emerging Organizational Challenges.* Ahmedabad: Indian Institute of Management, 1982.
O-HR

Montgomery, John D. "Allocation of Authority in Land Reform Programs: A Comparative Study of Administrative Processes and Outputs." *Administrative Science Quarterly* 17 (March 1972): 162-175.
MO-4

Montgomery, John D. "Decisions, Non-decisions and Other Phenomena: Implementation Analysis for Development Administrators." In *International Development Administration: Implementation Analysis for Development Projects* edited by George Honadle and Rudi Klauss. 55-72. New York: Praeger Publishers, 1979.
M-DM,PI

Montgomery, John D. "Planning to Cope: Administrative Consequences of Rapid Population Growth." In *Policy Science and Population* edited by W. Illchman. Lexington: DC Heath.
MO-2-PO

Montgomery, John D. "The Populist Front in Rural Development: Or Shall We Eliminate the Bureaucrats and Get on With The Job?" *Public Administration Review* 39, no. 1 (1979).
MO-1-TA

Montgomery, John D. *Technology and Civic Life: Making and Implementing Development Decisions.* Cambridge: MIT Press, 1974.
M-DM

Montgomery, John, and M. Esman. "Popular Participation in Development Administration." *Journal of Comparative Administration* 3, no. 3 (1971): 358-382.
no code

Montgomery, John D., John M. Cohen, and M.L.M. Perera. *CAFRAD's African Program for Training in the Management of Development Projects.* Summary of findings and recommendations from the Lusaka Workshop on project management for rural development CAFRAD. Tangier, Morocco, Aug 1975.
M-1-PI

Montjoy, Robert S., and L. O'Toole. "Toward a Theory of Policy Implementation: An Organizational Perspective." *Public Administration Review* 39, no. 5 (1979): 465-476.
O-PO,PI

Moris, Jon R. "The Transferability of Western Management Concepts and Programs, An East African Perspective." In *Education and Training For The Public Sector Management In Developing Countries* edited by Lawrence D. Stifel, James S. Coleman, and Joseph E. Black. New York: The Rockefeller Foundation, 1977.
M-TA

Morgan, Philip C. *Why Aid Fails: An Organizational Interpretation.* Gaborone Botswana: IDM, 1978.
O-TA

Morss, Elliott R., John K. Hatch, Donald R. Mickelwait, and Charles F. Sweet. *Strategies for Small Farmer Development* 2 vols. Boulder: Westview Press, 1976.
-1-PO,PI

Mosher, A.T. "Administrative Experimentation: As A 'Way of Life' for Development Projects." *Industrial Development Journal* 9 (June 1967): 38-41.
MO-PO,PI

Mosher, A.T. *Serving Agriculture as an Administrator.* New York: Agricultural Development Council, Inc., 1975.
M-1-

Moulik, T.K. "Entrepreneurship and Planning." *Mainstream* 20, no. 44 (July 1982): 21-22.
-3-PO

Moulik, T.K. "On Entrepreneural Achievements in an Industrially Progressive Rural Setting: Arand Gujarat." In *Administration for Rural Development* edited by D.R. Mehta and S.K. Batra Jaipar, India: Center for Administrative Change, 1981.
M-1-PI -3-HR,PO

Moursi, Mahmoud A. "The Applicability of Newer Management Training Techniques in Developing Countries." In *Proceedings of the Academy of Management* edited by A.G. Bedeian, A.A. Armenakis, W.H. Holky, and H.S. Field. New Orleans: Academy of Management, 1975.
M-HR

Mouton, J., and R. Blake. "Issues in Transnational Organizations Development." In *Managing for Accomplishment* edited by B.M. Bass, R.C. Cooper and J.A. Haas. Lexington: Heath Lexington, 1970.
MO-PI,PO

Mozumdar, S.N. "Training in Community Development." Indian Journal of Public Administration 9 (April-June 1963): 182-188.
M-4-

Murphy, Jerome T. Getting the Facts: A Fieldwork Guide for Evaluators and Policy Analysis. Santa Monica: Goodyear Publishing Co., Inc. 1980.
M-PI,DM,PO

Murray, F. "Export OD?" Training and Development Journal 36 (Oct. 82): 18-23.
O-TA,PI

Murrell, Kenneth L. "The Definition, the Literature and the Initial Conceptual Underpinning of Empowerment." Unpublished Working Paper, The University of West Florida, 1984.
M-HR

Murrell, Kenneth L. "Does O.D. Have a Role in the Third World?" O.D. Journal (Summer 1984): 16-20.
O-PO,PI

Murrell, Kenneth L. "Management Infrastructure Development in The Third World." Macau: International Organization Development Journal University of East Asia, forthcoming.
M-TA

Murrell, Kenneth L. "A Systems Approach to the Delivery of Technical Assistance for Management Development." In Managing Project-Related Technical Assistance: The Lessons of Success Staff Working Paper No. 586. Francis Lethem, and L. Cooper. Washington, DC: World Bank, n.d.
M-TA,PI

Murrell, Kenneth L. "Training and Development for Developing Countries." European Journal of Industrial Training 8, no. 4 (1984): 25-32.
M-

Murrell, Kenneth L. "Understanding the Egyptian Manager: A Third World Management Development Experience." Leadership and Organization Development Journal 2, no. 3 (Oct./Nov. 1981): n.p.
M-TA

Murthy, K.R.S. "Control Systems in Public Enterprises." In Public Enterprises in India: Focus on Researches edited by T.L. Shankar, R.K. Misra, and S. Ravishankar. Bombay: Himalaya Publishing House, 1983.
O-EM

Murthy, Nirmala, and J.K. Satia. Management Information and Evaluation Systems in Health and Family Planning Programs. India: PSG Group, Indian Institute of Management, 1983.
M-2-IS,EM

Narain, L. Principles and Practice of Public Enterprise Management. New Delhi: S. Chand and Co., 1980.
M-2-PO-PI

Narayanan, P.P. "Management and Worker Development Strategies." Malaysian Management Review 19 (Aug. 1984): 1-4.
M-HR

National Economic and Development Authority. A Guide to Project Development. Manila: NEDA, 1978.
-PI,PO

Neelamegham, S., ed. Management Development: New Perspectives and Viewpoints. Delhi: Kalyani, 1973.
M-

Newman, William H. "Is Management Exportable?" Columbia Journal of World Business 5 (Jan./Feb. 1970): 7-18.
M-PI

van Nieuwenhuijze, C.A.O. "A Subject Matter That Needs Attention: The Common Man's Participation in Development." Civilisations 19, 3 (1969): 359-370.
O-4-PO,PI

Nigerian Center for Management Development. "Programming for Improved Performance (P.I.P.) A Guideline for Managers of Public Enterprises, Management Educators, Trainers and Consultants." Lagos, Nigeria: 1976.
M-PI,PO

Noor, A. "Managing Adult Literacy Training." Prospects 12, no. 2 (1982): 163-84.
M-2-HR

Noranitipadungkarn, Chakrit, ed. The Role of the Public Enterprise in Development. Asia and Pacific Region. Manila: EROPA, 1979.
O-2-HR

Nylen, Donald J., Robert Mitchell, and Anthony Stout. Handbook of Staff Development and Human Relations Training: Materials Developed for Use in Africa. Washington, DC: National Institute for Applied Behavioral Science, 1967.
M-HR,PI

Oakley, Peter, and David Marsden. Approaches to Participation in Development Geneva: ILO, 1984.
MO-4

Ollawa, Patrick E. "On a Dynamic Model for Rural Development in Africa." Journal of Modern African Studies 15, no. 3 (1977): 401-423.
-1-PI,PO

Olsen, Peter. Management and Productivity. Gaborone, Botswana: IDM, 1983.
M-3

O'Regan, Fred. Eliciting Needs in Planning Urban-Based Services for Rural Development. Washington, DC: The Development Group for Alternative Policies, 1978.
-1-PO,PI

Owens, E., and R. Shaw. Development Reconsidered: Bridging the Gap Between Government and People. Lexington: D.C. Heath and Co., 1972.
O-4-PO

Overseas Development Institute. Institutions, Management, and Social Development. Agricultural Administration Unit Occ. Paper No. 3. London: ODI, 1979.
MO

Owens, Edgar. "Small Farmer Participation and World Agricultural Development." Public Administration Review 36, no. 2 (1976): 142-147.
O-1,4-PO

Ozgediz, S. Managing the Public Service in Developing Countries." Staff Working Papers 583. Management and Development Subseries no. 10. Washington, DC: The World Bank, 1983.
M-2-

Pandoy, I.M. Management Accounting: A Planning and Control Approach. New Delhi: Vikas Publishing House Private Ltd., 1983.
M-FB,EM

Pareek, Udai. Education and Rural Development Asian Experience. Ahmedabad: PSG Group, Indian Institute of Management, 1983.
-1,2-HR

Pareek, Udai and T.V. Rao. Learning from Action. Ahmedabad, India: The PSG Group, The Indian Institute of Management, 1983.
M-PI

Pareek, Udai, and T.V. Rao. Training of Education Managers: A Handbook for Trainers on Planning and Management of Education. Ahmedabad, India: PSG Group, The Indian Institute of Management, 1983.
M-2-PO,PI

Parks, Y.U. "Organizational Development and Culture Contact: A Case Study of Sokagakkai in America." Ethnic Studies 10 (1982): 1-16
O-

Parry, Scott B., and Edward J. Robinson. "Management Development: Training or Education?" Training and Development Journal 33, no. 7 (July 1979):8-13.
M-PO,PI,EM

Patel, V.C. "Innovations in Promoting and Developing New Enterprises." In Small Enterprise Development: Policies and Programmes, edited by P.A. Neck. Geneva: International Labour Office, 1977.
M-3-PO

Patil, S.S. "Choosing Chief Executives (For Government Undertakings)-- Ideologists, Specialists or Generalists?" Indian Journal of Public Administration 18, no. 1 (Jan.-Mar. 1972): 7-35.
M-DM

Paul, A.B. "The MBA in Indian Industry-- Some Observations." Indian Management 9, no. 7 (July 1970): 3-13.
M-3-

Paul, Samuel. "Managerial Behavior and Public Sector Performance." Integrated Management (April 1974): 19-26.
M-2-PI

Paul, Samuel. Managing Development Programmes: Lessons From Success. Boulder: Westview Press, 1982.
M-DM,EM,PO

Paul, Samuel. "Strategic Management of Development Programmes: Evidence from an International Study." International Review of Administrative Sciences 1 (1983): 73-86.
M-PI,PO

Paul, Samuel. Strategic Management of Public Programs. Ahmedabad, India: PSG Group, The Indian Institute of Management, 1983.
M-2-PI

Perrett, Heli and Francis Lethem. "Human Factors in Project Work." Staff Working Paper no. 397. Washington, DC: World Bank, 1980.
M-PI,PO

Peterson, R.E., and K.K. Seo. "Benefit-Cost Analysis for Developing Countries: A Decision-tree Approach." Economic Development and Cultural Change 24, no. 1 (1975): 185-197.
M-DM

Peterson, R.E., and K.K. Seo. "Public Adminstration Planning in Developing Countries: A Bayesian Decision-Making Theory Approach." *Policy Sciences* 3, no. 3 (1972): 371-78.
M-PO,DM

Pezeshkpur, Chanqiz. "Challenge to Management in the Arab World." *Business Horizons* 21, no. 4 (Aug 1978): 46-55.
M-PI

Pitt, David C. *Development from Below: Anthropologists and Development Situations*. The Hague: Mouton Publ., 1976.
M-4-

Pitt, David. *The Social Dynamics of Development*. Elmsford: Pergamon Press, 1976.
M-PO

Poland, Orville, F., ed. "A Symposium: Program Evaluation." *Public Administration Review* 34 (July/Aug. 1974): 299-338.
-EM,PI

Pollnac, Richard B. *Socio-cultural Aspects of Developing Small-Scale Fisheries: Delivering Services to the Poor*. Staff Working Paper 490. Washington, DC: World Bank, 1981.
-1-PI

Powelson, John P. *Institutions of Economic Growth: A Theory of Conflict Management in Developing Countries*. Princeton: Princeton Univ. Press, 1972.
M-PO

Prasad, S. Benjamin, and Anant R. Negandhi. *Managerialism for Economic Development*. The Hague: Marinus Nijhoff, 1968.
M-PI

Pratt, D.J., and M.D. Gwynne. *Rangeland Management and Ecology in East Africa*. London: Hodder and Stoughton, 1977.
M-1-PO

Provinse, John H. "Community Development Research and Evaluation." *Community Development Review* 5 (Dec. 1960):
-4-EM

Public Administration Service. *Organization for Agriculture-based Development*. Washington, DC: Public Administration Service, 1975.
O-1-PO

Pyle, D.F. *From Project to Programme: Structural Constraints Associated with Expansion*. Working Paper No. 3. Washington, DC: NASPAA 982.
O-PI,PO

Qamar, M.K. "Why Not an Interdisciplinary Rural Extension Service?" *Journal of Administration Overseas* 18, no. 4 (Oct 1979): 256-268.
O-1-PO

Rai, H. "Country Note for International Program in Training of Trainers in Development Administration." *Prashasan* 42 (March 1985): 123-132.
IM-M-HR

Rajana, C. "Third World Industrialization--Industrial Cooperation Under the Lowe Convention." *Journal of African Studies* 10, no. 2 (1983): 30-49.
-2-PO

Ralston, Lenore, James Anderson and Elisabeth Colson. *Voluntary Efforts in Decentralized Management: Opportunities and Constraints in Rural Development*. Berkely: Institute of International Studies, Univ. of California, 1983.
M-1-PI,PO

Raman, N. Pattabhi. "Project Implementation in the Context of a Plan: The Missing Links." *International Development Review* 20 (1978): 5-7.
-PO,PI

Rao, T.V. "HRD: The Now Approach." *Indian Journal of Industrial Relations* 1 (1982): 29-41.
-HR

Rao, T.V. "Managing Your Human Resources." *Malaysian Business* (Nov 1982): 51-54.
M-HR

Rao, T.V. "Performance Appraisals: How to Have Good, Happy Workers." *Malaysian Business* (Dec. 1982): 73-77.
M-HR,EM

Rao, T.V. "Potential Appraisal: Finding the Right Man." *Malaysian Business* (April 1983): 47-50.
M-EM,PO

Rao, T.V. "Should Good Performance Be Rewarded?" *Malaysian Business* (Jan. 1983): 45-48.
M-HR,PI,EM

Rapp, Brian W. and Frank M. Patitucci. *Managing Local Government For Improved Performance: A Practical Approach*. Boulder: Westview Press, 1977.
MO-PO,PI

Raveed, S.R., and W. Renforth. "State Enterprise--Multinational Corporation Joint Ventures: How Well Do They Meet Both Partners' Needs?" *Management International Review* 1 (1983):
O-3-

Reddin, W.J. "Effective International Training." *Training and Development Journal* 32, no. 4 (April 1978): 12-16, 18-20.
M-3-PI

Reilly, Wynn. *Training Administrators for Development*. London: Heineman Educational Books, 1979.
MO-2-PO,PI,EM

Reynolds, Agnes, ed. *Technology Transfer A Project Guide for International HRD*. Boulder: Westview Press, 1984.
M-HR

Reynolds, J.I. *Case Method in Management Development: Guide for Effective Use*. Geneva: International Labour Office, 1980.
M

Richman, Barry. "Ideology and Management: Commission and Compromise." *Columbia Journal of World Business* (June 1971): 45-58.
M-PO

Riggs, Fred W. "Administrative Development: An Elusive Concept." In *Approaches To Development: Politics, Administration and Usage* edited by J.D. Montgomery and W.J. Siffri. New York: McGraw Hill, Inc., 1966.
MO-EM,PO,PI

Ringbakk, K.A. "Strategic Planning in a Turbulent International Enviornoment." Longe Range Planning, 9, no. 3 (1976): 2-11.
M-PO

Rogers, Everett M. *Communication of Innovations: A Cross-Cultural Approach*. New York: The Free Press, 1969.
M-PI

Rondinelli, Dennis A. "Administration of Integrated Rural Development Policy: The Politics of Agrarian Reform in Developing Countries." *World Politics* 31, no. 3 (1979): 389-416.
O-1-PI

Rondinelli, Dennis A. "Designing International Development Projects for Implementation." In *International Development Administration Implementation Analysis for Development Projects* edited by George Honadle and Rudi Klauss. New York: Praeger Publishers, 1979.
O-PI,PO

Rondinelli, Dennis A. *Diagnostics for Project Implementation--Difficulties in the Administration Projects*. Mimeo, Syracuse: Syracuse University, 1977.
MO-OM

Rondinelli, Dennis A. "The Dilemma of Development Administration: Complexity and Uncertainty in Control Oriented Bureaucracies." *World Politics* 35 (Oct 82): 43-72.
MO-DM,PI,PO

Rondinelli, Dennis A. "Implementing Development Projects: The Problem of Management." *International Development Review* 20 (1978): 11
M-PI

Rondinelli, Dennis A. "International Assistance Policy and Development Project Administration: The Impact of Imperious Rationality." *International Organization* 30 (1976): 573-605.
MO-PO,PI

Rondinelli, Dennis A. "International Requirements for Project Preparation: Aids or Obstacles to Development Planning?" *Journal of the American Institute of Planners* 42, no. 3 (July 1976): n.p.
MO-HR,PO,TA

Rondinelli, Dennis A. "National Investment Planning and Equity Policy in Developing Countries: The Challenge of Decentralized Administration." *Policy Sciences* 10, no. 1 (1975): 105-118.
O-DM,PO

Rondinelli, Dennis A. *Planning Development Projects*. Stroudsburg: Dowden, Hutchinson and Ross, 1977.
M-PO,PI

Rondinelli, Dennis A. "Project as Instrument of Development Administration." Paper from APDC/ADB Regional Training Workshop on Project Planning and Management. *Prashasan* 42 (March 1985): 97-122.
IM-M-PI

Rondinelli, Dennis A. "Why Development Projects Fail: Problems of Project Management in Developing Countries." *Project Management Quarterly* 7 (1976): 10-15.
M-EM,PI

Rondinelli, Dennis A., and Barclay A. Jones. "Decision-making, Managerial Capacity and Development: An Entrepreneurial Approach to Planning." *African Administrative Studies* 13 (1975): 105-118.
M-3-PO

Rondinelli, Dennis A., and H.R. Radosevich. "Administrative Changes in International Assistance: Implications for Asian Cooperation." *The Asian Economic and Social Review* 1, no. 1 (1976).
MO-TA,PO,PI

Rondinelli, Dennis A. and Kenneth Ruddle. Appropriate Institutions for Rural Development: Organizing Services and Technology in Developing Countries. Syracuse: Syracuse University, Maxwell School of Citizenship and Public Affairs, 1978.
O-1-PO

Rondinelli, Dennis A., and Kenneth Ruddle. "Local Organizations for Integrated Rural Development: Implementing Equity Policy in Developing Countries." International Review of Administrative Science 43, no. 1 (1977): 20-30.
O-1-PI

Rondinelli, Dennis A. and Kenneth Ruddle. "Nonformal Education and Training for Rural Development." Productivity -- Quarterly Journal of the National Productivity Council. New Delhi (1978).
M-1,2-PO

Rondinelli, Dennis A. and Kenneth Ruddle. "Political Commitment and Administrative Support." Journal of Administration Overseas 20 (1977): 46-47.
MO-PI

Rondinelli, Dennis A., John R. Nellis and G. Shabbir Cheema. Decentralization in Developing Countries: A Review of Recent Experience. Staff Working Paper no. 581. Washington, DC: The World Bank, n.d.
O-PI O-PI

Rose, C.J. "Management Science in Developing Countries - Comparative Approach to Irrigation Feasibility." Management Science Series B Application 20, no. 4 (1973): 423-438.
M-1-PI

Rosenbaum, Walter A. "The Paradoxes of Public Participation." Administration and Society 8, no. 3 (1976): 355-383.
O-4-PI

Rosenthal, Steven M. and Bob Mezoff. "How to Improve the Cost-benefit Ratio of Management Training and Development." Training and Development Journal 34, no. 12 (Dec 1980): n.p.
M-PI,FB,EM

Rothman, Jack. Planning and Organizing for Social Change Action Principles from Social Science Reserch. New York: Columbia University Press, 1974.
MO-PO,PI

Rothwell, Kenneth J., ed. Administrative Issues in Developing Economies. Lexington: D.C. Heath, 1972.
M-PI

Roy, S.K. "Managing Large Organizations - A Comparative-Study In A Developing-Country." Economic and Political Weekly 17, no. 9 (1982).
MO-

Ruthenberg, Hans. "Types of Organization in Agricultural Production Development." Zeitschroft fur Auslandische Landwirtschaft 12 (1973): 3-4.
O-1-

Ruttan, V.W. "Integrated Rural Development Programs: A Skeptical Perspective." International Development Review 4 (1975): 9-16.
-1-EM

Ruttan, Vernon W. "Induced Institutional Change." In Induced Innovations: Technology, Institutions and Development edited by Hans P. Binswanger and Vernon W. Ruttan. Baltimore: The Johns Hopkins Univ. Press, 1978.
O-PI

Sahni, Balbir S. "Public Sectors in Less Developed Countries-Development Goals and Efficiency." Annals of Public and Coop Economy 54 (Sept. 1983): 325-35.
MO-2-PO

Sambrani, S., and K.R. Pichholia. Area Planning: Precepts and Practices. Ahmedabad: Centre for Management in Agriculture, Indian Institute of Management, 1983.
M-PO,PI

Samiuddin, Abida. "A Uniform Organizational Pattern for Development Administration." Indian Journal of Public Administration 23, no. 3 (1977): 768-780.
O-PO

Saunders, Robert S. Traditional Cooperation, Indigenous Peasants' Groups and Rural Development: A Look at Possibilities and Experiences. Background Paper Washington, DC: The World Bank, 1977.
O-1-PI

Savas, E.S. Alternatives for Delivering Public Services. Boulder: Westview Press, n.d.
MO-PO

Saxena, A.P. "Backward Area Development: Issues in Administrative Planning." Indian Journal of Public Administration 23, no. 3 (1977): 449-464.
MO-PO

Schein, Edgar H., ed. Organization Development. Reading.: Addison-Wesley, 1969.
MO-PI,PO

Schein, Edgar H. *Organizational Culture and Leadership. A Dynamic View.* San Francisco: Jossey-Bass, Inc., 1985.
MO

Schein, Edgar H. and Warner G. Bennis. *Personal and Organizational Change Through Group Methods: The Laboratory Approach.* New York: John Wiley and Sons, 1965.
MO-PI

Schluter, M.G.G., and T.D. Mount. "Some Management Objectives of the Peasant Farmer: An Analysis of Risk Aversion in the Choice of Cropping Pattern, Surat District, India." *Journal of Development Studies* 12, no. 3 (1976): 246-261.
M-Em,DM

Schaffer, Bernard. *Organizational Decisions and Policy Outcomes.* Discussion Paper No. 22 Brighton:IDS, 1973.
O-PO,PI

Schmid, A. Allan, and Ronald C. Faas. "A Research Approach to Institutional Alternatives in the Administration of Agrarian Development Programs." *Agricultural Administration* 2, no. 4 (1975): 285-305.
O-1-PO

Schnapper, Melvin. "Culture Simulation as a Training Tool." *International Development Review* 15, no. 1 (1973): 3-6.
M-TA

Schultzberg, G. "Management of Rural Water Supplies." *Water Supply and Management* 2, no. 4 (1978): 333-340.
M-1-PI

Schuster, I. "Recent Research on Women in Development (Review Article)." *Journal of Development Studies* 18 (July 82): 522-535.
-HR

Scott, M., J.D. MacArthur, and D.M. Newbury. *Project Appraisal in Practice.* London: Heinemann.--rev. *Journal of Developmental Studies*, 14 (1976): 254-256.
M-PI,EM

Senor, James M. "Applicability of Selected Consultation Concepts to Community Development." *Indian Journal of Social Work* 25 (Oct 1964): 261-267.
MO-4-TA

Seshadri, K. "Social Innovation and Development Administration." *Behavioral Sciences and Community Development* 5, no. 2 (Sept 1971): 79-87.
M-4-PI

Shaner, W.W. *Project Planning for Developing Economies.* New York: Praeger Publishers, 1979.
MO-PO

Sherif, A. Fouad. "A New Approach to Training for Improved Performance in Public Corporations." *Public Administration Newsletter* (April 1971): 7-8.
M-3-PI,PO

Sherwood, Frank P. "Devolution as a Problem of Organization Strategy." In *Comparative Urban Research: The Administration and Politics of Cities* edited by Robert T. Daland. Beverly Hills: Sage Publications, 1969.
O-PI,PO

Shetty, Y. K. "Transmitting Management Know-how to LDC: Experiences of U.S. Multinational Corporations." *Management International Review* 13, no. 1 (1973): 71-78.
M-3-TA

Shirley, Mary M. *Managing State-Owned Enterprises.* Staff Working Paper 557. Washington, DC: World Bank, 1983.
MO-3-PI

Shroff, M.R. "Some Aspects of Financial Management for Economic Planning and Revival." *Economic Trends* 12, no. 7 (Apr. 1983): 99-104.
M-PO,FB

Siffin, W. *Administrative Problems and Integrated Rural Development.* Bloomington: International Development Institute, Indiana University, 1979.
Mo-1-

Siffin, William D., ed. *Approaches to Development: Politics, Administration and Change.* New York: McGraw-Hill Book Co., 1966.
O-PO,PI

Silberston, Aubrey, ed. *Industrial Management: East and West; Papers from the International Economic Association Conference on Labor Productivity, 1971.* New York: Praeger Publishers, 1973.
M-3-PO,EM

Silverman, Jerry M. *Technical Assistance and Aid.* Technical Paper 28. Washington, DC: The World Bank, 1984.
MO-TA

Simpson, James R. "Uses of Cultural Anthropology in Economic Analysis: A Papago Indian Case." *Human Organization* 29, no. 3 (1970): 162-168.
M-EM

Singapore Institute of Management. "Managerial Manpower Survey: Summary." *Singapore Management Review* 6, no. 2 (July 1984): 11-17.
IM-M

Singh, Ajit. "The 'Basic Needs' Approach To Development Vs. The New International Economic Order." World Development 7 (1979): 585-606.
MO-4

Smith, Kenneth Alan, and Craig Tenney. Considerations for Microcomputer Use in Development Management: A Review of Selected Articles. College Park: International Development Management Center with the Development Program Management Center, 1985.
Im-M,O-IS

Smith, Theodore M. "Stimulating Performance in the Indonesian Bureaucracy: Gaps in the Administrator's Tool Kit." Economic Development and Cultural Change 23, no. 4 (1975): 719-738.
MO-PI

Smith, William E., Francis Lethem, and Ben A. Thoolen. "The Design of Organizations for Rural Development Projects: A Progress Report" Staff Working Paper no. 375. Washington, DC: World Bank, 1980.
MO-1-PO

Smith, William E. Organizing as a Power Process. The Creation and Testing of a Conceptual Framework and Its Application to the Design of Development Projects. Unpublished Ph.D Dissertation, University of Pennsylvania, 1983.
MO-PO,DM

Solomon, Darwin D. "Characteristics of Local Organizations and Service Agencies Conducive to Development." Sociologia Ruralis 12, no. 3-4 (1972): 334-360.
O-2-RO

Soloman, Morris J. Analysis of Projects for Economic Growth: An Operational System for Their Formulation, Evaluation, and Implementation. New York: Praeger Publishers, 1970.
M-PI,PO,EM

Soloman, Morris J. "An Organizational Change Strategy for Developing Countries." Copenhagen, Denmark: Paper delivered to the 26th International Meeting of the Institute of Management Sciences, June 17-21, 1984.
O-PO,PI

Squire, Lyn. Employment Policy in Developing Countries: A Survey Of Issues. New York: Oxford University Press for The World Bank, 1981.
2-PO

Srivastava, U.K. "Management of Change and Implementation Strategy." In Management of Rural Energy Systems edited by P.S. Satsangi and Vinayshil Gautam. New Delhi: Galgotia Publications, 1983.

Srivastava, U.K.; Reddy M. Dharma, and V.K. Gupta. Management of Marine Fishing Industry: An Analysis of Problems in Harvesting and Processing. Ahmedabad, The Center for Management in Agriculture, The Indian Institute of Management, n.d.
M-1-PI,EM

Srivastava, U.K., G.V. Shenoy, and S.C. Sharma. Quantitative Techniques for Managerial Decision Making. New Delhi: Wiley Eastern Ltd., 1983.
M-PI,EM

Stahl, O. Glenn. "Managerial Effectiveness In Developing Countries." International Review of Administrative Sciences 45, no. 1 (1979): 1-5.
M-

Staudt, Kathleen. Women and Participation in Rural Development: A Framework for Project Design and Policy-Oriented Research. n.p., 1979.
M-1-HR,PO

Stifel, L.D., J.S. Coleman, and J.E. Black. Education and Training for Public Sector Management in Developing Countries. Special Report from the Rockefeller Foundations. March 1977.
MO-2-TA

Stokes, Bruce. Helping Ourselves: Local Solutions To Global Problems. New York: W.W. Norton and Co., 1981.
MO-4

Stokes, Bruce. Local Responses to Global Problems: A Key to Meeting Basic Human Needs. Paper No. 17, Washington, DC: World Watch Institute, 1977.
O-4-HR,PI

Stockton, Ronald R. "A Tale of Two Locations: Mobilization, Innovation and Resistance to Change." Rural Africana 18 (1972): 30-39.

Stone, D., and A. Stone. "Creation of Administrative Capability: The Missing Ingredient in Development Strategy." In Strategy for Rural Development edited by J. Barratt. London: Macmillan, 1976.
MO-1-PO

Stone, D.C. The Development of Methods for the Evaluation of Education and Training Programs and Courses in Public Administration. Ife, Nigeria: Institute of Administration, University of Ife, 1970.
MO-2-EM

Stout, Russell, Jr. Management or Control? The Organizational Challenge. Bloomington: Indiana University Press, 1980.
MO

Stover, William James. <u>Information Technology in the Third World: Can I.T. Lead to Human National Development?</u>" Boulder: Westview Press, 1984.
M-IS

Strachan, Harry W. "Side Effects of Planning in the AID Control Systems." <u>World Development</u> 6 (1978): 467-478.
MO-PO-PI.

Strand, Stephen H. "Implementation Alternatives and Economic Analysis." In <u>International Development Administration. Implementation Analysis for Development Projects</u>" edited by George Honadle and Rudi Klauss. New York: Praeger Publishers, 1979.
MO-EM,PI,PO

Streeten, Paul. "The Distinctive Features of a Basic Needs Approach to Development." <u>International Development Review</u> 19, no. 3 (1977): 8-16.
O-EM,PI

Stuckenburck, Linn C., ed. <u>The Implementation of Project Management. The Professional Handbook.</u> Reading: Addison-Wesley Publ. Co., 1981.
M-PI,PO

Subramanian, Ashok. <u>New Roles in Hospitals: Organizational Innovations in the Voluntary Sector.</u> Ahmedabad, India: The PSG Group, the Indian Institute of Management, n.d.

Subramanian, Ashok; Onderjit Khanna, Anil Bhatt, and Anil K. Singh. <u>Managing and Adult Education Projects.</u> Ahmedabad, India: The PSG Group, The Indian Institute of Management, 1983.
M-2-PI

Subramaniam, V. "Some Administrative Aspects of Federalism in the Third World." <u>International Review of Administrative Sciences</u> 50, no. 1 (1984): 47-59.
M-

Sundarem, K. "<u>Social and Human Problems in Introducing Technological Change.</u>" Proceedings of CIOS 13 International Management Congress 6 (1963): 495-498.
M-PI

Sushma. "Informational Needs of Backward Area Entrepreneurs." <u>Vikalpa</u> 6 (Jan. 1981): 25-33.
3-HR,IS

Sutherland, John W. <u>Management Handbook for Public Administrators.</u> New York: Van Nostrand, Reinhold, 1978.
MO-PI

Swee, Goh Keng. "Social, Political and Institutional Aspects of Development Planning." <u>The Malayan Economic Review</u> 10 (April 1965): 1-15.
O-PO

Sweet, Charles F., and Peter F. Weisel. "Process Versus Blueprint Models for Designing Rural Development Projects." In <u>International Development Administration: Implementation Analysis for Development Projects</u> edited by George Honadle and Rudi Klauss. New York: Praeger Publishers, 1979.
MO-PI,PO

Swerdlow, Irving, and Marcus Ingle, eds. <u>Public Administration Training for the Less Developed Countries.</u> Syracuse: Maxwell School, 1974.
M-HR

Swinth, Robert. <u>Organizational Systems for Management: Designing, Planning and Implementation.</u> Columbus: Grid, Inc. 1974.
MO-PO,PI

Sycip, W.Z. "The Need for Management Education in the Third World Countries." <u>Malaysian Management Review</u> 11 (Dec. 1976): 31-37.
M-HR

Szal, Richard J. "Popular Participation, Employment and the Fulfillment of Basic Needs." International Labour Review, 118 (1979): 27-38.
O-4

Takahashi, Akira. "Mobilizing Peasants for Irrigation Development." In <u>Farm Water Management for Rice Cultivation</u> n.a. Tokyo: Asian Productivity Organization, 1977.
-4-PI

Takaji, Kenjiro. "Some Approaches to the Problems of Management Development in Developing Countries." <u>Productivity Digest</u> 2 (Dec. 1966): 12-20.
M-PI

Taylor, B.O and G.L. Lippitt, eds. <u>Management Development and Training Handbook.</u> London: McGraw-Hill Book Co., 1975.
M-HR,PI,PO

Taylor, James C. "Strategies for Organizational Change." In <u>The Conditioning Effects of Technology on Organizational Behavior in Planned Social Change.</u> Technical Report Contract No. N00014-67-A-0181- 0013, NR 170-719/29-68 (Code 452) Office of Naval Research, Group Psychology Programs (Sept. 1969): 16-29.
O-PI,PO

Taylor, Max. <u>Coverdale on Management.</u> London: Wm. Heinemann Ltd., 1979.
M-PO,PI

Teheranian, Majid; F. Hakimzadeh, and M.L. Vidale, eds. Communications Policy for National Development: A Comparative Perspective. London: Routledge and Kegan Paul--rev Journal of Development Administration 12 (1977): 357-359.
MO-IS,PI

Teune, Henry, and Zdravko Mlinar. "Development and Participation." In Local Politics, Development and Participation F.C. Bruhns. Pittsburgh: University of Pittsburgh, Center for International Studies, 1974.
O-4-PI

Thakur, C.P., and K.C. Sethi, eds. Industrial Democracy: Some Issues and Experiences. New Delhi: Shri Ram Centre for Industrial Relations and Human Resources, 1973.
O-4-PI,PO

Thamain, Hans J., and David L. Wileman. "Conflict Management in Project Life Cycles." Sloan Management Review (Spring 1975): 31-50.
M-PI

Thamain, Hans J., and David L. Wileman. "Diagnosing Conflict Determinants in Project Management." IEEE Transactions on Engineering Management EM-22 no. 1 (1975): n.p.
M-DM,PI

Thomas, K.S. Communication and Decision Making in International Organization: A Cross Cultural Perspective on Organizational Behavior in the World Bank. Ann Arbor: University Microfilms International, 1980.
O-IS-DM

Thiagarajan, K.M., and C.K. Prahalad. Some Problems in the Behavioral Science Education of Managers and Management Instructors in Developing Nations. Technical Report No. 31. Rochester: Management Research Center, University of Rochester, Sept. 1, 1969.
M-2-HR,PI,EM

Thomas, James T. "Public Choice Analysis of Institutional Constraints on Firewood Production Strategies in the West African Sahel." In Public Choice and Rural Development edited by C.S. Russel and N.K. Nicholson, n.p., 1981.
MO-4-PI,EM

Thomas, Rosamund M. "The Rejuvenation of Public Administration in Developing Countries." Journal of Admiinistration Overseas 13 (April 1974): 366-373.
MO-PI

Thomas, Theodore H. "People Strategies for International Development: Administrative Alternatives to National, Political and Economic Ideologies." Journal of Comparative Administration (1973): 87-107.
MO-2,4,-HR-,PO

Thomas, Theodore H. Reorienting Bureaucracy Performance: A Social Learning Approach to Development Action. Working Paper No. 8, Washington, DC: NASPAA, July 1983.
MO-PI,PO

Thomas, Theodore H., and Derick E. Brinkerhoff. Semi-Autonomous Partnership Organizations for Development: Lessons from the JCRR Experience. Working Paper No. 8. Los Angeles: USC, School of Public Administration, n.d.
O-4

Thompson, Kenneth W., and Barbara R. Fogel. Higher Education and Social Change: Promising Experiments in Developing Countries. New York: Praeger Publishers, 1976.
MO-2-PI

Thornton, D.S. "Some Aspects of the Organisation of Irrigated Areas." Agricultural Administration 2, no. 3 (1975): 179-194.
O-1-PO

Tichy, Noel M. "Managing Change Strategically: The Technical, Political, and Cultural Keys." Organizational Dynamics (1982): 59-80.
MO-PO,PI

Tilman, Robert O. "Emergence of Black Market Bureaucracy: Administration, Development and Corruption in the New States." Public Administration Review 28, no. 5 (1968): 437-444.
MO-PI-EM

Timmer, Peter C., John W. Thomas, Louis T. Wells, and David Morawetz. The Choice of Technology in Developing Countries (Some Cautionery Tales). Cambridge: Harvard University, Center for International Affairs, 1975.
M-PI,PO,DM

Tinker, Irene, M.B. Bramsen, and M. Buvinic. Women and World Development, with an Annotated Bibliography 2 vols. New York: Praeger Publishers for Overseas Development Council, n.d.
-HR

Tomasetti, W.E. "Development Administration and Community Development." Community Development Journal 9, no. 1 (1974): 47-63.
MO-4-

Trifunovic, Bogden. "Self Management and Peoples Participation - A Demand and Perspective of Our Time." Translated by S. Petnicki. Socialist Thought and Practice: (A Yugoslav Monthly) 10 (Oct. 1981): 25-38.
MO-4

Trist, Eric. "Planning the First Steps Toward Quality of Working LIfe in a Developing Country." In The Quality of Working Life vol. 1 edited by Lou Davis and Al Cherns. New York: Free Press, 1975.
MO-PI,PO

United Kingdom, Foreign and Commonwealth Office, Overseas Devleopment Administration. A Guide to Project Appraisal in Developing Countries. London: United Kingdom HMSO, 1972.
M-EM,FB,PI

United Nations. Administration of Development Programmes and Projects: Some Major Issues. New York: United Nations, 1971.
MO-PI,PO

United Nations. Changes and Trends in Public Administration and Finance for Development. Second Survey 1977-79, New York: United Nations, 1982.
MO-2-FB

United Nations. Planning in Developing Countries. Theory and Methodology. New York: United Nations, n.d.
M-PO

United Nations. "Popular Participation in Development." In Social Change and Social Development Policy in Latin America. New York: United Nations, 1970.
O-4-

United Nations. Public Service Delivery Systems for the Rural Poor. Bangkok, UN: ESCAP, 1980.
O-1,2-PI

United Nations. Strengthening Public Administration and Finance for Development. Issues and Approaches. New York: United Nations, 1978.
MO-FB

United Nations. Women and Development: Guidelines for Programs and Project Planning. New York: United Nations, 1983.
-HR,PI

United Nations Asia Development Institute. An Approach to Evolving Guidelines for Rural Development. Prepared by Yusuf A. Ahmad. Discussion Paper Series no. 1, New York: United Nations, 1975.
M-1-PO,PI

UNCRD. Planned Development and Self Management UNCRD Working Paper NO. 82-8. New York: United Nations, 1983.
M-PI,PO

United Nations. Department of Economic and Social Affairs. A Practical Guide to Performance Improvement Programming in Public Organizations. ST/ESA/SER.E/9, New York: United Nations, 1977.
M-PO,PI

United Nations. Appraising Administrative Capability for Development. New York: United Nations Department of Economic and Social Affairs, ST/TAO/46, 1969.
MO-EM

United Nations. Department of Economic and Social Affairs. Development Administration: Current Approaches and Trends in Public Administration for National Development ST/ESA/SER.E/3, New York: 1975.
MO-PO,PI

United Nations. Department of Economic and Social Affairs. Local Government Reform: Analysis of Experience in Selected Countries. ST/ESA/SER.E/2, New York: United Nations, 1975.
O-PO,PI

United Nations. Department of Economic and Social Affairs. New Approaches to Personnel Policy for Development. ST/TAO/M/66, New York: United Nations, 1975.
M-PI,EM

United Nations. Department of Economic and Social Affairs. Organization, Management and Supervision of Public Enterprises in Developing Countries. ST/TAO/M/65, New York: United Nations, 1974.
MO-2-PI,EM

United Nations. Department of Economic and Social Affairs, Popular Participation in Decision Making for Development. New York: UN 1975.
O-4-PI

United Nations. Department of Economic and Social Affairs, Popular Participation in Development: Emerging Trends in Community Development. ST/SOA/106. New York: UN, 1971.
O-4-PO,PI

UNESCO. Adaptation of Public Administration and Management to Different Sociocultural Contexts. Final Report of an Expert Meeting Held in Tangier, Morocco, in Sept. 1977. Paris: UNESCO, 1979.
M-

UNESCO. International Social Science Journal 20, no. 1 (1968). An issue devoted to theory, training, and practice in management.
M-PI,PO

UNESCO. Public Administration and Management: Problems of Adaptation in Different Socio-cultural contexts. New York: UNESCO, 1982.
MO-PI

UNESCO. The Right to Education: What Kind of Management. New York: UNESCO, 1982.
M-2-EM

United Nations. FAO. Improving the Organization and Administration of Agricultural Development in the Near East. Rome: FAO, 1981.
MO-1

United Nations. Industrial Development Organization. Contract Planning and Organization. New York: UNIDO, 1974.
O-3-PO

United Nations. Industrial Development Organization. Guidelines for Project Evaluation Project Formulation and Evaluation Series No. 2. New York: United Nations, 1972.
M-3-EM,PO

UNIES. Strengthening Public Administration and Finance For Development In The 1980s. New York: United Nations.
M-FB

United Nations. Institute for Training and Research. Criteria and Methods of Evaluation: Problems and Approaches. New York: United Nations, 1969.
M-PI,EM,PO

United Nations. Organization for Economic Cooperation and Development, The Evaluation of Technical Assistance. Paris: United Nations, 1969.
-TA,EM

UNRISD. Rural Cooperatives as Agents of Change: A Research Paper and a Debate. Geneva: United Nations Research Institute for Social Development.
MO-1-PI

UNTCD. Changes and Trends in Public Administration and Finance for Development--Second Survey, 1977-79. New York: United Nations, 1982.
MO-FB

UNTCD. Elements of Institution-Building for Institutes of Public Administration and Management. ST/ESA/SER.E/25. New York: United Nations, 1982.
MO-TA

UNTCD. Enhancing Capabilities for Administrative Reform in Developing Countries. New York: United Nations, 1983.
MO-PI,PO

UNTCD. Handbook on the Improvement of Administrative Management in Public Administration. New York: United Nations, 1979. ST/ESA/SER.E/19, 1979.
MO-PI

UNTCD. Issues and Priorities in Public Administration and Finance in the Third U.N. Development Decade. New York: United Nations, 1984.
MO-FB

UNTCD. Priority Areas for Action in Public Administration and Finance in the 1980's. New York: United Nations, 1981.
MO-FB

UNTCD. Public Administration Institutions and Practices in Integrated Rural Development Programmes. New York: United Nations, 1980.
MO-1-PI

UNTCD. Survey of Changes and Trends in Public Administration and Finance for Development. New York: United Nations, 1978.
O-TA,FB

Uphoff, Norman T., and Warren R. Ilchman. The Political Economy of Development. Berkely: University of California Press, 1972.
O-PI

Uphoff, Norman T., John M. Cohen and Arthur A. Goldsmith. Feasibility and Application of Rural Development Participation: A State-of-the-Art Paper. Ithaca: Cornell University, Center for International Studies, Rural Development Committee, 1979.
O-1-PI

USAID. A Guide for Team Leaders in Technical Assistance Projects. Washington: Agency for International Development, 1973.
M-TA

USAID. Implementation of "New Directions" in Development Assistance. Report prepared for the Committee on International Relations on Implementation of the Foreign Assistance Act of 1973, 94th Congress, 1st Session, July 22, 1975.
MO-TA

USAID. Improving the Public Service Through Training. Washington, DC: Agency for International Development, 1962.
M-2-HR

USAID. "Managers Guide to Data Collection." AID, Program Design and Evaluation Methods. Washington, DC: 1979.
M-IS,EM

USAID. Managing Planned Agricultural Development. Washington, DC: Governmental Affairs Institute, Agricultural Sector Implementation Project, Oct. 1976.
MO-TA,PI

Utton, Albert G., and Ludwick A. Teclaff, eds. Water in a Developing World: The Management of a Critical Resource. Boulder: Westview Press, 1978.
M-PI

Vakil, C.N., and P.E. Brahmanand. "Technical Knowledge and Managerial Capacity as Limiting Factors on Industrial Expansion in Underdeveloped Countries." In Social Change and Economic Development. UNESCO. London: Sijthoff, 1963.
M-3-PI

Valsan, A.H. "Development, Decentralization and Leadership: A Discussion." Nagralok (Municipal Quarterly) (Jan./Mar. 1972).
MO-PO,DM

Valsan, A.H. "Positive Formalism: A Desideratum for Development." Philippine Journal of Public Administration (1968): 3-6.
O-PI,PO

Vandenput, Michel A.E. "The Transfer of Training: Some Organisational Variables." European Training 2, no. 3 (1973): 251-262.
M-PI

Vanek, Jaroslav. The Participatory Economy: An Evolutionary Hypothesis and a Strategy for Development. Ithaca: Cornell Univ. Press, 1974.
O-4-PO

Vanek, Jaroslav, and T. Bayard. "Education Toward Self-Management: An Alternative Development Strategy." International Development Review 18, no. 4 (1975): 17-23.
M-4-PO

Van Heck, Bernard. "The Involvement of the Poor in Development Through Rural Organizations." Rome: Rural Organization Action Programme, FAO, 1977.
O-2,4-

Vansina, L.S. "Integrating Different Nationality Groups." In Managing the Multinational Firm: A Behavioral Approach edited by K.M. Thiagarajan, G.V. Barratt, L.S. Vansina, and B.M. Bass. New York: Prentice-Hall, 1971.
M-3-PO

Van Wagenen, R.W. "Training as an Element in Bank Group Projects." Finance and Development 9, no. 3 (Sept. 1972): 34-39.
M-PI,PO

Varga, Karoly. "Who Gains From Achievement Motivation Training." Vikalpa 2 (July 1977): 187-199.
-HR

Varma, M.K. "Worker's Participation in Management." Indian Management 9, no. 10 (Oct. 1970): 29-36.
M-PI,PO

Vengroff, Richard. Simulation: Development Planning and the Local Budget in the Republic of Pedegogia West Hartford: Kumarian Press, 1983.
M-FB,PI

Vepa, Ram P. "Implementation: The Problem of Achieving Results." Indian Journal of Public Administration 20 (April-June 1974): 257-292.
M-PI

Vera, Hernan, and R. Santoyo. "The Unequal Exchange of Mutual Expectations: A Neglected Dimension of Rural Development." Rural Sociology 43, no. 4 (1978): 610-617.
M-1-

Von der Embse, Thomas J. "Choosing a Management Development Program: A Decision Model." Personnel Journal 52, no. 10 (1973): 907.
M-OM

Vrancken, Fernand. Technical Assistance in Public Administration: Lessons of Experience and Possible Improvements. Brussels: International Institute of Administrative Sciences, 1963.
MO-TA,PI

Waldo, Dwight, ed. Temporal Dimensions in Development Administration. Durham: Duke Univ. Press, 1970.
MO-PI

Walsh, John E. Guidelines for Management Consultants in Asia. New York: United Nations, 1973.
M-TA

Warren, Richard D., Charles L. Mulford, and Mervin J. Yetley. "Analysis of Cooperative Organizational Effectiveness." Rural Sociology 41, no. 3 (1976): 330-353.
O-4-DM,PO

Waterson, Albert. "A Viable Model for Rural Development." Development Digest 13, no. 3 (July 1975): 3-11.
O-1-PO

Waterson, Albert. "Helping Bridge the Gap Between Planners and Farmers." IDR/Focus 2 (1976): 25-27.
MO-1-PO

Waterson, Albert. Managing Planned Agricultural Development. Washington, DC: Government Affairs Institute, 1976.
M-1-PO

Watson, Charles E. Management Development Through Training. Reading: Addison-Wesley Publ. Co., 1979.
M-PI,PO

Webster, R. Lyle, ed. Integrated Communication: Bringing People and Rural Development Together. Honolulu: East-West Communication Institute, East-West Center, 1975.
MO-4-IS

Weidner, Edward W. Technical Assistance in Public Administration Overseas: The Case for Development Administration. Chicago: Public Administration Service, 1964.
MO-TA

Weisel, Peter. Designing Rural Development Projects: An Approach. Washington, DC: Development Alternatives, Inc., 1978.
MO-1-PI

Weiss, Wayne, Albert Waterston, and John Wilson. "The Design of Agricultural and Rural Development Projects." In Planning Development Projects edited by Dennis A. Rondinelli. Stroudsburg: Dowden, Hutchinson and Ross, 1977.
MO-1-PO

Wells, Louis T., Jr. Third World Multinationals: The Rise of Foreign Investment from Developing Countries. Cambridge: The MIT Press, 1983.
MO-3-

Wheeler, David. Human Resource Development and Economic Growth in Developing Countries: A Simultaneous Model. Washington, DC: World Bank, 1980.
M-HR

Whetien, David A., and Thomas K. Leung. "The Instrumental Value of Interorganizational Relations: Antecedents and Consequences of Linkage Formation." Academcy of Management Journal 22, no. 2 (1979): 325-344.
O-PI

W.H.O. Community Involvement in Primary Health Care: A Study of the Process of Community Motivation and Continued Participation. Geneva: Joint WHO/UNICEF Study on Health Policy, 1977.
O-4,2-PI

W.H.O. Modern Management Methods and the Organization of Health Services, Geneva: World Health Organization, 1974.
MO-2-PO

Whyte, W.F. Building Better Organizational Models. Ithaca: Cornell Univ, 1969.
O-PO

Whyte, W.F. Organizing for Agricultural Development. New Brunswick: Transaction Books.
O-1-PO

Whyte, W.F., and Lawrence K. Williams. Toward an Integrated Theory of Development. Ithaca: Cornell Univ., 1968.
O-PI

Wichelmann, S. "Promoting Re-integration in Their Developing Countries of Origin of Professionals and Skilled Personnel Trained in an Industrialized Country." International Migration 15, nos. 2-3 (1977): 236-242.
MO-PI

Wickham, T., and K. Takase. Some Management Issues in Irrigation Development. Paper presented at the CPDS-UPLB-NWRC-NIA workshop on water resources, Los Banos, Philippines, 1976.
M-1-

Wigglesworth, David C. "Management Development Overseas-Some Thoughts." Training and Development Journal 35 (Oct. 1981): 73-6.
M-

Wilmon, E.T. "Rural Development Projects: The Farmer and the Community as Decision Makers." Agricultural Administration 4 (1977): 293-305.
O-1,4-DM

Wilson, H.T. "Innovation; the Practical Uses of Theory." In Social Change, Innovation and Politics in East Asia edited by Y.S. Yim, H.T. Wilson, and R.W. Wilson. Hong Kong: Asian Research Service, 1980.
M-PO,PI

Wood, G.P., and A.T. Mosher, eds. Readings in Agricultural Administration. New York: Agricultural Development Council, 1980.
MO-1-

Woodworth, W., and R. Nelson. "Witch Doctors, Messianics, Sorcerers, and OD Consultants: Parallels and Paradigms." Organizational Dynamics 8, no. 2 (Autumn 1979): 17-33.
O-TA

The World Bank. *Appropriate Technology in World Bank Activities*. Washington, DC: World Bank, 1976.
M-PI

The World Bank. *Institution Building for Traffic Management*. Washington, DC: World Bank, 1983.
O-2-PO

Wu, Chi-Yuen. "Public Enterprise as an Instrument of Development." *Journal of Administration Overseas* 6, no. 3 (July 1967): 149-158.
MO-

Wu, Chi-Yuen. "Training in Public Administration for Development: Some Lessons of International Cooperation." *Journal of Administration Overseas* 10, no. 1 (Jan 1971): 12-21.
M-TA

Yamazawa, I., and A. Hirata. "Industrialization and External Relations-Comparative Analysis of Japan's Historical Experience and Contemporary Developing Countries Performance." *Hitotsubashi Journal of Economics* 18, no. 2 (1978): 33-61.
O-3-

Yawer, Duraid. *Rural Industrialization for Developing Countries*. New Delhi: Chetana Publications, 1978.
1-3

Yin, Robert K. "Production Efficiency versus Bureaucratic Self-Interest: Two Innovative Processes." *Policy Sciences* 8, no. 4 (1977): 381-399.
O-PO

Yudelman, Montague. "Integrated Rural Development Projects: The Bank's Experience." *Finance and Development* 14, no. 1 (1977): 15-18.
O-1-

Zald, M.N., and M.A. Berger. "Social Movements in Organizations: Coup d'etat, Insurgency and Mass Movements." *American Journal of Sociology* 83 (1978): 823-861.
O-PI

Zaltman, Gerald, and Robert Duncan. *Strategies for Planned Change.* New York: Wiley-Interscience, 1978.
M,O-PO

Zaman, M.A. "Integrated Rural Development: FAO/SIDA Expert Consultation on Policies and Institutions." *Agricultural Administration* 5 (1978): 239-273.
O-1-TA,PO

Zaman, M.A. "Some Experiences in the Implementation of Integrated Rural Development (IRD) Programmes." *Agricultural Administration* 4 (1977): 307-316.
M,O-1-PI

Zelter, R. "Imported or Indigenious Planning Education: Some Observations on the Needs of Developing Countries." *Ekistics* 47 (Nov./Dec. 1980): 410-415.
M-2-PO

SECTION IV

GEOGRAPHIC CASE STUDIES

This section is not limited to formal case writeups, but rather includes analyses and reports of what has been done, as well as descriptions of aspects of current country situations and strategies. The user of this volume will note some overlap with the implementation section, as the distinctions within the literature are not always as clear as in our bibliographic sections.

The classification used is geographic, as this is the one predominantly used by the cited authors or editors. A country and region index follows. The current editors did not bias their search toward any specific region, and so the high numbers for some reflect, to a degree, the relative activity within those areas. Latin American citations are less reported due to our decision to focus on English language publications. Institutions that responded to our literature search have made possible a broader representation of their respective countries.

These citations are just a small representation of a vast wealth of cases and reports that exist. Unfortunately, much of the literature remains inaccessible to professionals, because it is buried in institutional files, or is indexed on only a regional basis. In order to effectively utilize this rich resource, a more comprehensive indexing must be established, as well as a viable system for the procurement of documents.

INTERNATIONAL   (19)

AFRICA, EUROPE AND THE MIDDLE EAST (267)		ASIA AND THE PACIFIC (336)		LATIN AMERICA AND THE CARIBBEAN (95)	
Africa-general	23	Asia-general	21	General	24
Algeria	3	Afghanistan	1	Argentina	1
Botswana	11	Bangladesh	30	Bolivia	2
East Africa	6	Bhutan	1	Brazil	9
Egypt	17	Burma	3	Chile	5
Ethiopia	7	China	24	Colombia	2
Gambia	2	Hong Kong	1	Costa Rica	3
Ghana	11	India	108	Cuba	1
Guinea	1	Indonesia	8	Dominican Republic	2
Guinea Bissau	1	Iran	6	Ecuador	1
Hungary	1	Korea	9	El Salvador	1
Iraq	3	Laos	1	Guatamala	3
Israel	1	Malaysia	18	Guyana	1
Ivory Coast	5	Nepal	14	Haiti	1
Kenya	31	New Guinea	3	Honduras	2
Kuwait	1	Pacific Islands	5	Jamaica	7
Liberia	4	Pakistan	9	Mexico	13
Madagascar	1	Philippines	35	Panama	1
Malawi	2	Seychelles	1	Paraguay	1
Mali	3	Singapore	2	Peru	9
Middle East-general	3	South East Asia	4	Puerto Rico	1
Morocco	1	Sri Lanka	7	Surinam	1
Niger	1	Taiwan	1	Venezuela	4
Nigeria	42	Thailand	25		
Saudi Arabia	5	Vietnam	2		
Senegal	2				
Sierra Leone	2				
Somalia	3				
Sudan	12				
Tanzania	30				
Tunisia	4				
Turkey	7				
Uganda	3				
Yemen Arab Republic	2				
Yugoslavia	4				
Zaire	2				
Zambia	8				
Zimbabwe	2				

INTERNATIONAL

Dore, Ronald, and Zoe Mars, eds. Community Development. New York: Unesco, 1981.

F.A.O. Participation of the Poor in Rural Organizations: A Consolidated Report on Studies in Selected Countries of Asia, the Near East and Africa. New York: F.A.O., 1979.

Fernandez, Raul. "Third World Industrialization: A New Panacea?" Monthly Review 32 (1981):10-18.

Gran, Guy. Learning from Development Success: Some Lessons from Contemporary Case Histories. Working Paper No. 9. Washington, DC: NASPAA, 1983.

Harper, Malcom, and Tan Thiam Soon. Small Enterprises in Developing Countries. Case Studies and Conclusions. London: Intermediate Technology Publishers, 1979.

Hunter, Guy. "The Daudzai Project: Some Practical Implications for Agricultural Administration." Agricultural Administration 3, 1 (1976): 29-32.

Khan, Shoaib Sultan. "The Daudzai Project: A Case Study." Agricultural Administration 3 (1976): n.p.

King, John A., Jr. Economic Development Projects and Their Appraisal: Cases and Principles from the Experience of the World Bank. Baltimore: The John Hopkins Univ. Press, 1967.

Knudson, H.R., Jr. Organizational Behavior: Cases for Developing Nations. Reading: Addison-Wesley Publ. Co., 1967.

Lambert, C.M., ed. Village Studies Data Analysis and Bibliography. Vol. 2. Africa, Middle East and North Africa, Asia, Pacific Islands, Latin America, West Indies and the Caribbean, 1950-1975. London: Mansell/IDS, 1978.

Mayo-Smith, Ian. Managing People: Five International Case Studies. West Hartford: Kumarian Press, 1981.

Mayo-Smith, Ian, and Nancy L. Ruther. Managing Information: International Case Studies with Notes for Case Leaders. West Hartford: Kumarian Press, 1984.

McCollom, I. "Industrial Psychology Around the World: Part II. Eastern Europe, Africa, Asia, and Australia" International Review of Applied Psychology 17 (1968): 17.

Morss, Elliott R., John K. Hatch, Donald R. Mickelwait, and Charles F. Sweet. Strategies for Small Farmer Development: An Empirical Study of Rural Development Projects in the Gambia, Ghana, Kenya, Lesotho, Nigeria, Bolivia, Columbia, Mexico, Paraguay and Peru. Boulder: Westview Press, 1976.

Nelson, N., ed. "African Women in the Development Process." Journal of Development Studies (special issue). 17 (Apr. 1981): 1-136.

Niehoff, Arthur H., ed. A Case Book of Social Change. Chicago: Aldine Publ. Co.,1967.

Palmer, I. The Nemow Case, 4th ed. West Hartford: Kumarian Press, 1985.

Safavi, Farrokh. Management Education and Business Systems and Environments in Africa, S.E. Asia and the Far East. Bellingham: Western Wash. Univ. College of Business and Economics, 1978.

Schaffer, B. Administrative Training and Development: A Comparative Study of East Africa, Zambia, Pakistan, and India. New York: Praeger, 1974.

Strange, L.R.N. "Ecological Management of Arid and Semi-Arid Rangelands in Africa, the Near and Middle East (EMASAR Phase 2)." Grassland Education and Training 5 (1978).

Subramaniam, V. "Politicized Administration in Africa and Elsewhere: A Socio-historical Analysis." International Review of Administrative Sciences 43, no. 4 (1977): 297-308.

AFRICA, EUROPE AND THE MIDDLE EAST

AFRICA GENERAL

Adamolekun, Lapido. "Towards Development Oriented Bureaucracies in Africa." International Review of Administrative Sciences 42 (1976): 257-265.

Barker, Jonathan. The Politics of Agriculture in Tropical Africa. Toronto: Univ. of Toronto,1984.

Bellamy, M. A. ed. African Agriculture and Rural Development 1-5 (1975).

Blunt, P. "Social and Organizational Structures in East Africa: A Case for Participation." Journal of Modern African Studies 16, no. 3 (1978): 433-449.

Burke, Fred G. "Public Administration in Africa: The Legacy of Inherited Colonial Institutions." Journal of Comparative Administration 1 (Nov. 1969): 345-378.

Fortman, Louise. "Pitfalls in Implementing Participation: An African Example." Rural Development Participation Review 1 (1979): n.p.

Gordenker, Leon. International Aid and National Decisions: Development Programs in Malawi, Tanzania and Zambia. Princeton: Princeton University Press, 1976.

Halpern, Manfred. The Politics of Social Change in the Middle East and North Africa. Princeton: Princeton University Press, 1969.

Heyer, Judith, Pepe Roberts, and Gavin Williams. Rural Development in Tropical Africa. New York: St. Martins Press, 1981.

Hickson, D. J., and C. J. McMillan, eds. Organization and Nation: The Aston Programme IV. Farmborough: Gower Publ., 1981.

Jiggins, Janice. "Regional Alternatives to Ministries of Agriculture: Agricultural Development Projects in Malawi, Nigeria and Ghana." Agricultural Administration 6 (1979): 89-97.

Killick, Tony. "The Role of the Public Sector in the Industrialization of African Developing Countries." Industry and Development 7 (1983): 57-88.

McLouglin, P.F.M. "Business and Its Management in Africa." California Management Review 5 (1963): 43-50.

Morgan, Philip, ed. The Administration of Change in Africa: Essays in the Theory and Practice of Development Administration in Africa. New York: Dunellen Publ. Co., Inc., 1974

Muwanga-Barlow, C. H. "The Development of Administrative Sciences in English-speaking Africa." International Review of Administrative Sciences 44 (1978): 93-105.

Nelson, N. ed. "African Women in the Development Process." Journal of Development Studies (special issue) 17 (Apr. 1981): 1-136.

Nurmi, R., and U. Uda-Aka. "Management Research for Management Development in a Developing Country. A Model and Case." Management International Review 20, no. 2 (1980): 90-95.

Onyemelukwe, C. Men and Management in Contemporary Africa. London: Longmans, 1973.

Oyenuga, V.A. Industrial versus Agricultural Development in Africa, in The Challenge of Development. Nairobi: East African Publishing House, (1968): 93-105.

Rweyemamu, Anthony H., and Goran Hyden, eds. A Decade of Public Administration in Africa. Management and Administrative Series No. 5. Nairobi: East African Literature Bureau, 1975.

Safavi, Farrokh. "A Model of Management Education in Africa." Academy of Management Review 6 (Apr. 1981): 319-331.

USAID, Office of the Auditor General. An Evaluation of the Management of Technical Assistance Projects in Three African Countries. Washington, DC: USAID, 1972.

The World Bank. Accelerated Development in Sub-Saharan Africa: An Agenda for Action. Washington, DC: The World Bank, 1981.

Yaeger, Rodger. "Micropolitical Dimensions of Development and National Integration in Rural Africa: Concepts and an Application." African Studies Review 15, no. 3 (1972): 367-402.

ALGERIA

Blair, Thomas. The Land to Those Who Work It: Algeria's Experiment in Workers' Management. Garden City: Doubleday, 1970.

Harbron, J.D. "Emphasis on Cultural Cross Fertilization with Algeria's Technocrats." Business Quarterly 45, no. 7 (Winter 1980): 45-47.

Nellis, John R. "Socialist Management in Algeria." Journal of Modern Africa Studies 15, no. 4 (1977): 529-554.

BOTSWANA

Ho, John D. "Rural Development in Botswana: Three Basic Political Trends." Rural Africana 18 (1972): 80-92.

Hunter, John. The Successful and Unsuccessful Enterprise: An Analysis of Fifty Small Business Enterprises Supported by the Botswana Enterprise Development Unit. Gaborone, Botswana: IDM, 1979.

Kingshotte, Alan. The Organization and Management of Agricultural Extension and Farmer Assistance in Botswana. Agricultural Administration Network Discussion Paper No. 1, Overseas Development Institute, London: 1979.

Mushonga, B.L.B. "African Small Scale Entrepreneurship with Special Reference to Botswana. Working Paper No. 34, National Institute of Development and Cultural Research. Botswana: 1981.

Ochieng, Washington. Annotated Bibliography of IDM Publications (Botswana, Lesotho and Swaziland). Gaborone, Botswana: Institute of Development Management, 1983.

Picard, Louis A. "Rural Development in Botswana: Administrative Structures and Public Policy." Journal of Developing Areas 13, no. 3 (1979): 283-300.

Raphaeli, Nimrod, Jacques Roumani, A.C. McKellan. "Public Sector Management in Botswana: Lessons in Pragmatism." World Bank Staff Working Papers, No. 709. Washington, DC: The World Bank, 1984

Snyder, Hugh. Integrated Rural Development in Botswana: The Village Area Development Programme, 1972-1978. IRD Project Working Paper No. 2. Washington, DC: Development Alternatives, Inc., December, 1979.

Tordoff, William. "Local Administration in Botswana." Journal of Administration Overseas 12, no. 4 (1973): 293-304.

Vengroff, Richard. "Popular Participation and the Administration of Rural Development: The Case of Botswana." Human Organization 33, no. 3 (1974): 303-309.

Wass, P. "Policy Issues for Community Development in Africa: Lessons from Botswana." Community Development Journal 10, no. 1 (1975): 14-23.

EAST AFRICA

Abramson, R. A Revised Concept of Organization Development as Illustrated by a Case Study of OD in an African Community Public Corp. Arusha: East African Community Management Institute, 1973.

Deboeck, Guido, and Bill Kinsey. Managing Information for Rural Development: Lessons from Eastern Africa. Staff Working Paper No. 379 Washington, DC: World Bank, 1980.

Fleming, William G. "Authority, Efficiency, and Role Stress: Problems in the Development of East-African Bureaucracies." Administrative Science Quarterly 11 (1966): 386-404.

Hyden, Goran. Efficiency Versus Distribution in East African Cooperatives: A Study in Organizational Conflicts. Nairobi: East African Literature Bureau, 1973.

Inukai, Ichiro. "African Socialism and Agricultural Development Strategy: A Comparative Study of Kenya and Tanzania." The Developing Economies 12, no. 1 (1974): 3-22.

Morris, J.R. "Administrative Authority and the Problem of Effective Agricultural Administration in East Africa." African Review 2, no. 1 (1972): 105-146.

Sherif, A. Fouad. "Improving Performance of East African Community Corporations." Public Administration Newsletter (Oct. 1971): 23-24.

Widstrand, Carl Gosta, ed. Co-operatives and Rural Development in East Africa. Uppsala: Scandinavian Institute of African Studies, 1970.

EGYPT

Abo-khalil, Z.M. Public Sector Administration in Egypt. Ann Arbor: University Microfilms International, 1983.

Afifi, H., Fahmy, S.B. "Training in Egypt as an Approach for Management Development" in Management Development in Egypt. F. Ismail. Cairo: American University in Cairo Press, 1979.

Ayubi, N.N.M. "Bureaucratic Inflation and Administrative Inefficiency: The Deadlock in Egyptian Administration." Middle East Studies 18 (July 1982): 286-99.

Badran, M., and B. Hinings. "Strategies of Administrative Control and Contextual Constraints in a Less Developed Country: The Case of Egyptian Public Enterprises." Organization Studies 21, no.1 (1981): 3-21.

Okdah, E.L. A Test of the Effects of Interactive Planning on Selected Behavioral Variables of Egyptian Managers and Work Environment. Ann Arbor: University Microfilms International, 1983.

Ikram, Khalid, Egypt: Economic Management in a Period of Transition. Baltimore: The John Hopkins Univ. Press, 1980.

Ismail, F. "Management Development in Egypt: An Inside Look." In <u>Management Development In Egypt</u> Cairo: American University in Cairo Press, 1979.

Langenderfer, Harold Q. "The Egyptian Executive: A Study in Conflict." <u>Human Organization</u> 24 (Spring 1965): 89-95.

Mayfield, James B. <u>Local Institutions and Egyptian Rural Development.</u> Ithaca: Cornell Univ., Center for International Studies, Rural Development Committee, 1974.

Murrell, K.L. "A Cultural Analysis of the Egyptian Management Environment." In <u>Innovation in Global Consultation</u> edited by Philip R. Harris and Garld H. Malin. Copenhagen, Denmark, 1979.

Murrell, K. L. "Team Building in Egypt." In <u>Systems Thinking: A Resource for Organization Diagnosis and Intervention.</u> Washington, DC: International Consultants Foundation, July 1981.

Murrell, K.L. "Understanding the Egyptian Manager: A Third World Management Development Experience." <u>Leadership and Organization Development Journal</u> 2, no. 3 (Oct./Nov. 1981).

Rycroft, Robert W., and J. Szyliowiez. "The Technological Dimension of Decision Making: The Case of the Aswan High Dam." <u>World Politics</u> 33, no. 1 (1980): 36-61.

Schrier, David, and K.L. Murrell. <u>Comparison of Organization Development in Ecuador and Egypt from a Western Perspective.</u> Seattle: Proceedings of OD Network Conference, (Oct. 1981).

Valsan, A.H. "An Essay on Egyptian Experience in Development Administration." <u>Journal of the Social Sciences</u> (Oct. 1979).

Valsan, A.H. "Challenges to Development Administration in Egypt." <u>Middle East Management Review</u> (April 1976).

The World Bank. <u>Egypt, Economic Management in a Period of Transition.</u> Baltimore: John Hopkins University Press, 1980.

Zahra, S.A. "Egyptian Management at the Crossroads." <u>Management International Review</u> 20, no. 3 (1980): 118-124.

ETHIOPIA

Clark, Ronald, J. "Ethiopian Land Reform: Scope, Accomplishments and Future Objectives." <u>Land Reforms, Land Settlement, and Cooperatives</u> 2 (1975): 65-68.

Cohen, John M. "Effects of Green Revolution Strategies on Tenants and Small Scale Landowners in the Chilalo Region of Ethiopia." <u>Journal of Developing Areas</u> 9, no. 3 (1975): 335-358.

Cohen, John M. "Rural Change in Ethiopia: The Chilalo Agricultural Development Unit." <u>Economic Development and Cultural Change</u> 22 (1974): 580-614.

Meshesha, A.W. <u>Manpower Training for Development Administration: The Case of Ethiopia and Kenya in the Quest for Open Model Approach.</u> Ann Arbor: University Microfilms International, 1983.

Korten, D.C. <u>Planned Change in a Traditional Society: Psychological Problems of Modernization in Ethiopia.</u> New York: Praeger Publishers, 1972.

Rosen, Charles B. "The Dynamics of Provincial Administration in Haile Selassie's Ethiopia: 1930-1974." In <u>Hieraarchy and Society.</u> Philadelphia: I.S.H.I. Publ., 1980.

Stommes, Eileen, and Seleshi Sisaye. "The Administration of Agricultural Development Programmes: A Look at the Ethiopian Approach -- Part 2." <u>Agricultural Administration</u> 6, no. 4, (1979).

GAMBIA

Dey, J. "Development Planning in the Gambia: The Gap Between Planners' and Farmers' Perceptions, Expectations and Objectives." <u>World Development</u> 10 (May 1982): 377-396.

Kargbo, A.M. <u>An Economic Analysis of Rice Production Systems and Production Organization of Rice Farmers in the Gambia.</u> Ann Arbor: University Microfilms International, 1983.

GHANA

Beckman, Bjorn. <u>Organizing the Farmers: Cocoa Politics and National Development in Ghana.</u> Uppsala: Scandinavian Institute of African Studies, 1976.

Harris, Richard L. "The Effects of Political Change on the Role Set of the Senior Bureaucrats in Ghana and Nigeria." <u>Administrative Science Quarterly</u> 13 (1968): 386-401.

Hyndman, Albert. "Management Education in Developing Countries: The Case of Ghana." <u>Journal of Management Studies</u> 7, no. 1 (1974): 25-33.

Management Development and Productivity Institute. <u>Improving Effectiveness of Public Enterprises in Ghana.</u> D-211 Accra, Ghana, 1979.

Management Development and Productivity Institute. *Proposals on the Role of the Peoples Defense Committees in the Management of Organizations*. Accra, Ghana, 1982.

Mendosa, Eugene L. "Elders, Officeholders and Ancestors Among the Sisalsa of Northern Ghana." *Africa* 46 (1976): 57-65.

Opare, K. Dua. "The Role of Agricultural Extension in the Adoption of Innovation by Cocoa Growers in Ghana." *Rural Sociology* 42, no. 1 (1977): 71-82.

Owen, Wilfred, Jr. *Teacher Participation in Community Development: Comparative Case Studies in Central Ghana*. Unpublished Ph.D. dissertation, Northwestern Univ., 1976.

Price, Robert M. *Society and Bureaucracy in Contemporary Ghana*. Berkeley: Univ. of California Press, 1975.

Quansah, S.T. "The Gonja Settlement and Development Scheme, Ghana." *Economic Bulletin of Ghana* 2, no. 1 (1972): 14-24.

Sarpong, Kwame, and James R. Rawls. "A Study of the Transfer of Training from Developed to Less Developed Countries: The Case of Ghana." *Journal of Management Studies* 13, no. 1 (1976): 16-31.

Steel, William F. *Small Scale Employment and Production in Developing Countries: Evidence from Ghana*. New York: Praeger Publishers, 1977.

GUINEA

Adamolekun, Ladipo. "Politics and Administration in West Africa: The Guinean Model." *Journal of Administration Overseas* 8, no. 4 (1969): 235-242.

GUINEA-BISSAU

Rudebeck, Lars. "Political Mobilization for Development in Guinea-Bissau." *Journal of Modern African Studies* 10 no. 1 (1972): 1-18.

HUNGARY

Lauter, Greza Peter. *The Manager and Economic Reform in Hungary*. New York: Praeger Publishers, 1972.

IRAQ

Fernea, Robert A. *Shaykh and Effendi: Changing Patterns of Authority Among the El Shaban of Southern Iraq*. Cambridge: Harvard University Press, 1970.

Simmons, John L. "Agricultural Development in Iraq: Planning and Management Failures," *The Middle East Journal* 19 (Spring 1965): 129-140.

ISRAEL

Weitz, Raanan, and Aushalom Rokach. *Agricultural Development: Planning and Implementation (Israel Case Study)*. Dordrecht, Holland: D. Reidel Publ. Co., 1968.

IVORY COAST

den Tuinder, Bastiaan. *Ivory Coast: The Challenge of Success*. Baltimore: The John Hopkins Univ. Press, 1978.

Harbron, J.D. "In Ivory Coast: A Mix of Management Methods." *Business Quarterly* 46 (Summer 1981): 16-18.

Mushi, Mugumorhagerwa. *The Promotion of Entrepreneurship for National Development: A Study of Public Policies in Kenya and the Ivory Coast*. Ann Arbor: University Microfilms International, 1983.

Ova Hara, K.S. *Managerial Attitudes of Ivorian Banking Managers*. Ann Arbor: University Microfilms International, 1982.

Staniland, Martin. "Colonial Government and Populist Reform: The Case of the Ivory Coast: Local Administration at Independence and After." *Journal of Administration Overseas* 10, nos. 1, 2 (1971): 33-42; 113-126.

KENYA

Ay, S.W., and Philip Mbithi. "Local Involvement in the SRDP." In *An Overall Evlauaiton of the Special Rural Development Program*. Development Studies Occassional Paper No. 8. Nairobi: Univ. of Nairobi, 1973.

Barclay, A.H. *The Development Impact of Private Voluntary Organizations: Kenya and Niger*. Washington, DC: Development Alternatives, Inc., 1979.

Blunt, Peter. "Bureaucracy and Ethnicity in Kenya. Some Conjectures for the Eighties." *The Journal of Applied Behavioral Science* 16, no. 3 (1980): 336-353.

Brokensha, David, and John Nellis. "Administration in Kenya, A Study of Mbere." *Journal of Administration Overseas* 13, no. 4 (1974): 510-523; 14, no. 1 (1975): 17-29.

Chabala, H.H.A., D.H. Kiru, and S.W. Mukuna. *A Further Evaluation of the Programming and Implementation Management (PIM) System*, Working Paper 119. Nairobi, Kenya: Institute for Development Studies, University of Nairobi, 1973.

Chambers, R. "Managing Rural Development." *Bulletin of the Institute of Development Studies* 6, no. 1 (1974): 4-12.

Clayson, J.E. "How Relevant is Operational Research to Development? The Case of Kenyan Industry." *Journal of the Operational Research Society* 31, no. 4 (Apr. 1980): 293-299.

Faruqee, Rashid. *Kenya: Population and Development*. Washington, DC: World Bank, 1980.

Godfey, E.M., and G.C.M. Mutiso. "The Political Economy of Self-Help: Kenya's 'Harambee' Institutes of Technology." *Canadian Journal of African Studies* 8, no. 1 (1974): 109-133.

Henley, John S. "The Personnel Professionals in Kenya." *Personnel Management* 9, no. 2 (1977): 10-14.

Hyden, Goran, Robert Jackson, and John Okumu, eds. *Development Administration: The Kenyan Experience*, New York: Oxford Univ. Press, 1970.

Institute for Development Studies, University of Nairobi, *An Overall Evaluation of the Special Rural Development Programme*, Occasional Paper No. 8. Nairobi: IDS (1972):1-22.

Keller, Edmond J. "Harambee! Educational Policy, Inequality, and the Political Economy of Rural Community Self-Help in Kenya." *Journal of African Studies* 4, no. 1 (1977): 86-106.

Lamb, Geof P. *Peasant Politics: Conflict and Development in Muranga (Kenya)*. New York: St. Martin's Press, 1974.

Leach, J.W. "The Kenya Special Rural Development Programme," *Journal of Administration Overseas* 13, no. 2 (1974): 358-365.

Leonard, David K., ed. *Rural Administration in Kenya: A Critical Appraisal*. Nairobi: East African Literature Bureau, 1973.

Leonard, David K. "Organization Theory in Kenya." In *Reading the Peasant Farmer*. Chicago: University of Chicago Press, 1977.

Mbithi, P.M. and R. Rasmusson. *Self-Reliance in Kenya: The Case of Harambee*. Leiden: E.J. Brill, 1978.

Miller, Norman N. *Kenya, The Quest for Prosperity*. Boulder: Westview Press, 1984.

Mugyenyi, Meddi. *A Trichotomy of Elite Participation in Decision-Making: The Case of Municipal Kisumu in Kenya*. Unpublished Ph.D. Dissertation, Northwestern University, 1976.

Muthama, J.K., and J.O. Otieno. "The Challenge of Rural Development in Kenya." *Cahiers Africains d'Administrative Publique* 17 (1977): 85-94.

Nellis, J.R. "The Administration of Rural Development in Kenya: Plan Formulation and Implementation in the Special Rural Development Programme." In *Issues in African Development*. Waterloo Univ., Division of Environmental Studies, Department of Geography (Feb. 1972).

Nellis, J.R. "Is the Kenyan Bureaucracy Developmental? Political Considerations in Developmental Administration." *African Studies Review* 14, 3(1971):389-401.

Pala, A.O. "Women's Access to Land and Their Role in Agriculture and Decision-Making on the Farm: Experiences of the Juluo of Kenya." IDS Discussion Paper No. 263. Nairobi: Institute for Development Studies, Univ. of Nairobi, 1978.

Rasmusson, R. "Social Emphasis of Peoples' Priorities in Rural Development: Case Studies in Kenya on Results of Decentralized Planning." *Agricultural Administration* 2, no. 4 (1975): 263-284.

Staudt, Kathleen. "Administrative Resources, Political Patrons and Redressing Sex Inequities: A Case from Western Kenya." *Journal of Developing Areas* 12, no. 4 (1978): 399-414.

Steeves, Jeffrey. *The Politics and Administration of Agricultural Development in Kenya: The Kenya Tea Development Authority*. Unpublished Ph.D. dissertation, University of Toronto, 1975.

Trapman, Christopher. *Change in Administrative Structures: A Case Study of Kenyan Agricultural Development*. London: Overseas Development Institute, Ltd., 1974.

Wallis, Malco. "Community Development in Kenya: Some Current Issues." *Community Development Journal* 11, no. 3 (1976): 192-198.

Wass, Peter. "Developing Research Skills in Professional Staff: A Study of Adult Education Training in Kenya." Convergence 9, no. 2 (1976): 63-72.

Weisel, Peter F. Some Issues Related to District Development (in Kenya). Washington, DC. Kenya Ministry of Finance and Planning and Development Alternatives, Inc., 1977.

Winans, Edgar V., and A. Haugerud. "Rural Self-Help in Kenya: The Harambee Movement." Human Organizations 36, no. 4 (1977): 334-351.

KUWAIT

Al Shamali, A.M.A. A Study of the Impact of Culture on Organizational Communication of a Kuwaiti Government Organization. Ann Arbor: University Microfilms International, 1983.

LIBERIA

Honadle, George H. Organization Design for Development Administration: A Liberian Case Study of Implementation Analysis for Project Benefit Distribution. Unpublished Ph.D. Dissertation, Syracuse University, 1978.

Howell, P., J. Strauss, and P. F. Sornesen. "Research Note: Cultural and Situational Determinants of Job Satisfaction Among Management in Liberia." Journal of Management Studies 12 (1975): 225-227.

Nimley, Anthony J. The Liberian Bureaucracy: An Analysis and Evaluation of the Environment, Structure and Functions. Washington, DC: University Press of America, 1977.

Siebel, Hans Dieter, and Andreas Massing. Traditional Organizations and Economic Development: Studies of Indigenous Cooperatives in Liberia. New York: Praeger Publishers, 1974.

MADAGASCAR

Joshi, P.C. Madagascar: Recent Economic Development and Future Prospects. Washington, DC: World Bank, 1980.

MALAWI

Honadle, George. Manpower for Rural Development in Malawi: An Integrated Approach to Capacity-Building. A draft report prepared for the Agency for International Development. Washington, DC: Development Alternatives, Inc., 1980.

Kydd, J., and R. Christiansen. "Structural Change in Malawi Since Independence: Consequences of a Development Strategy Based on Large Scale Agriculture." World Development 10 (May 1982): 355-375.

MALI

Bingen, R. James. Food Production and Rural Development in the Sahel. Lessons from Malis Operation Riz-Segou. Boulder: Westview Press, 1984.

Hopkins, Nicholas S. "Leadership and Consensus in Two Malian Cooperatives." In The Anthropology of Development in Sub-Saharan Africa edited by D. Brokensha and Marian Pearsall. Lexington: Society for Applied Anthroplogy, 1969.

Hopkins, Nicholas S. "Participatory Decision Making and Modern Cooperatives in Mali: Notes Toward a Prospective Anthropology." In Popular Participation in Social Changes (1976): 99-111.

MIDDLE EAST - GENERAL

Ferris, John P. "Organization for Regional Economic Development Projects. A Middle East Experience." Public Administration Review 25 (June 1965): 128-134.

Salzman, Philip Carl. "The Study of 'Complex Society' in the Middle East: A Review Essay." International Journal of Middle East Studies 9 (1978):539-557.

Wright, P. "Organizational Behavior in Islamic Firms." Management International Review 21 (1981): 86-94.

MOROCCO

Merat, Christian. Morocco: Economic and Social Development Report. Washington, DC: World Bank, 1981.

NIGER

Laucoin, G. ("Management of Hydro-Agricultural Projects in Niger") "La gestion des amenagements hydro-agricoles au Niger: analyse et bilan d'un processus de participation provoquee," Developement et Civilisations 51 (1973): 21-31.

NIGERIA

Adamolekun, Ladipo. "Local Government Reform in the Benue Plateau State of Nigeria." Journal of Administration Overseas 16, no. 1 (1977): 30-42.

Adebayo, Augustus. Principles and Practice of Public Administration in Nigeria. New York: John Wiley and Sons, 1981.

Agbonifo, Peter, and Ronald Cohen. "The Peasant Connection: A Case Study of the Bureaucracy of Agri-Industry." *Human Organizations* 35 (1976): 367-380.

Akinsanya, Adeoye. "Local Government Reforms in Western Nigeria." *Journal of Administration Overseas* 15, no. 2 (1976): 100-104.

Akinsanya, Adeoye. "Reforming a Public Enterprise Through Management Audit: Any Lessons from the Former Western Nigeria Development Corporation?" *Indian Journal of Public Administration* 24, no. 4 (1978): 1016-1031.

Aluko, M.A. *Work Motivation and Perceptions of Academic Organizational Climate: A Nigerian Study.* Ann Arbor: University Microfilms International, 1983.

Armor, Thomas H. *Addressing Problems of Middle-Level Management: A Workshop Held at the Lofa County Agricultural Development Project.* Washington, DC: Development Alternatives, Inc., 1979.

Arua, E.: "Improving Rural Development Administration in Nigeria." *Agricultural Administration* 5, no. 4 (1978): 285-286.

Ay, P. "Differences in the Effects of Agricultural Development Programmes: The Example of the Ibadan East Area in Nigeria." *Akrika Spectrum* 13, no. 2 (1978): 179.

Balogun, M. J. "Security of Tenure in Nigerian Public Administration: A Brief History and Recent Developments." *International Review of Administrative Sciences* 42 (1976): 375-381.

Berry, Sara S. *Cocoa, Custom, and Socio-Economic Change in Rural Western Nigeria.* Oxford: Clarendon Press, 1975.

Bowden, Edgar. "Mal-administration: A Thematic Analysis of Nigerian Case Studies in the Context of Administrative Initiative." *Human Organization* 35, no. 4 (1976): 391-394.

Cohen, Ronald. "The Blessed Jobs in Nigeria." In *Hierachy and Society* edited by G. Britan and R. Cohen. Philadelphia: I.S.H.I. Publications, 1980.

D'Silva, Brian C., and M.R. Raza. "Integrated Rural Development in Nigeria--The Funtua Project." *Food Policy* 5 (Nov. 1980): 282-297.

Harrison, R. "Work and Motivation: A Study of Village-Level Agricultural Extension Workers in the Western State of Nigeria." Ibadan: Nigerian Institute of Social and Economic Research, 1969.

Iboko, J.I. "Management Development and Its Developing Patterns in Nigeria." *Management International Review* 3 (1976): 97-104.

Igbozurike, M. "Problem-Generating Structures in Nigeria's Rural Development." Uppsala: Scandinavian Inst. of African Studies, 1976.

Ijere, M.O. "The Planning experience in Nigerian Agriculture." *Journal of Administration Overseas* 16, no. 1 (1977) 17-23.

Jibowo, Abraham Adegboyega. *Leadership Structure and Participation in Development Programs of Some Communities in Ife Divison, Western State, Nigeria.* Unpublished Ph.D. Dissertation, University of Wisconsin, 1973.

Kerr, Graham Burrell. *Leadership and Communication in the Collective Adoption Process of Development Associations in Eastern Nigeria.* Unpublished Ph.D. Dissertation, Michigan State University, 1970.

Mijindadi, Ndanusa. "Staff Organization for Agricultural Planning: The Case of Nigeria." *Agricultural Administration* 3, no. 4 (1976): 239-247.

Murray, D. *The Work of Administration in Nigeria: Case Studies.* London: Hutchinson, 1970.

Nafziger, E. Wayne. *African Capitalism: A Case Study in Nigerian Entepreneurship.* Stanford: Hoover Institution Press, 1977.

Nalmburdiri, C.N.S., and M.S. Saiyadain. *Management Problems and Practices-- India and Nigeria. Columbia Journal of World Business* 4 (1978).

Nwadike C.G.S. *A Study of Administrative and Leadership Behavior of Secondary School Principals in Nigeria.* Ann Arbor: University Microfilms International, 1982.

Nwaeke, L.I. *The Empirical Examination of Classified Staff Participation in Decision Making with Regard to Policy Determination, Administrative Practices and Influence on Working Conditions in Nigerian Universities*. Ann Arbor: University Microfilms International, 1983.

Nurmi, R., and U. Udo-Aka. "Management Research for Management Development in a Developing Country: A Model and Case." *Management International Review* 20, no. 2 (1980): 90-95.

Odenigwe, G.A. "Divisional Administration in East Central Nigeria." *Journal of Administration Overseas* 12 (1973): 106-111.

Ogaba Otokpa, A.G., Jr. "Nigerian OD: The Work of the Business Research Management Center." *Leadership and OD Journal* 2, no. 3 (1980): 13-16.

Ogunnika, Z.O. *Mechanics of Tension Management in a Plural Society: A Study of Inter Ethnic Relations in Kano City, Nigeria*. Ann Arbor: University Microfilms International, 1982.

Ogunu, M.A. *The Development of a Model Training Program in Education Planning and Management for the Preparation of School Administrators in Nigeria*. Ann Arbor: University Microfilms International, 1983.

Okoli, F.C. "Dilemma of Premature Bureaucratization in the New States of Africa. The Case of Nigeria." *African Studies Review* 23 (Sept. 1980): 1-16.

Okpala, Donatus, C.I. "Towards a Better Conceptualization of Rural Community Development: Empirical Findings from Nigeria." *Human Organization* 39, no. 2 (1980): 161-169.

Onibokun, Adepoju. "Directions for Social Research on Self-Help Projects and Programmes in Nigeria." *Community Development Journal* 11 (1976): 60-69.

The Quarterly Journal of Administration (University of Ife, Nigeria) 10, no. 1 (Oct. 1975). Special issue: "Management Education and Training."

Rimlinger, Gaston V., and Carolyn C. Stremlau. *Indigenization and Management Development in Nigeria*. Lagos: Nigerian Institute of Management, 1973.

Silverstein, S.B. *Sociocultural Organization and Locational Strategies of Transportation Entrepreneurs: An Ethnoeconomic History of the Nnewi Igbo of Nigeria*. Ann Arbor: Univeristy Microfilms International, 1983.

Smock, D.Q. "Cultural and Attitudinal Factors Affecting Agricultural Development in Eastern Nigeria." *Economic Development and Cultural Change* 18, no. 1 (1969): 110-124.

Sote, G.A. *An Investigation of Organizational Types Among Nigerian Banks (Banking)*. Ann Arbor: University Microfilms International, 1982.

Sullivan, B.C. "Structural Dependency: The Nigerian Economy as a Case Study." *Journal of Asian and African Studies* 14 (Jan.-Apr. 1979): 44-55.

Ukandi, G.D., and H.D. Seibel, eds. *Social and Economic Development in Nigeria*. New York: Praeger Publishers, 1973.

Uzoigwe, C.N. *A Model for Establishing a Higher Education Administrative Degree at a Nigerian University*. Ann Arbor: University Microfilms International, 1982.

SAUDI ARABIA

Al Mazroa, S.A. *Public Administration and Prospects in the Context of Development in Saudi Arabia*. Ann Arbor: University Microfilms International, 1980.

Anastos, Denis, Alexis Bedos, and Bryant Seaman. "Development of Modern Management Practices in Saudi Arabia." *Columbia Journal of World Business* 15 (Summer 1980): 81-92.

DeNisi, A, M. Watson, A. Al-Jafary, and A. Hollingsworth. *Management in Transition: A Study of Management Styles in Saudi Arabia*. Accepted, Academy of Management Meeting, Dallas, 1983.

Gohaidan, M.S.S *Organizational Innovations in Developing Countries: The Case of Saudi Arabia*. Ann Arbor: University Microfilms International, 1982.

Looney, Robert E. *Saudi Arabia's Development: Potential Application of an Islamic Growth Model*. Lexington: Lexington Books, 1981.

SENEGAL

Markovitz, Irving L. "Traditional Social Structure, the Islamic Brotherhoods, and Political Development in Senegal." *Journal of Modern African Studies* 8, no. 1 (1970): 73-96.

Schumacher, Edward J. *Politics, Bureaucracy and Rural Development in Senegal*. Berkeley: University of California Press, 1975.

SIERRA LEONE

Barrows, Walter L. Grass Roots Politics in an African State: Integration and Development in Sierra Leone. New York: Africana Publ. Co., 1974.

Spencer, Dustan, and Derek Byerlee. "Technical Change, Labor Use, and Small Farmer Development: Evidence from Sierra Leone." American Journal of Agricultural Economics 58, no. 5 (1976): 874-880.

SOMALIA

Haaland, G., and W. Keddeman. "Poverty Analysis: The Case of Rural Somalia." Economic Development and Cultural Change 32 (July 1984): 843-860.

Hindle, D. "Cluster Analysis and the Organizational Structure: The Ministry of Health, Somalia." Omega 9, no. 2 (1981): 205-6.

I.L.O./JASPA. Economic Transformation in a Socialist Framework: An Employment and Basic Needs Oriented Strategy for Somalia. Addis Ababa: JASPA, 1977.

SUDAN

Adams, Martin E., and John Howell. "Developing the Traditional Sector in the Sudan." Economic Development and Cultural Change 27, no. 3 (1979): 505-518.

Barnett, T. The Gezira Scheme: An Illusion of Development. London: Frank Cass, 1977.

Gabir, D.A. Assessing Organizational Effectiveness: Two Sudanese Cases. Ann Arbor: University Microfilms International, 1983.

Hanson, A.H. "Nile and Niger: Two Agricultural Projects," Public Administration 38 (Winter 1960): 339-352.

Howell, John. "Administration and Development Planning: A Sudanese Case." Agricultural Administration, 4 (1977): 99-120.

Howell, John. "Local Government Reform in the Sudan." Journal of Administration Overseas 12, no. 1 (1973): 28-36.

Khalil, H.M.M. "The Sudan Gezira Scheme. Some Institutional and Administrative Aspects." Journal of Administration Overseas 9, no. 4 (1970): 273-285.

McLoughlin, Peter F.M. "Business and Its Managers in the Sudan." California Management Review 6 (Fall 1983): 81-88.

Rondinelli, D.A. "Administrative Decentralization and Economic Development: The Sudan's Experiment with Devolution." Journal of Modern African Studies 19 (Dec. 1981): 595-624.

Sharma, B.S. "Local Government and Community Development in the Sudan." Journal of Develoment Overseas 8, no. 1 (1969): 46-52.

UNESCO, Cultural Policy in the Sudan. New York: UNESCO, 1982.

Zein, K.M. The Practice of Public Administration in the Sudan: A Study of a District Center. Unpublished Ph.D. Dissertation, Rotterdam, 1978.

TANZANIA

Bomani, Paul. "Tanzania's Road to Development: Bringing Development to the People." International Development Review 16, no. 2 (1974): 2-9.

Cliffe, Lionel, Peter Lawrence, William Luttrell, Shem Migot-Adholla, and John S. Saul, eds. Rural Cooperation in Tanzania. Dar es Salaam: Tanzania Publishing House, 1975.

Collins, Paul. "Decentralization and Local Administration in Tanzania." Africa Today 21, no. 3 (1974): 15-25.

East African Posts and Telecommunications Corporation. "Planning for Performance: Lessons of Experience." In Management's Role in Promoting Productivity in the East African Community and the East African Corporations. Report of the UNDP/FAC Tharp Sonton Executive Seminar, Arusha, Tanzania, October 26-27, 1972.

El-Namaki. "The Effectiveness and the Managerial Behavior of Company Boards in Tanzania." International Review of Administrative Sciences 42, no.3 (1976): 241-247.

Finucane, J.R. "Hierarchy and Participation in Development: A Case Study of Regional Administration in Tanzania." African Review 2, no.4 (1972): 573-597.

Finucane, J.R. Rural Development and Bureaucracy in Tanzania: The Case of Mwanza Region. Uppsala: Scandinavian Institute of African Studies, 1974.

Hill, Francis. Ujamaa: Mobilization and Participation in Tanzania. London: Frank Cass, 1978.

Honadle, George, and Richard McGarr. "Organizing and Managing Technical Assistance: Lessons from the Maasai Range Mangement Project." IRD Project Field Report Prepared for the United States Agency for International Development. Washington, DC: Development Alternatives, Inc., 1979.

Hyden, Goran. Beyond Ujamaa in Tanzania. London: Heinemann, 1980.

Kanawaty, G., and E. Thorsrud. "Field Experiences with New Forms of Work Organization." International Labour Review 120, no. 3 (1981): 263-276.

McHenry, Dean E., Jr. "Peasant Participation in Communal Farming: The Tanzanian Experience." African Studies Review 20, no. 3 (1977): 43-63.

McHenry, Dean E., Jr. "The Underdevelopment Theory: A Case Study from Tanzania." Journal of Modern African Studies 14, no.4 (1976): 621-36.

McHenry, Dean E., Jr. "The Utility of Compulsion in the Implementation of Agricultural Policies: A Case Study from Tanzania." Canadian Journal of African Studies 7, no. 2 (1973): 305-316.

Maeda, Humphrey J. Popular Participation, Control and Development: Unpublished Ph.D. Dissertation, Yale University, 1976.

Malhotra, D.D. "Decentralization Strategy for Nation Building and Development--The Tanzanian Approach." Indian Journal of Public Administration 24, no. 3 (1978): 779-799.

Monishi, G.K.K. Development Administration in Tanzania: Public Service Planning and Utilization. Ann Arbor: Univ. Microfilms International, 1982.

Msekwa, P. "Workers' Participation in Management in Tanzania: A Background." The African Review 5, no. 2 (1975): 127-140.

Mukandala, R.S. "Organizational Form and Control of Parastatals in Tanzania." Africa Development 8 (1983): 58-72.

Mutaha, A.Z. Cooperatives in Tanzania: Problems of Organization. Studies in Political Science No. 4. Dar es Salaam: Tanzania Publishing House, 1976.

Mutahaba, F. "Local Autonomy and National Planning: Complementary or Otherwise? A Case Study from Tanzania." The African Review 4, no. 4 (1974): 509-530.

Nellis, J.R. "Prelude to Arusha: A Study of Productivity Problems on a Rural Development Scheme in Tanzania." Journal of Administration Overseas 11, no. 3 (1972): 169-181.

Omari, C.K. Strategy for Rural Development. Nairobi: East African Literature Bureau, 1976.

Proctor, D.H., ed. Building Ujamaa Villages in Tanzania. Studies in Political Science No. 2. Dar es Salaam: Univ. of Dar es Salaam, 1971.

Rural Development Research Committee, University of Dar es Salaam. Rural Cooperation in Tanzania. Dar es Salaam: Tanzania Publ. House, 1975.

Silver, M.S. The Growth of the Manufacturing Industry in Tanzania. Boulder: Westview Press, 1984.

Swantz, Marja Liisa. Women in Development: A Creative Role Denied? The Tanzanian Experience. London: C. Hurst, 1980.

Tanzanian Government Management Development in Tanzania. Report of the Management Training Study of the President's Office. Dar Es Salaam, April, 1975.

USAID. Terminal Evaluation of the Maasai Livestock and Range Management Project. Submitted to The Agency for International Development, Tanzania, DEVRES, Inc., Oct. 19, 1979.

Yeager, Rodger. Tanzania: An African Experiment. Boulder: Westview Press, 1982.

TUNISIA

Parsons, Kenneth H. "The Tunisian Program of Cooperative Farming." Land Economics 41, no. 4 (1965): 303-316.

Popper, Robert, and Tom McKee. Evaluation of USAID/Tunisia's Seliana Rural Development Project and the Save the Children Foundation Project. Washington, DC: Practical Concepts, Inc., 1980.

Tessler, Mark A., and L. Hawkings. "Acculturation, Socio-Economic Status, and Attitude Change in Tunisia: Implications for Modernization Theory." Journal of Modern African Studies 17, no. 3 (1979): 473-495.

Wolfson, Margaret. Aid Management in Developing Countries: A Case Study: The Implementation of Three Aid Projects in Tunisia. Paris: The Development Center of the Organization for Economic Cooperation and Development, 1972.

TURKEY

Ashford, Douglas E. Local Government and Agricultural Development in Turkey. Special Series on Rural Local Government. Ithaca: Cornell University, Center for International Studies, Rural Development Committee, 17, 1974.

Copur, Halil. Organizational Dimensions of Rural Development: A Turkish Case. Unpublished Ph.D. Dissertation, Cornell University, 1976.

Foundation for Management Education Survey on the Present State and Potentials for Future Development of Management Education in Turkey, 4 vols.. Istanbul: Foundation for Management Education, 1973.

Hinderink, Jan, and Mubeccel Kiray. Social Stratification as an Obstacle to Development: A Study of Four Turkish Villages. New York: Praeger Publishers, 1970.

Lauter, G.P. "Advanced Management Processes in Developing Countries: Planning in Turkey." California Management Review 12, no. 3 (Spring 1970): 7-12.

Terrill, William A. "Management Organization and Methods in Turkey," Human Organization 24 (Spring 1965): 96-104.

Walstedt, Bertil. State Manufacturing. Enterprise in a Mixed Economy: the Turkish Case. Baltimore: John Hopkins University Press for the World Bank, 1980.

UGANDA

Apter, David E. The Political Kingdom in Uganda: A Study in Bureaucratic Nationalism. Princeton: University Press, 1969.

Gartrell, B. "British Administrators, Colonial Chiefs and the Comfort of Tradition: An Example of Uganda." African Studies Review 26 (Mar. 1983): 1-24.

Kasfir, Nelson. "Organizational Analysis and Ugandan Cooperative Unions." In Cooperatives and Rural Development in East Africa, edited by Carl Gosta Widstrand. Uppsala: Scandinavian Institute of African Studies, 1970.

YEMEN ARAB REPUBLIC

Maiss, Otto. Yemen Arab Republic: Development of a Traditional Economy. Washington, DC: World Bank, 1979.

YUGOSLAVIA

Kavcic, Bogdan, Veljko Rus, and Arnold S. Tannenbaum. "Control, Participation, and Effectiveness in Four Yugoslav Industrial Organizations." Administrative Science Quarterly 16 (1971): 74-86.

Pusic, Eugene. "Territorial and Functional Administration in Yugoslavia." Administrative Science Quarterly 14 (1969): 62-72.

Schrenk, Martin, Cyrus Ardalan, and Nawal A. El Tatawy. Yugoslavia: Self-Management Socialism and the Challenges of Development. Baltimore: Johns Hopkins University Press, 1979.

Tannenbaum, Arnold, Stane Mozna, Janez Jcrousek, and Rensis Likert. "Testing a Managment Style." European Business, 27 (Autumn 1970).

ZAIRE

Mitchnik, David A. "The Role of Women in Rural Development in the Zaire. New York: Oxfam Publications, 1972.

Rimlinger, Gaston V. "Administrative Training and Modernization in Zaire." Journal of Development Studies 12, no. 4 (1976): 364-382.

ZAMBIA

Administration for Rural Development Project. Organization for Participation in Rural Development in Zambia. Lusaka: National Institute of Public Administration, 1977.

Lungu, Gatian F. "Administrative Responsibility in a Developing Country: Theoretical Considerations and the Case of Zambia." Public Administration and Development 3 (Oct.-Dec. 1983): 361-371.

Metaferia, G. Manpower Training for National Development: The Training of Zambian Civil Servants at the National Institute of Public Administration. Ann Arbor: University Microfilms International, 1983.

Oxenham, John. "Community Development and Village Employment in Zambia, 1948-1962." African Affairs 52, no. 228 (1976): 55-66.

Quick, Stephen A. "Bureaucracy and Rural Socialism in Zambia." Journal of Modern African Studies 15, no. 3 (1977): 379-400.

Scott, I. "Ideology, Party, and the Cooperative Movement in Zambia." <u>Journal of Administration Overseas</u> 19, no. 4 (1980): 228-238.

Taylor, P.L. "The Training of Elected Councillors in Zambia." <u>Journal of Administration Overseas</u> 6, no. 4 (1967): 252-255.

Tordoff, William, ed. <u>Administration in Zambia</u>. Manchester: Manchester University Press, 1981.

ZIMBABWE

Bratton, M. "Development in Zimbabwe: Strategy and Tactics." <u>Journal of Modern African Studies</u> 19 (Sept. 81): 447-475.

Lester, T. "Zimbabwe's British Lessons." <u>Management Today</u> (Feb. 1982): 74-77.

ASIA AND THE PACIFIC

ASIA-GENERAL

<u>The Asian Manager: Recruiting, Training and Retraining Executives</u>. Hongkong: Business International Asia/Pacific, 1982.

Bruch, Mathias, and Ulrich Hiemenz. <u>Small- and Medium- Scale Industries in the Asian Countries: Agents or Victims of Economic Development</u>. Boulder: Westview Press, 1984.

Cernea, Michael M., John K. Coulter, and John F. A. Russell. <u>Agricultural Extension by Training and Visit: The Asian Experience</u>. Washington DC: The World Bank, 1982.

Gable, Richard W., and J. Fred Springer. <u>Administering Agricultural Development in Asia. A Comparative Analysis of Four National Programs</u>. Boulder: Westview Press, 1977.

Gable, Richard W., and J. Fred Springer. "Administrative Implications of Development Policy: A Comparative Analysis of Agricultural Programs in Asia." <u>Economic Development and Cultural Change</u> 27 (1979): 687-703.

Gaikwad, V. R., and V. K. Gupta. <u>Managing Paddy-rice Business of Small Farmers' Integrated Cooperatives in Asia: Case Studies</u>. Ahmadabad: Centre for Management in Agriculture, Indian Institute of Management, 1983.

Hsieh, S. C. "Agricultural Development in Asia: Problems and Strategies, Part I." <u>Asia Research Bulletin</u> 2, no. 1 (1972): 915-917.

Iglesias, Gabriel U., et. al., eds. <u>Training Public Enterprise Managers Curricula and Country Studies</u>. Kuala Lumpur: Asian and Pacific Developemnt Centre, 1980.

Inayatullah, M. <u>Cooperatives and Development in Asia: A Study of Cooperatives in Fourteen Rural Communities of Iran, Pakistan and Ceylon</u>. Geneva: United Nations Research Institute for Social Development, 1972.

Inayatullah, M., ed. <u>Management Training for Development: The Asian Experience</u>. Kuala Lumpur: Asian Center for Development Administration, 1975.

International Labor Office. <u>Rural Development and Women in Asia: Proceedings and Conclusions of the ILO Tripartite Asian Regional Seminar, Maharashtra, India</u>. Geneva: ILO, 1982.

Jain, S.K. "Management Education to the End of this Century: The Asian Scene." <u>Malaysian Management Review</u> 19 (Aug. 1984): 5-19.

Raksasataya, Amara. "Development of the Administrative Sciences in Southeast Asia and Oceania." <u>International Review of Administrative Sciences</u> 44 (1978): 50-60.

Raksasataya, Amara, and Heinrich Siedentopf, eds. <u>Asian Civil Services: Developments and Trends</u>. Kuala Lumpur: Asian and Pacific Development Administration Center. Bonn: Konrad Adenauer Stiftung, 1980.

Redding, S.G., and T.W. Casey. "Managerial Beliefs Among Asian Managers." In <u>Proceedings Academy of Management 36th Meeting</u> edited by R.L. Taylor. Kansas City: Academy of Management, 1976.

Redding, S.G. "Some Perceptions of Psychological Needs Among Managers in East Asia." In <u>Basic Problems in Cross-Cultural Psychology</u> edited by Y.H. Poortinga. Amsterdam: Swets and Zeitlinger, n.d.

Rondinelli, Dennis A., John R. Nellis, and G. Shabbir Cheema. <u>Decentralization in Developing Countries: A Review of Recent Experience</u>. Staff Working Paper 581. Washington, DC: World Bank, 1983.

Taira, Koji. "Foreign Direct Investment, Personnel Structure and Working Conditions in Less Developed Countries in Asia." In <u>Foreign Investment and Labor in Asian Countries</u>, Tokyo: The Japan Institute of Labor, 1976.

Uphoff, N., ed. *Training and Research for Extended Rural Development in Asia. A Report of the Rural Development Committee.* Ithaca: Center for International Studies, Cornell University, 1974.

Uphoff, Norman T., and Milton J. Esman. *Local Organization for Rural Development: Analysis of Asian Experience.* Ithaca: Center for International Studies, Rural Development Committee, Cornell University 1974.

Weidner, Edward W. *Development Administration in Asia.* Durham: Duke University Press, 1980.

AFGHANISTAN

O'Connor, Ronald W., ed. *Mangaging Health Systems in Developing Areas. Experiences from Afghanistan.* Lexington: D.C. Heath, 1980.

BANGLADESH

Ahmed, S. "Management of Public Enterprises/Public Corporations in Bangladesh." *Management Development* 9 (1980): 15-29.

Anisuzzaman, M. *Bangladesh Public Administration and Society.* Dacca: Bangladesh Books Int. Ltd., 1979.

Bezdudni, F. "Organization and Planning of the Enterprises of the Textile Industry (II)." *Management Development* 6 (1975): 18-27.

Blair, Harry W. "Rural Development, Class Structure and Bureaucracy in Bangladesh." *World Development* 6, no. 1 (1978): 65-82.

Choldin, H. M. "An Organizational Analysis of Rural Development Projects at Comilla, East Pakistan." *Economic Development and Cultural Change* 20, no. 4 (1972): 671-690.

Choudhury, G.S. "Managerial Problems of Nationalized Industries in Bangladesh." *Management Development* 6 (1975): 15-24.

Chowdhury, S.A. "Management Consultancy in Bangladesh." *Management Development* 12 (1983): 15-24.

Coward, E. Walter, Jr., and B. Ahmed. "Village, Technology, and Bureaucracy: Patterns of Irrigation Organization in Comilla District, Bangladesh." *Journal of Developing Areas* 13, no. 4 (1979): 431-440.

Faaland, Just, and J. R. Parkinson. *Bangladesh: The Test Case for Development.* Boulder: Westview Press, 1976.

Fairchild, H. W. "The Comilla Rural Modernization Experiment, Its Philosophy, Underlying Hypotheses, and Usefulness as a Rural Development Model." *Monthly Bulletin of Agricultural Economics and Statistics* 17, no. 6 (1968): 1-6.

Hoong, Yip Yat. *Role of Universities in Management Education for National Development in Southeast Asia.* Regional Institute of Higher Education and Development, 1972.

Huq, M. Ameerul. *The Characteristics of the Managers of the Agricultural Cooperatives in Comilla.* Bangladesh: Academy for Rural Development, n.d.

Huq, M. Ameerul. *Five Years of a Workmans Cooperative: A Case Study of the Kashinathpur, Balarampur, Deeder Sramick Samabaya Samity, Ltd.* Comilla: Pakistan Academy for Rural Development, 1965.

Huq, M. Ameerul. "Reorganization of Rural Settlement in Bangladesh." *The Journal of Asiatic Society of Bangladesh* 22, no. 2 (Aug. 1977).

Hussain, Z. "Management Thoughts in Bangladesh." *Journal of Management, Business and Economics* 8 (1982): 392-413.

Inayuatullah, M. "An Analysis of the Emergence of a Rural Development Innovation in Comilla, Bangladesh." *Journal or Developing Areas* 11, no. 1 (1976): 79-90.

Jannuzi, F. and James T. Peach. *The Agrarian Structure of Bangladesh: An Impediment to Development.* Boulder: Westview Press, 1980.

Jayarajah, Carl A.B. *Bangladesh: Current Trends and Development Issues.* Washington DC: World Bank, 1979.

The Journal of Management, Business and Economics. *Index to Volume 1-9, 1975-1983.* Dhaka: Institute of Business Administration, University of Dhaka, 1983.

Kamal, M. "Evaluation of Management Training and Its Classification Levels." *Management Development* 11 (1982): 1-7.

Khan, Akhter H. "The Comilla Projects - A Personal Account." *International Development Review* 16 (Mar. 1974): 2-7.

Khan, Azizin Rahman. "The Comilla Model and the Integrated Rural Development Programme of Bangladesh: An Experiment in Cooperative Capitalism." World Development 7, nos. 4/5 (1979): 397-422.

Khan, Obaidullah. "Rural Development and Administrative Reorganization." Journal of the Pakistan Academy for Rural Development 4 (Apr. 1964): 190-202.

Quasem, Abul. "Agricultural Administration in Bangladesh--A Note." Agricultural Administration 4, no. 3 (1977): 159-165.

Rahim, Syed A. "Nonformal Aspects of the Comilla (Bangladesh) Project." In Nonformal Education and The Rural Poor, edited by R. O. Neihoff. East Lansing: Michigan State University College of Education, 1977.

Rahman, M. "Management Decision Making in a Developing Country: A Case Study in Bangladesh." Journal of Management, Business, and Economics 5 (1979): 332-344.

Rahman, Shamaur. "Bangladesh." In Farm Water Management for Rice Cultivation, Tokyo: Asian Productivity Organization, 1977.

Raper, Arthur, et. al Rural Development in Action: The Comprehensive Experiment at Comilla, East Pakistan. Ithaca: Cornell University Press, 1970.

Teel, J. H. Dynamic Social Systems Model for Population Management in Bangladesh. Ann Arbor: University Microfilms International, 1983.

Thomas, W.T. "Development Institutions, Projects and Aid: A Case Study of the Water Development Programme in East Pakistan," Pakistan Economic and Social Review 12 (1974): 87-103.

Waliullah, Syed. Modernity Characteristics of Local Leaders and the Family Planning Program in Bangladesh. Unpublished Ph.D. Dissertation, Utah State University, 1974.

BHUTAN

Bhutan: Development in a Himalayan Kingdom. Washington, DC: World Bank, 1983.

BURMA

Guyot, James F. "Bureaucratic Transformation in Burma." In Asia Bureaucratic Systems Emergent from the British Tradition edited by Ralph Braibanti. Durham: Duke Univ. Press, 1966.

Kyi, K.M., and H.B. Moore, eds. Cases in Management and Administration: Series I, Rangoon: Case Research Program, University of Rangoon, n.d.

McKay, Q.G. and K.M. Kyawe, eds. Cases in Management and Administration: Series 2, Burma: Case Research Program, University of Rangoon, n.d.

CHINA

Bennett, Gordon, K. Kieke, and K. Yoffy. Huadong: The Story of a Chinese People's Commune. Boulder: Westview Press, 1978.

Braddick, B. and N. Foy. "Management After Mao." Management Today (Aug. 1980): 46-49.

Chan, W.K.K. "The Organizaitonal Structure of the Traditional Chinese Firm and Its Modern Reform." Business History Review 56 (Summer 1982): 218-35.

Chang, King-yuh, ed. Perspectives on Development in the PRC. Boulder: Westview Press, 1984.

Chastain, C.G. "Management, The Key to China's Development." Management International Review 22, no. 1 (1982): 5-12.

Chen, Jack. Self Management in China's Communes. Paper presented to Second International Conference on Self-Management, Ithaca: Cornell University, 1975.

Dernberger, Robert, ed. China's Development Experience in Comparative Perspective. Cambridge: Harvard University Press, 1980.

Falkenheim, Victor C. "County Administration in Fukien." China Quarterly, 59 (1974): 518-543.

Kim, S.T. Changing Policies of Rural Commune Management in China: 1975, 1977 and 1979. Ann Arbor: University Microfilms International, 1983.

Lau, S. Managerial Style of Traditional Chinese Firms. Unpublished dissertation, University of Hong Kong, 1977.

Lasdon, L.S. "Operations Research in China." Interfaces 10 (Feb. 1980): 23-27.

Lowe, J. "China's Managerial Revolution." Management Today (Mar. 1983): 68-73.

Nelson, Harvey W. The Chinese Military System: An Organizational Study of the People's Liberation Army. Boulder: Westview Press, 1977.

Nickum, James E. Irrigation Management in China: A Review of the Literature. Staff Working Paper 545. Washington, DC: World Bank, 1983.

Perkins, Dwight H., and Shahid Yusuf. Rural Development in China. Baltimore: The John Hopkins Univ. Press, 1984.

Schram, Stuart R., ed. Authority, Participation and Cultural Change in China. New York: Cambridge University Press, 1973.

Schurmann, Franz. Ideology and Organization in Communist China, 2nd ed. Berkeley: University of California Press, 1969.

Sinha, R. P. "Chinese Agriculture: Past Performance and Future Outlook," Journal of Agricultural Economics 25, no. 1 (1974): 37-52.

Stavis, Benedict. "China's Rural Local Institutions in Comparative Perspective." Asian Survey 26, 4 (1976): 381-396.

Stavis, Benedict. People's Communes and Rural Development in China. Ithaca: Rural Development Committee, Cornell Univ. Press, 1977.

Tung, R.L. "Patterns of Motivation in Chinese Industrial Enterprises." Academy of Management Review 6 (July 1981): 481-89.

Whyte, Martin K. "Bureaucracy and Anti-Bureaucracy in the Peoples Republic of China," in Hierarchy and Society edited by G.M. Briton, and R. Cohen. Philadelphia: I.S.H.I. Publications, 1980.

Whyte, Martin King. Small Groups and Political Rituals in China. Berkeley: University of California Press, 1975.

Wong, J. "Some Aspects of China's Agricultural Development Experience: Implications for Developing Countries in Asia," World Development 4, no. 6 (1976): 485.

HONG KONG

Mok, Victor. The Organization and Management of Factories in Kwun Tong. Hong Kong: Social Research Center, University of Hong Kong, 1973.

INDIA

Aggarwal, Partap C. Caste, Religion and Power: An Indian Case Study. New Delhi: Shri Ram Centre for Industrial Relations, 1971.

Agarwala, A.N. The Emerging Dimensions of Indian Management. New York: Asia Publishing House, 1970.

Alexander, K.C. Rural Organizations in South India: The Dynamics of Laborer and Tenant Unions and Farmer Associations in Kerala and Tamil Nadu. Rural Development Committee Center for International Studies, Ithaca: Cornell University Press, 1980.

Alliband, T. Catalysts of Development, Voluntary Agencies in India. West Hartford: Kumarian Press, Inc., 1983.

Avasthi, Amreshwar. Central Administration, New York: McGraw Hill, 1980.

Baviskar, Baburao S. "Opportunity and Response: Social Factors in Agricultural Development in Maharashtra," Institute of Development Studies Bulletin 8 no. 2 (1976): 22-26.

Bedi, I. S. and R. P. Saxena. "Improved Agricultural Practices: Behavioristic Pattern of Farmers in Punjab and Uttar Pradesh" A.I.C.C. Economic Review 21 (1965): 27-33.

Benner, Jeffrey. The Indian Foreign Policy Bureaucracy. Boulder: Westview Press, 1984.

Bergmann, T. "Resource Mobilization and Obstacles to Development in Indian Farming," Pacific Viewpoint 14, no. 1 (1973): 1-22.

Bhatt, Anil, Arun Monappa, and Amla Subramangam. City Management: A Study of Some Aspects of Municipal Administration in Ahmedabad and Baroda. Ahmedabad, India: PSG Group, The Indian Institute of Management, 1983.

Bjorkman, James Warner. The Politics of Administrative Alienation: Relations Among Civil Servants and Political Leaders in Rural India's Development Programs. Unpublished Ph.D. Dissertation, Yale University, 1976.

Broehl, Wayne, Jr. The Village Entrepreneur: Change Agents in India's Rural Development. Cambridge: Harvard University Press, 1978.

Chandrakant, L.S. Management Education and Training in India. Bombay: D.B. Taraporevala Sons, 1973.

Dasgupta, S. "Community Factors in Agricultural Development: A Case Study in Six Indian Villages." International Review of Community Development 19-20 (1968): 285-308.

Dayal, Ishwar. "Directions of Change in Administration." Indian Management 13, no. 7 (July 1974): 3-15.

Desai, D.K. "Managing Agricultural System in India: The Role of Agricultural Economists." Indian Journal of Agricultural Economics 38, no. 4 (Oct.-Dec. 1982): 426-453.

Desal, Padma. The Bokaro Steel Plant: A Study of Soviet Economic Assistance, New York: American Elsevier, 1972.

Draper, J.A., and Y.K.N. Unnithan, "The Sociology of Citizen Participation: A Case Study of Citizen Awareness of the Jaipur City Plan." International Review of Community Development, 37-38, (1977): 259-272.

Dubey, S.N. "Organizational Analysis of Panchayati Raj Institutions in India" Indian Journal of Public Administration 19, no. 1 (1972): 54-81

Dugan, John J., Jr. The Relationship Between Culture and Managers' Behavioral Decisions: A Two Country Study of the Preference Formation and Choice Processes. Ann Arbor: University Microfilms International, 1984.

Elder, Robert E., Jr. Development Administration in a North Indian State: The Family Planning Program in Uttar Pradesh. Carolina Population Center, Monograph No. 18. Chapel Hill: Carolina Population Center, 1972.

Fritz, Dan. "Bureaucratic Commitment in Rural India: A Psychological Application." Asian Survey 16, no. 4 (1976): 338-354.

Gaikwad, V.R., and D.S. Parmar. Serving Small Farmers: A Study of the Farmers' Service Cooperative Society, Bidadi. Mono. No. 94 Ahmedabad: Centre for Management in Agriculture. Indian Institute of Management, 1983.

Ganesh, S.R., and Neera Sethi. Retrospective Case Analyses of Organization Development in Public Systems in a (State) Government in India, Mono. No. 50 Ahmedabad: Public Systems Group. Indian Institute of Management, 1982.

Garg, Pulin. "Organization Structure, Design and Development. Case Material, OB-121. Ahmedabad: Indian Institute of Management, 1980.

Gupta, T. "Land and Forest Resource Management for Economic Betterment of the Poor in Rural India." Indian Economic Aanac, 2 (1982):76-81

Hale, Sylvia M. "Stratificaton and Local Organization: The Case of Rural Development in India." In Contributions to Asian Studies edited by K. Ishwaran. Leiden: E.J. Brill, 1977.

Heginbotham, Stanley J. Cultures in Conflict: The Four Faces of Indian Bureaucracy. New York: Columbia University Press, 1975.

Hill, T.M., W. W. Haynes, and H. Baumgartel. Institution Building in India: A Study of International Collaboration in Management Education. Boston: Harvard Univ. Press, 1973.

Hunter, Guy. The Administration of Agricultural Development: Lessons from India. London: Oxford Univ. Press, 1970.

Index of Case Studies. Training Monograph No. 8. New Delhi: Training Division, Department of Personnel, Cabinet Secretariat, (Feb 1971).

Jaggi, Bikki. "Analysis of Perceived Need Importance of Indian Managers." Management International Review 19, no. 1 (1979): 107-112.

Jaggi, Bikki. "Job Satisfaction and Leadership Style in Developing Countries: The Case of India." International Journal of Contemporary Sociology 14 (July-Oct.): 230-235, 1977.

Jain, Sagar C. Indian Manager: His Social Origin and Career. Bombay: Somaiya Publications, 1971.

Johl, S.S. The Dynamics of Institutional Change and Rural Development in Punjab, India. Ithaca: Rural Development Committee Center for International Studies, Cornell University, Nov., 1974.

Kakar, Sudhir. "Authority Patterns and Subordinates' Behavior in Indian Organizations." Administrative Science Quarterly 16 (Sept. 1971): 298-307.

Kakar, Sudhir. "Authority Relations in Indian Organizations." Management International Review 12 (1972): 51-56.

Kapp, W.K., Hindu Culture: Economic Development and Economic Planning in India. New York: Asia Publishing House, 1963.

Karunaratne, Garvin. "The Failure of the Community Development Programme in India." Community Development Journal 11, no. 2 (1976): 95-119.

Khandwalla, Pradip N. "Management in Our Backyard." *Vikalpa* 5 (July 1980): 173-184.

Khanna, I. *External Aid and Development Strategy in Rajasthan.* Ahmedabad: Public Systems Group, Indian Institute of Management, 1982.

Khanna, I., and A. Subramanian. *Bureaucracy and Development Programmes: Notes and Cases.* Ahmedabad: Public Systems Group, Indian Institute of Management, 1982.

Khanna, I., and A. Subramanian. "Lessons from Antyodaya for Integrated Rural Development Programmes." *Vikalpa* 7, no. 3 (July-Sept. 1982): 227-234.

Krishnamurthy, V. "Management of Organizational Change. The Bharat Heavy Electricals Ltd. Experience." *Vikalpa* 2 (1977): 113-119.

Long, W. A., and K. K. Seo. *Management in Japan and India with Reference to the U.S.* New York: Praeger Publishers, 1977.

Maddick, Henry. *Panchayati Raj: A Study of Rural Local Government in India.* London: Longman, 1970.

"Management of Public Enterprises in India." *The Indian Worker* (Aug 1974):35-39.

Maru, Rushikesh, Nirmala Murthy, and J.K. Safia. "Management Intervention in Established Bureaucracies: A Case Study." *Economic and Political Weekly* 18, no. 35 (1983): 998-110.

Mascarenhas, R.C. "A System View of the Measurement of the Performance of Public Enterprises in India." *Policy Sciences.* 5 (March 1974): 29-46.

Mathur, D.P., and V.K. Gupta. *Management in Cooperative Rice Mills.* Ahamedabad: The Center for Management in Agriculture, The Indian Institute of Management. n.d.

Mathur, D.P. and V.K. Gupta. *Management in Small Poultry Farms (A Study in Maharashtra and Giyaret Regions).* Ahmedabad: The Center for Management in Agriculture, The Indian Institute of Management, n.d.

Mathur, Hari Mohan. "Training of Senior Agricultural Experts and Administrators: The Case of Rajasthan, India." *Agricultural Administration* 4, 1 (1977): 29-35.

Matthai, Ravi J., Udai Pareek, and T.V. Rao. *Managment Process in Universities: A Study of Decision Making and Organizational Health in Two Agricultural Universities.* Ahmedabad, India: PSG Group, Indian Institute of Management, 1983.

Mehta, D.R., and S.K. Batra, eds. *Administration for Rural Development.* Jaipur, India: Center for Administrative Change, 1981.

Mellor, J.W. *Developing Rural India: Plan and Practice.* Ithaca: Cornell University Press, 1968.

Mohanan, N. "The Cooperative Organizations in India." *Lok Udyog*, 16, 8 (Nov. 1982): 37-44.

Mohanan, N. "Participative Management: I - Dinesh Beedi Workers Society's Model." *Economic Times* (Dec. 1982): 7.

Mohanan, N. "Participative Management: II - Decision Making Models in Dinesh." *Economic Times*, (December 14, 1982): 5 & 8.

Mukherji, Partha Nath. "A Study on Induced Social Change: An Indian Experiment." *Human Organization* 29, no. 3 (1970): 169-177.

Murthy, Nirmala, ed. *Experiments in Management Development: Experience of India Population Project - I.* Ahmebadad, India: PSG Group, The Indian Institute of Management, 1983.

Murthy, Nirmala. *Management Information and Evaluation Systems for Maternity Homes and Urban Family Welfare Centers.* Ahmedabad, India: PSG Group, The Indian Institute of Management, 1983.

Murthy, Nirmala, and Bharat V. Upadhyaq. *Family Size and Absentieeism and Textile Workers.* Ahmedabad, India: PSG Group, The Indian Institute of Management, 1980.

Nair, Kusum. *Blossoms in the Dust: The Human Factor in Indian Development*, New York: Praeger Publishers, 1962.

Nambudiri, C.N.S., and S. Saiyadain Mirza. "Management Problems and Practices - India and Nigeria." *Columbia Journal of World Business* 20 (Summer 78): 62-70.

Narain, Laxmi. "Top Level Organization Planning in Indian Private Enterprise." *Indian Management* 13, no. 6 (June 1974): 5-10.

Niehoff, Arthur. "Caste and Industrial Organization in North India." *Administrative Science Quarterly* 3 (1959): 494-508.

Nobe, K.C. "Irrigation Management: Delivery System and Training Needs for India." *Vikalpa:* 7 (July/Sept. 1982).

Oommen, T.K. "Problems of Building Agrarian Organizations in Kerala." *Sociologia Ruralis* 16, no. 3 (1976): 177-196.

Oommen, T.K. "Rural Community Power Structure in India." *Social Forces* 49, no. 2 (1970): 226-239.

Orpen, C. "Risk Taking Attitudes Among Indian, U.S. and Japanese Managers." *Journal of Social Psycology* 120 (Aug 83): 283-284.

Panchanadikar, K.C., and J. Panchanadikar. *Rural Modernization in India: A Study of Developmental Infrastructure.* Bombay: Popular Prakashan, 1978.

Patel, V.C. *Indentifying and Developing Indigenous Entrepreneurs: The Gujarat Experience* Ahmedabad: The Centre for Entrepreneur Development, 1982.

Pestonjee, D.M., and Udai Bhan Singh. *An Intervention on Job Satisfaction As A Function of Role Stress, Locus of Control, Participation and Organisational Climate in an Electricity Supply Company.* PSG Monograph No. 47. Ahmedabad: Public Systems Group, Indian Institute of Management, 1982.

Pestonjee, D.M., and Udai Bhan Singh. "The EDP Managers: An Organisational Behavior Study." *Indian Institute of Management Ahmedabad,* n.d.

Prahalad, C.K., and P.S. Thomas. "Turnaround Strategy: Lessons from Hindustan Photo Films Experience." *Vikalpa* 2 (1977): 99-111.

Rao, Lakshamana. *Communication and Development: A Study of Two Indian Villages,* Minneapolis: University of Minnesota Press, 1966.

Rao, T.V. "HRD in India: A Review and Reflections About Expectations from ABS." *ISABS Journal* 1, no. 2 (1982): 48-54.

Rao, T.V., and P. Vijagashree. *Psychological Maturity and Motivational Students.* Ahmedabad, India: PSG Group, Indian Institute of Management, 1983.

Reddy, G. Ram. *Panchayati Raj and Rural Development in Andhra Pradesh.* Ithaca: Rural Development Committee, Cornell University, 1974.

Rice, A.K. *Productivity and Social Organization, The Ahmedabad Experiment.* London: Tavistock, 1958.

Richman, M.B. "A Firsthand Study of Industrial Management and Economic Development in India." *AID Research Paper* Los Angeles: University of California, 1969.

Rosser, Colin. "Action Planning in Calcutta: The Problem of Community Participation." *Journal of Development Studies* 6, no. 4 (1970): 121-129.

Roy, S.K. "Personnel Management in Indian Business and Industry." *Personnel Administration* 34, no. 2 (March-April 1971): 14-19.

Saghir, Ahmad, ed. *Class and Power in a Punjabi Village.* New York: Monthly Review Press, 1977.

Saran, Parmatma. *Rural Leadership in the context of India's Modernization.* Unpublished Ph.D. Dissertation, City University of New York, 1975.

Sarkar, N. *Social Structure and Development Strategy in India.* New Delhi: People's Publishing House, 1978.

Schluter, Michael G., and Timothy D. Mount. "Some Management Objectives of the Peasant Farmer: An Analysis of Risk Aversion in the Choice of Cropping Pattern, Surat District, India" *Journal of Development Studies* 12, 3(1976):246-261.

Seetharaman, S.P. "Surface Irrigation Co-operative: A Case Study." *Indian Journal of Public Administration* (Oct.-Dec. 1982): 815-831.

Sen, Lalit K. *Planning Rural Growth Centers for Integrated Area Development: A Study of Miryalguda Taluka.* Hyderabad, India: National Institute of Community Development, 1971.

Sen, P.K. "Role of Social and Economic Factors in Agricultural Administration and Organization in India." *Agricultural Administration* 1, no. 2 (1974): 89-102.

Seshadri, K. "Administration of Rural Small-Scale Industry Development Schemes in Andhra Pradesh, India." *Journal of Local Administration Overseas* 4, no. 4 (October 1965): 260-269.

Sharan, Girja, and P.V. Krishna. Identification of Problems in Management of Custom Hiring Centers. (Gujaret). Ahmedabad, India: Center for Management in Agriculture, The Indian Institute of Management, n.d.

Sharma, Baldev Raj. The Indian Industrial Worker: Issues in Perspective. Delhi: Vikas, 1974.

Sharma, S.K. "Administrative Decentralization in Punjab: The Village Cluster Development Programme." Indian Journal of Public Administration 24, no. 3 (1978): 837-847.

Shingi, P.M., S. Wadwalkar, and G. Kaur. Management of Agricultural Extension: Training and Visit System in Rajasthan. Mono. 96 Ahmedabad: Centre for Management in Agriculture, Indian Institute of Management, 1982.

Shiviah. "Decentralization and Panchayati Raj: A Development Perspective." Indian Journal of Public Administration 24, no. 3 (1978): 678-689.

Singh, G., T. Gupta, and A. Guleria. Economic and Management Aspects of Sugarbeet Cultivation and Processing in India. Mono. 105 Ahmedabad: Centre for Management in Agriculture, Indian Institute of Management, 1983.

Sinha, A.K. "Organization Building in a Developing Country: A Study of the Central Department of Food in India." International Review of Administrative Sciences 45 (1979): 176-182.

Srivastava, U.K. Management of Drought Prone Areas Programme (Analysis and Case Studies from Jhabva District). Mono. 71 Ahmedabad: The Centre for Management in Agriculture, The Indian Institute of Management, n.d.

Srivastava, U.K., and M.D. Reddy, eds. Fisheries Development in India: Some Aspects of Policy Management. New Delhi: Concept Publishing Co., 1983.

Taylor, Carl C. India's Roots of Democracy: A Sociological Analysis of Rural India's Experience in Planned Development Since Independence. New York: Praeger Publishers, 1966.

Tripathy, A. "Project Management Practices in India." In Proceedings of 7th Internet World Congress, 1982 edited by J.O. Riis. Copenhagen: The Danish Project Management Society, Projektphan, 1983.

UN. Poverty, Unemployment and Development Policy: A Case Study of Selected Issues with Reference to Kerela. New York: United Nations, 1975.

UNCRD. India: An Annotated Bibliography on Regional Development. New York: UNCRD, 1976.

Valsan, A.H. Community Development Programs and Rural Local Government: Comparative Case Studies of India and the Philippines. New York: Praeger Publishers, 1970.

Wade, Robert. "Leadership and Integrated Rural Development: Reflections on an Indian Success Story." Journal of Administration Overseas 17, no. 4 (1978): 245-255.

Waghmare, S.K., and A. U. Patel. "Indian Community Development Administration at the Crossroads," International Review of Administrative Sciences 37, no. 3 (1971): 277-279.

Wood, Geof. "Rural Development and the Post-Colonial State: Administration and the Peasantry in the Kosi-Region of North-East Bihar, India." Development and Change 8, no. 3 (1977): 307-323.

Zamara, Mario D. "Tradition, Social Control, and Village Administration: An Indian Case." Journal of Public Administration 6 (Oct. 1965): 303-313.

INDONESIA

Geertz, Clifford. Peddlers and Princes: Social Change and Economic Modernization in Two Indonesian Towns. Chicago: University of Chicago Press, 1963.

Habri, M. "Lessons for Leaders." Far East Economic Review 122 (Oct. 1983): 82.

Hansen, G.E. "Indonesia's Green Revolution: The Abandonment of a Non-Market Strategy Toward Change" Asian Survey 12, no. 11 (1972): 932-946.

Hesseling, P. Transfer of Knowledge for Economic Organization, The Indonesian Case. Rotterdam: Erasmus University, Center for Research in Business Economics, 1984.

Honadle, George. "Managing Institution Building: An Action-Oriented Model Based on the Provincial Area Development Program in Indonesia. Washington, DC: Development Alternatives, Inc., Unpublished draft, Nov 1979.

Horikoshi, Hiroko. *A Traditional Leader in a Time of Change: The Kijaji and Ulama in West Java.* Unpublished Ph.D. Dissertation, University of Illinois, Urbana-Champaign, 1976.

Liddle, R. William. "Evolution from Above: National Leadership and Local Development in Indonesia." *Journal of Asian Studies* 32, no. 2 (1973): 287-309.

VanSant, Jerry, and Peter F. Weisel. "Community Based Integrated Rural Development (CBIRD) in The Special Territory of Aceh, Indonesia." IRD Project Field Report. Prepared for United States Agency for International Development. Research Triangle Park: Research Triangle Institute and Development Alternatives, Inc., 1979.

IRAN

Jacobs, Norman. *The Sociology of Development, Iran as an Asian Case Study.* New York: Praeger Publishers, 1966.

Khalili, M.H. *U.S. Technical Assistance in Iranian Public Administration: An Evaluation of Performance.* Ann Arbor: University Microfis International, 1982.

Seitz, J.L. "The Failure of U.S. Technical Assistance in Public Administration: The Iranian Case." *Public Administration Review* 40 no. 5 (Sept./Oct. 1980): 407-413.

Seitz, J.L. "Iran and the Future of U.S. Technical Assistance: Some Afterthoughts." *Public Administration Review* 40, no. 5 (Sept./Oct. 1980): 432-433.

Sherwood, Frank P. "Learning from the Iran Experience" *Public Administration Review* 40, no. 5 (1980): 413-421.

Siffin, W.J. "The Sultan, The Wise Men, and the Fretful Mastodon: A Persian Fable." *Public Administration Review* 40, no. 5 (Sept./Oct. 1980): 418-421.

KOREA

Aqua, Ronald. *Local Institutions and Rural Development in South Korea.* Special Series on Rural Local Government, No. 13. Ithaca: Cornell University, Center for International Studies, Rural Development Committee, 1974.

Hasan, Parvez, and D.C. Rao. *Korea: Policy Issues for Long-Term Development.* Baltimore: The Johns Hopkins University Press, 1979.

Harbron, J.D. "Korea's Executives Are Not Quite the New Japanese." *Business Quarterly* 44, nos. 16, 17 (1979).

Hong, Sung Chick. *The Intellectual and Modernization: A Study of Korean Attitudes.* Seoul: Daehan Textbook Co., 1967.

Kim, L., and Utterback. "The Evolution of Organizational Structure and Technology in a Developing Country." *Management Science* 29 (Oct. 83): 1185-1197.

Lee, Hahn-Been. *Korea: Time, Change, and Administration.* Honolulu: East-West Center Press, 1968.

Lee, J.M. *Problems of Late-Late Industrialization: An Interpretation from an Industrial Organization Perspective.* Ann Arbor: University Microfis International, 1983.

Shin, D.C. "Concept of Quality of Life and the Evaluation of Developmental Effort: Some Applications to South Korea." *Comparative Politics* 11 (Apr. 1979): 299-318.

Shinohara, Miyohei, Toru Yanagihara, and Kwang Suk Kim. *The Japanese and Korean Experiences in Managing Development.* Staff Working Paper No. 574. Washington, DC: The World Bank, 1984.

LAOS

Halpern, Joel J. "Culture Change in Laos and Serbia: Possible Tendencies Toward Universal Organizational Patterns." *Human Organization* 20 (Spring 1961): 11-14.

MALAYSIA

Ahmed, Latheef N. *New Thinking for Malaysia Public Administration.* Kuala Lumpur: Dewan Bahasa Dan Pastaka, 1975.

Alcser, K.H. *Administrative Culture and Organization: State Level Variance in the Performance of the Malaysian National Family Planning Program.* Ann Arbor: University Microfis International, 1983.

Bell, Clive, Peter Hazel, and Roger Slade. *Project Evaluation in Regional Perspective: A Study of an Irrigation Project in N.W. Malaysia.* Baltimore: John Hopkins University Press, 1982.

Chee, Stephen. *Rural Development and Development Administration in Malaysia.* New York: Asia Society, 1974.

Deruah, Harun bin. Membership Participation, Organizational Performance and Developmental Change: A Comparative Study of Selected Farmers' Associations in West Malaysia. Unpublished Ph.D. Dissertation, University of Kentucky, 1976.

Fredericks, L.J. "Ideology and Organizations in Agricultural Development: The Case of Malaysia." Sociologia Ruralis 17, no. 3 (1977): 191-202.

Gripstra, G.B. Common Efforts in the Development of Rural Sarawak, Malaysia. Asen, Netherlands: Royal Vangoreum, 1976.

Jackson, James C., and M. Rudner, eds. Issues in Malaysian Development. Singapore: Heinemann Educational Books (Asia), 1980.

Lim, D. "Malaysian Development Planning" Pacific Affairs 55 (Winter 82/83): 613-639.

Mah, G.C. "Management Climate and The Manager of Tomorrow." Malaysian Management Review 14 (Aug. 1979): 32-34.

Malaysian Management Review 15 (Aug. 1980). Proceedings of the 7th AAMO Conference held on Oct. 19-23, 1980. Contents include excellent articles on management training skills and management-organization relationships.

Rao, T.V., and M. Iqbal. "HRD Practices in Malaysian Banks." Bankers Journal-Malaysia 14 (1982): 24-27.

Rudner, M. "Changing Planning Perspectives of Agriculture Development in Malaysia" Modern Asian Studies 17 (July 1983): 413-35.

Schwenk, R. "Sarawak: Working Backwards to Development." Reading Rural Development and Communication Bulletin (Nov. 1979).

Seri, D., and M. Mohd. "Malaysia in the 1980's: the Management Challenge. Malaysian Management Review 15 (Apr. 1980): 1-5.

Sich, M.L. "Managerial Revolution in Malaysia." Malaysian Management Review 12 (April 1977): 40-47.

Wikkramatileke, R. "The Jengka Triangle, West Malaysia: A Regional Development Project." Geographical Review 62, no. 4 (1972): 479-500.

Young, Kevin, Willem Bussink, and Parvez Hasan. Malaysia: Growth and Equity in a Multiracial Society. Baltimore: The Johns Hopkins University Press, 1980.

NEPAL

Agrawal, Hem Narayan. The Administration System of Nepal: From Tradition to Modernity. New Delhi: Vihas Publishing House PVT LTD, 1976.

Bhatta, Bhim Dev. An Evaluation of the Executive Development Training Program in Nepal. Kathmandu: Center for Ecology Development and Administration, Tribhavan University, 1978.

Huang, Yukon. Nepal: Development Performance and Prospects. Washington, DC: World Bank, 1979.

Joshi, Nanda Lall. Evolution of Public Administration in Nepal. Katmandu: Shanti Printing Press, 1973.

Joshi, Shyam. "Private Enterprise: Has It Been Neglected in Nepal?" PRASHASAN The Nepalese Journal of Public Administration 40 (July 1984): 83-91.

Lohani, Madhu S.; Nilkantha R. Paohya, Mahesh Banskota, and Krishna R. Khadka. "The Problems of Planning Cells (Nepal)." PRASHASAN, The Nepanese Journal of Public Administration, 40 (July 1984): 119-133.

Poudyal, Madhab Prasad. "Social Administration in Nepal: Historical Perspectives." PRASHASAN, The Nepanese Journal of Public Administration, 40 (July 1984): 93-101.

Poudyal, Madhab P. Public Administration and Nation Building in Nepal. Delhi: NBO Publishers Distributors, (1984): 128.

Pradhan, Prachanda. "Baglung Suspension Bridges: Outcome of People's Participation in Nepal." Rural Development Participation Review 1 (1979).

Pradhan, Prachanda. Local Institutions and People's Participation in Rural Public Works in Nepal. n.p., 1980.

Rajbhandary, Achyut B. "Motivation in the Public Service in Nepal." PRASHASAN, The Nepalese Journal of Public Administration 40 (July 1984): 51-55.

Schloss, A. "Stages of Development and the Uses of Planning: Some Nepali Experiences." Asian Survey 23 (Oct. 1983): 1115-1127.

Uphoff, Norman T. "Excerpts from a Presentation by Dr. Norman Uphoff on 'Problems Inhibiting Achievement of Broader People's Participation'" in People's Participation in Rural Development in Nepal. Katmandu: Agricultural Projects Service Center, 1978.

Wildavsky, Aaron. "Why Planning Fails in Nepal." Administrative Science Quarterly 17 (1972): 508-528.

NEW GUINEA

Baldwin, George B., et. al. Papua New Guinea: Its Economic Situation and Prospects for Development. Baltimore: The Johns Hopkins University Press, 1978.

Finney, Ben R. Big-Men and Business. Entrepreneurship and Economic Growth in New Guinea Highlands. Honolulu: University Press of Hawaii, 1973.

Galenson, Alice, et. al. Papua New Guinea: Selected Development Issues. Washington, DC: World Bank, n.d.

PACIFIC ISLANDS

Campbell, M.J. "Devolution in the Solomon Islands: A Study of Major Reforms." Journal of Administration Overseas 16, no. 4 (1977): 228-239.

Davies, B.V. "Administration of the Rural Development Programme in Fiji." Journal of Administration Overseas 10, 4 (1971): 252-267.

Murray, David J. "Microstates: Public Administration for the Small and Beautiful." Public Administration and Development 1 (July-Sept. 1981): 245-256.

Oliver, Douglas L. A Solomon Island Society: Kinship and Leadership Among the Sinai of Bouganville. Boston: Beacon Press, 1967.

Traynor, William, and Manik Wadwani. Aspects of Training. Fiji: University of the South Pacific, 1981.

PAKISTAN

Birkhead, Guthrie S., ed. Administrative Problems in Pakistan. Syracuse: Syracuse Univ. Press, 1966.

Honigmann, John J. "A Case Study of Community Development in Pakistan." Economic Development and Cultural Change 8 (Apr. 1960): 288-303.

Khan, Afzal. "Thoughts on Problems of Rural Development." Journal of Rural Development and Administration 4 (Sept. 1964): 19-26.

Mahbub-ul-Haq, "The Strategy of Economic Planning: A Case Study of Pakistan." Karachi: Oxford Univ. Press, 1966.

Nicholson, Norman, and Dilawar Ali Khan. Basic Rural Democracies and Rural Development in Pakistan. n.p., 1974.

Radosevich, George E. Water User Organizations for Improving Irrigated Agriculture: Application to Pakistan. Water Management Technical Report No. 44. Fort Collins: State University, 1975.

Raza, M. Ali. "Management Ideologies and Resources in Pakistan." Journal of Industrial Relations. (Mar. 1965): 50-73.

Sayeed, Khalid Bin. "Religion and Nation Building in Pakistan." The Middle East Journal 17 (Summer 1963): 279-291.

UNCRD. Pakistan: An Annotated Bibliography on Local and Regional Development. New York: UNCRD, 1981.

PHILIPPINES

Anderson, Dennis, and Farida Khambata. Small Enterprises and Development Policy in the Philippines: A Case Study. Staff Working Paper No. 468. Washington, DC: World Bank, 1981.

Carner, G., and DC Korten. People-Centered Planning: The USAID/Philippines Experience. NASPAA Working Paper No. 2. Washington, DC: National Association of Schools of Public Affairs and Administration, 1982.

de Guzman, Raul P., ed. Patterns in Decision-Making, Case Studies in Philippine Public Administration. Manila: Graduate School of Public Administration, Univeristy of the Philippines, 1963.

dela, Paz, R.S. The Development of Central Luzon State University into a Regional Agriculture University: A Comparative Case Study in Institution Building. Ann Arbor: University Microfilms International, 1983.

de los Reyes, R.P. Socio Cultural Patterns and Irrigation Organization: The Management of a Philippines Community Irrigation System. Ann Arbor: University Microfilms International, 1982.

Einsiedel, L.A. *Success and Failure in Selected Community Development Projects in Batangas.* Quezon City, Philippines: Community Development Research Council, University of the Philippines, 1968.

Flores, P. *The Applicability of American Management Know-How to Developing Countries: A Case Study of American Firms Operating in the U.S. and the Philippines in Comparison with Philippino firms.* Unpublished Ph.D. dissertation, University of California, Los Angeles, Graduate School of Business, 1968.

Garilao, Ernesto. "*Laguna Rural Society Development Project.*" Case Study No. 1. Case Studies in Public Policy Implementation and Project Management Honolulu: East-West Technology and Development Institute, 1977.

Honadle, George. "Beneficiary Involvement in Project Implementation: Experience in the Bicol." *Rural Development Participation Review* 1, no. 1 (1979): 12-13.

Honadle, George. "*Implementing Integrated Area Development in the Bicol.*" A report prepared for the U.S. Agency for International Development and the Bicol River Basin Coordinating Committee, Washington, DC: Development Alternatives, Inc., 1977.

Iglesias, G. "Marcos' Rice Self-Sufficiency Program: Leadership Role in Implementation." In *Implementation: The Problem of Achieving Results,* G. Iglesias. Manila: Eastern Regional Organization for Public Administration, 1976.

Korten, David. "*People-Centered Planning: The USAID/Philippines Experience.*" NASPAA Working Paper No. 2. Washington, DC: NASPAA, 1982.

Korten, David C. *The Working Group as a Mechanism for Managing Bureaucratic Reorientation: Experience from the Philippines.* Working Paper No. 4, Washington, DC: NASPAA, 1982.

Korten, Frances F. *Building National Capacity to Develop Water User's Associations: Experience from the Philippines.* Washington, DC: World Bank Sociological Workshop, 1981.

Lacson, Zenaida C., and Francisca C. Bataclan. *Philippine Public Administration, 1969-1977.* Manilla: Univ. of the Philippines, College of Public Administration, 1980.

Leuterio, Mariano P. "Philippines." In *Farm Water Management for Rice Cultivation,* Asian Productivity Organization. Tokyo: 1977.

Machado, K.G. "From Traditional Faction to Machine: Changing Pattern of Political Leadership and Organization in the Rural Philippines." *Journal of Asian Studies* 33, no. 4 (1974): 523-548.

Manrique, G.G. *Multi National Corporations, Advertising and Industrial Organization in Economic Development: A Case Study of the Philippines.* Ann Arbor: University Microfilms International, 1982.

Mariano, S.M. *The Relationship of Decision Participation with Job Satisfaction and Organizational Commitment in the University of the Philippines at Los Banos Extension.* Ann Arbor: University Microfilms International, 1982.

Misajon, M.J. *Toward Improved Rural Development Management in the Philippines: A Management Education Program.* Ann Arbor: University Microfilms International, 1983.

Ng, R., and F. Lethem. *Monitoring Systems and Irrigation Management: An Experience from the Philippines.* Monitoring and Evaluation Case Studies Series, Washington, DC: The World Bank, 1983.

Panganiban, L.C. *Land Reform Administrative Procedures in the Philippines: A Critical Analysis,* Madison: Land Tenure Centre, University of Wisconsin, 1972.

Parco, Salvador A. "In-Service Training Needs of Barrio Development Workers in the Philippines." *Philippine Sociological Review* 14 (Apr 1966): 93-109.

Ramos, C.P. "The Use of Modern Management Techniques in the PUblic Administration of Developing Countries: The Philippine Experience." *Philippine Journal of Public Administration* 15, no. 1 (January, 1971).

Ray, J.J. "Achievement Motivation and Authoritarianism in Manila and Some Anglo-Saxon Cities." *Journal of Social Psychology* 115 (Oct. 81): 3-8.

Sibley, Willis E. "Social Organization, Economy and Directed Cultural Change in Two Philippine Barrios." *Human Organization* 28, no. 2 (1969): 148-154.

Sibley, Willis E. "Social Structures and Planned Change: A Case Study from the Philippines." *Human Organization* 19 (Winter 1960-61): 209-211.

Simpas, Santiago S., Ledvina Carino, and Arturo Pacho. Local Government and Rural Development in the Philippines. n.p. 1974

Siy, R.Y. Jr. Rural Organizations for Community Resource Management: Indigenous Irrigation System in the Northern Philippines. Ann Arbor: University Microfilms International, 1982.

Siy, R.Y. Jr., Rural Development and Community Resource Management: Lessons from the Zanjera. Honolulu: University of Hawaii Press for University of Philippines Press, 1983.

Takahashi, Akira. Land and Peasants in Central Luzon: Socio-economic Structure of a Philippine Village. Honolulu: East-West Center Press, 1970.

UNCRD. Philippines: An Annotated Bibliography on Regional Development. New York: UNCRD, 1979.

University of the Philippines, College of Public Administration Bicol Studies Project Staff. CPA Bicol Studies: Regional Planning, Local Governments, and Service Accessibility in the Bicol River Basin. Manila: College of Public Administration, University of the Philippines, 1978.

Villanueva, A.B. "Policy Articulation of Local Autonomy in Filipino Municipal Reform." Journal of Administration Overseas 18 (1979): 123-134.

Varela, Amelia P. "The NIA-UNDP Groundwater Development Project: A Case Study in Transnational Development Administration." Philippine Journal of Public Administration 16 (1972): 186-203.

SEYCHELLES

Maubouche, Robert, and Naimeh Hadjitarkhani. Seychelles: Economic Memorandum. Washington, DC: World Bank, 1980.

SINGAPORE

Deyo, Frederic C. "Local Foremen in Multinational Enterprise: A Comparative Case-study of Supervisory Role-tensions in Western and Chinese Factories in Singapore." Journal of Management Studies 15 (1978): 308-317.

Elliott, T.H. "Work Enrichment for Singapore?" Free Labour World 273 (1973): 11.

SOUTH EAST ASIA

Deboek, Guido, and Ronald Ng. Monitoring Rural Development in East Asia. Staff Working Paper 439. Washington, DC: World Bank, 1980.

International Rice Research Institute. Irrigation Policy and Management in S.E. Asia. Washington, DC: Int. Rice Research Institute, 1978.

Taylor, Donald C., and T. Wickham, eds. Irrigation Policy and the Management of Irrigation Systems in Southeast Asia. Bangkok: Agricultural Development Council, Inc., 1979.

SRI LANKA

Ariyaraine, A.T. "Sarvodaya Shramadana in Sri Lanka." Development Digest 14 (1976): 87-90.

Farmer, B.H., ed. Green Revolution?: Technology and Change in Rice Growing Areas of Tamil Nadu and Sri Lanka. Boulder: Westview Press, 1977.

Matthews, B. "District Development Councils in Sri Lanka." Asian Survey 22 (Nov 82): 1117-1134.

Rajendra, M. "The Rajangana Colonization Project-Sri Lanka." In Implementation: The Problem Achieving Results edited by Gabriel Iglesias. Manila: Eastern Regional Organization for Public Administration, 1976.

United Nations. Planning for the Poor: A Case Study of Malaweli Sri Lanka. UNCRD Working Paper Series #82-2. New York: UN, 1982.

UNCRD. Sri Lanka: An Annotated Bibliography on Regional Development. New York: UNCRD, 1981.

Weerekon, Bradman. "Role of Administrators in a Changing Agrarian Situation: The Sri Lanka Experience." Journal of Administration Overseas 16, no. 3 (1977): 148-161.

TAIWAN

Negandhi, Anani R. Management and Economic Development: The Case of Taiwan. The Hague: Martinus Nijhoff, 1973.

THAILAND

Calavan, Michael M. "Local Resource Management: Some Development Principles for Rural Thailand." Washington: Development Studies Program. USAID, n.d.

Deyo, F.C. "The Cultural Patterning of Organizational Development: A Comparative Case Study of Thai and Chinese Industrial Enterprise. *Human Organization* 37 (n.d.): 68-73.

Haas, David F. *Interaction in the Thai Bureaucracy: Structure, Culture, and Social Exchange.* Boulder: Westview Press, 1979.

Ingle, Marcus. *Local Governance and Rural Development in Thailand.* Ithaca: Cornell University, Center for International Studies, Rural Development Committee, Special Series on Rural Local Government, No. 16, 1974.

Jacobs, N. *Modernization Without Development: Thailand as an Asian Case Study.* New York: Praeger Publishers, 1971.

Juasiripukdee, Orapun. *A Case Study of the American Technical Assistance to the National Institute of Development Administration (NIDA) in Thailand.* Ann Arbor: University Microfilms International, 1983.

Kangsanan, K. *Politics and Public Organization in Thailand: A Case Study of Organizational Change in the National Institute of Public Administration (NIPA), Bangkok.* Ann Arbor: University Microfilms International, 1983.

Karnjanaprakorn, Choop. "The Role of Informal Organization in Community Development: Thai Experience." *Thai Journal of Public Administration* 6, no. 2 (1965).

Krannich, R.L. "Administrative Leadership of Mayors. The Politics of Mayor-Manager Relationships in Thailand." *Public Administration Review* 40, no. 4 (1980): 330-340.

Lim, E.R., John Shilling et. al. *Thailand: Toward A Development Strategy of Full Participation.* Washington, DC: World Bank, 1980.

Linn, Johannes. *Thailand: Managing Public Resources for Structural Adjustment.* Washington, DC: The World Bank, 1983.

Mickelwait, Donald R., Charles A. Murray, and Alan Roth. *Rural Development Strategies in Thailand: A Review of the Organization and Administration of Rural Development for AID.* IRD Project Field Report. Prepared for the USAID, Washington, DC: Development Alternatives, Inc., 1979.

Mosel, J. "Thai Administrative Behavior." In *Toward the Comparative Study of Public Administration*, edited by W. Siffin. Bloomington: Dept. of Government, Indiana Univ., 1957.

Murray, Charles A. *A Behavioral Study of Rural Modernization: Social and Economic Change in Thai Villages.* New York: Praeger Publishers, 1977.

Neher, C. *The Dynamics of Politics and Administration in Rural Thailand.* S.E. Asia Series No. 30. Athens: Ohio University Press, 1974.

Piker, Steven. "The Relationship of Belief Systems to Behavior in the Rural Thai Society." *Asian Survey* 8 (May 1968): 386-399.

Pramomsook, Suwit. "Thailand." In *Farm Water Management for Rice Cultivation*, Asian Productivity Organization, Tokyo: 1977.

Pratumnopharati, T. *An Assessment of the Administration of the Student Activity Program in Thailand.* Ann Arbor: Univ. Microfilms International, 1982.

Riggs, F.W. *Thailand: The Modernization of a Bureaucratic Polity.* Honolulu: East-West Center Press, 1966.

Rubin, Herbert J. "Modes of Bureaucratic Communication: Examples from Thai Local Administration." *Sociological Quarterly* 15 (1974): 212-230.

Rubin, Herbert J. "Will and Awe: Illustrations of Thai Villager Dependency upon Officials." *Journal of Asian Studies* 32 (1973): 425-444.

Rubin, Herbert J., and Irene S. Rubin. "Effects of Institutional Change Upon A Dependency Culture: The Commune Council 275 in Rural Thailand." *Asian Survey* 13 (1973): 270-287.

Scoville O.J., and J.J. Dalton. "Rural Development in Thailand: The ARD Program," *Journal of Developing Areas* 9 (1974): 53-68.

Siffin, William J. *The Thai Bureaucracy: Institutional Change and Development.* Honolulu: East-West Center Press, 1966.

Siffin, William J. *The Thai Institute of Public Administration: A Case Study in Institution Building,* Pittsburgh: Inter-University Program in Institution Building, Mar 1967.

VIETNAM

Fox, Guy H., and Charles A. Joiner. "Perceptions of the Vietnamese Public Administration System." *Administrative Science Quarterly* 8 (1964): 443-481.

Rondinelli, Dennis A. "Community Development and American Pacification in Vietnam." *Philippine Journal of Public Administration* 15, 2 (1971): 162-174.

LATIN AMERICAN AND THE CARIBBEAN

GENERAL

Bourgeois, L.G., and Manuel Boltvinik. "OD in Cross-cultural Settings: Latin America." *California Management Review* 22, no. 3 (1981): 75-81.

Brundenius, Claes, and Mats Lundahl eds. *Development Strategies and Basic Needs in Latin America*. Boulder: Westview Press, 1982.

Central American Institute of Public Administracion. *Casos de Administracion de Entidades Publicas Descentralizadas del Istmo Centroamericano*. Washington, D.C.: Interamerican Development Bank, 1979.

Cortes, Mariluz, and Peter Bocock. *North-South Technology Transfer: A Case Study of Petrochemicals in Latin America*. Baltimore: The John Hopkins Univ. Press (for the World Bank), 1984.

Departamento de Desarrollo Instituicional y Recursos Financieros. *Problemas y Estrategias de Implementacion de Proyectos en America Latina*. Washington, DC: Organization of American States, 1981.

Form, W.H., and A.A. Blum. *Industrial Relations and Social Change in Latin America*. Gainesville: University of Florida Press, 1965.

Formacion de Administradores para el Sector Publico en America Latina. Centro Latinoamericano de Administracion para el Desarrolo, Caracas: 1979.

Garcia-Zamour, Jean Claude G. *The Ecology of Development Administration in Jamaica, Trinidad, Tobago and Barbados*. Washington, DC: Organization of American States, 1977.

Kriesberg, Martin, ed. *Public Administration in Developing Countries*, Washington, DC: Brookings Institute, 1965.

Hammergren, Linn. *Development and the Politics of Administrative Reform: Lessons from Latin America*. Boulder: Westview Press, 1983.

Honey, John C. *Toward Strategies for Public Administration Development in Latin America*. Syracuse: Syracuse Univ. Press, 1968.

Lauterbach, A. *Enterprise in Latin American*. Ithaca: Cornell University Press, 1966.

Lumban, N. Paul, Efraim Turban, and Alvin Cohen. "Implementation of Management Science in Latin America; A Case Study and Generalization." *Management Science* 14, no. 12 (Aug. 1968): 695-704.

Nelson, Michael. *The Development of Tropical Lands: Policy Issues in Latin America*. Baltimore: The Johns Hopkins University Press for Resources for the Future, Inc., 1973.

Nelson, Michael. "Twenty-Four Settlement Projects in Latin America." *Development Digest* 15, no. 4 (1977): 91-103.

Orlove, Benjamin, and G. Custred, eds. *Land and Power in Latin America. Agrarian Economies and Social 76 Processes in the Andes*. New York: Hoes and Meier, 1980.

Potobsky, Geraldo von. "Participation by Workers' and Employers' Organizations in Planning in Latin America." *International Labour Review* 45, no. 6 (1967): 533-552.

Rubinger, Marcos M. "Social Participation as an Instrument for the Development and Formation of Society in Latin America." *International Labour Review* 47, no. 6 (1968): 551-570.

Sloan, J.W. "Bureaucracy and Public Policy in Latin America." *Inter America Economic Affairs* 34 (Spring 1981): 17-47.

Tendler, Judith. *Intercountry Evaluations of Small Farmer Organizations: Ecuador and Honduras. Final Report*. Washington, DC: U.S. Agency for International Development (1976).

Thurber, Clarence E., and Lawrence S. Graham eds. *Development Administration in Latin America: Comparative Administration Group Series*, Durham: Duke University Press for Comparative Administration Group of the American Society for Public Administration, 1973.

Valle, V.M. *A Study for Personnel Needs in Management Training for Personnel Working at the Managerial Levels Within Ministries of Education in Three Selected Latin American Countries: Columbia, Costa Rica and Panama.* Ann Arbor: University Microfilms International, 1983.

Woodworth, W., and R. Nelson. "Information in Latin American Organizations." *Management International Review* 20, no. 2 (1980): 61-69.

Wynia, Gary W. *Politics and Planners: Economic Development Policy in Central America.* Madison: Univ. of Wisconsin Press, 1972.

ARGENTINA

Frederick, Kenneth P. *Water Management and Agricultural Development: A Case Study of the Cuyo Region of Argentina.* Baltimore: The John Hopkins University Press, 1975.

BOLIVIA

Tendler, J. *"What To Think About Cooperatives: A Guide from Bolivia.* Washington: IAF, 1983

Widerkeher, Doris E. "Autonomy Overshadowed: A Bolivian Cooperative within the Nationalized Mining Industry." *Human Organization* 39, no. 2 (1980): 153-160.

BRAZIL

Cehelsky, Marta. *Land Reform in Brazil: The Management of Social Change.* Boulder: Westview Press, 1979.

Daland, Robert E., ed. *Brazilian Public Administration: Perspectives.* Rio de Janeiro: Brazilian School of Public Administration and USC School of Public Administration, 1963.

Frohlich, E.R. *The Role That Voluntary Farm Organiztions Exert As Communication Linkages Between Members, Government Agencies and Private Enterprises (A Brazilian Case Study).* Ann Arbor: University Microfilms International, 1983.

Knight, Peter T., Ricardo J. Moran, et. al. *Brazil: Human Resources Special Report.* Vol. 1 and 2, Washington, DC: The World Bank, 1979.

Mahar, Dennis J., et. al. *Brazil: Integrated Development of the Northwest Frontier.* Washington, DC: The World Bank, 1981.

Prasad, S.B. "Managers' Attitudes in Brazil: National vs. Expatriates." *Management International Review* 21, no. 2 (1981): 78-85.

Schmitz, Hubert. *Manufacturing in the Backyard. Case Studies on Accumulation and Employment in Small-Scale Brazilian Industry.* London: Frances Printer, 1982.

Siegel, Gilbert B. "The Strategy of Public Administration Reform: The Case of Brazil," *Public Administration Review* 26 (March 1966): 45-55.

Taylor, Donald A. *Institution Building in Business Administration: The Brazilian Experience,* East Lansing: Michigan State Univ., Graduate School of Business Administration, 1968.

CHILE

Chonchol, Jacques. "The Peasants and the Bureaucracy in Chilean Agrarian Reform." In *Popular Participation in Social Change*, edited by June Nash. The Hague: Mouton Publishers, 1976: 353-364.

Davis, Stanley M. "Politics and Organizational Underdevelopment in Chile." In *Comparative Management*, Stanley M. Davis, Englewood Cliffs: Prentice-Hall, 1971.

Davis, Stanley M. "The Politics of Organizational Underdevelopment: Chile." *Industrial and Labor Relations Review* (Oct. 1970): 23-83.

Estafan, Bernard D. *"The Comparative Management of Firms in Chile."* Indiana University: Foundation for the School of Business, Indiana University, 1972.

Petras, James F. "Chile: Nationalism, Socio-economic Change and Popular Participation." *Studies in Comparative International Development* 8, no. 1 (1973): 24-51.

COLOMBIA

Hunt, Richard M., and Nancy Truitt. "The Proder Project in Colombia: The Successes and Failures of a Pilot Popular Participation Project." *International Development Review* 13, no. 4 (1971): 14-19.

Ruhl, Mark J., and Everett Egginton. "The Influence of Agrarian Reform Participation on Peasant Attitudes: The Case of Colombia." *Inter-American Economic Affairs* 28 (1974): 27-43.

COSTA RICA

Barlett, Peggy F. "Agricultural Change in Paso: The Structure of Decision-Making in a Costa Rican Peasant Community." Unpublished Ph.D. Dissertation, Columbia University, 1975.

Seligson, Mitchell A. "The Impact of Agrarian Reform: A Study of Costa Rica." *Journal of Developing Areas* 13, no. 2 (1979): 161-174.

Seligson, Mitchell A. *Peasants of Costa Rica and the Development of Agrarian Capitalism.* Madison: University of Wisconsin Press, 1980.

CUBA

Barkin, David. "Popular Participation and the Dialectics of Cuban Development." *Latin American Perspectives* 2, no. 4 (1975): 42-59.

DOMINICAN REPUBLIC

Pazos, Felipe. "Development and the Under-utilization of Labour. Lessons from the Dominican Republic Employment Mission." *International Labour Review* 3, no. 2 (1975): 235-49.

Walker, Malcolm T., and J. Hanson. "The Voluntary Associations of Villalta: Failure with a Purpose." *Human Organization* 37, no. 1 (1978): 64-68.

ECUADOR

Nowicki, Alexander G., *Ecuador: Development Problems and Prospects.* Washington, DC: The World Bank, 1979.

EL SALVADOR

The World Bank. *El Salvador: Monitoring and Evaluation of Urban Development Projects - Analysis of the Level of Demand for Low-Cost Housing in Usulutan.* Washington, DC: The World Bank, 1978.

GUATEMALA

Departamento de Desarrollo Institucional y Recursos Financieros. *Diseno y Evaluacion del Funcionamiento de un Sistema de Siguimiento de Proyectos de Desarrollo.* Washington, DC: Organization of American States, 1981.

Hildebrand, John R. "Guatemalan Colonization Projects: Institution Building and Resource Allocation." *Inter-American Economic Affairs* 19 (Spring 1966): 41-51.

O'Sullivan-Ryan, Jeremiah. *Rural Development Programs Among Marginal Farmers in the Western Highlands of Guatemala.* Stanford University, California Institute of Communication Research, 1978.

GUYANA

Hope, Kempe R. *Development Policy in Guyana: Planning, Finance, and Adminstration.* Boulder: Westview Press, 1979.

HAITI

Maguire, Robert. "*Bottom-up Development in Haiti.*" 2nd edition. Washington: Inter-American Foundation, 1981.

HONDURAS

Smith, Richard L., et. al. "*Honduras Small Farmer Technologies: A Review of the Organization and Administration of Rural Development for USAID.*" IRD Project Field Report. Prepared for the United States Agency for International Development. Washington, DC: Development Alternatives, Inc., 1979.

Srinivasan, Chris. "Honduras: 'We Won't Be Here Forever'." Case Presentation of Save the Children Federation/Community Development Foundation. *Criteria for Evaluation of Development Projects Involving Women.* Prepared by the Subcommittee on Women in Development of the Committee on Development Assistance, ACVAFS, Technical Assistance Information Clearing House, 1975.

JAMAICA

Fever, Carl Henry. *Jamaica and the Sugar Worker Cooperatives.* Boulder: Westview Press, 1984.

Goldsmith, Arthur A., and Harvey S. Blustain. *Local Organization and Participation in Integrated Rural Development in Jamaica.* Ithaca: Cornell University, Rural Development Committee, Center for International Studies, 1980.

Hamilton, B.L. St. John. *Problems of Administration in an Emergent Nation.* New York: Praeger Publishers, 1964.

Haye, Winston I.S. *A Model for a Leadership Development Component of Vocational Agriculture Programs in Jamaica.* Unpublished Ph.D. Dissertation, Iowa State Univ., 1976.

Mills, G.E. "Administration of Public Enterprise - Jamaica and Trinidad - Tobago." *Social and Economic Studies* 30 (Mar. 1981): 45-74.

Stone, Carl. "Class, Community and Leadership on a Jamaican Sugar Plantation." Economic Development and Cultural Change 24, no. 4 (1976): 787-798.

United States Department of Agriculture. Development Project Management Center. Action-Training in Project Planning and Management. Washington, DC: Government Printing Office, 1980.

MEXICO

Benito, C.A. "'Peasants' Response to Modernization Projects in Minifundio Economies" American Journal of Agricultural Economics 58, no. 2 (1976): 143-151.

Boseman, F.G. "Management Policy, Structure and Effectiveness of Firms Operating in Mexico." Management International Review. 19, no. 4 (1979): 61-67.

Boseman, F.G. "Management Policy Toward Task Environment Agents: A Longitudinal Study in Mexico." Management International Review 22, no. 3 (1982): 74-78.

Boseman, F.G., and Arvind Phatak. "Management Practices of Industrial Enterprises in Mexico: A Comparative Study." Management International Review 18, no. 1 (1978): 43-48.

Carlos, Manuel L. Politics and Development in Rural Mexico: A Study of Socio-Economic Modernization. New York: Praeger Publishers 1974.

Cernea, Michael M. Measuring Project Impact: Monitoring and Evaluation in the PIDER Rural Development Project - Mexico. Staff Working Paper no. 332, Washington, DC: World Bank, 1979.

Grindle, Merilee S. Bureaucrats, Politicians and Peasants in Mexico. Berkeley: University of California Press, 1977.

Grindle, Merilee. "Power, Expertise and the Mexican Case Study." Journal of Politics 30 (1977): 399-426.

McCann, Eugene. "Anglo American and Mexican Management Philosophies." MSU Business Topics (Summer 1970: 28-37.

Neubauer, Robert J. "Job-evaluation--The Mexican Encounter.: Personnel 55, no. 5 (1978): 52-56.

Poitras, Guy E. "Welfare Bureaucracy and Clientele Policies in Mexico." Administrative Science Quarterly 18 (1973): 18-26.

Scott, Michael F. "Self-Help in Rural Mexico: Santa Maria's Well." Community Development Journal 12, no. 2 (1977): 116-121.

Simon, Barbara D. R. Power, Privilege and Prestige in a Mexican Town: The Impact of Industry on Social Stratification. Unpublished Ph.D. Dissertation, University of Minnesota, 1974.

Toth, Csanad. "A Comment on the PIDER Project." International Development Review 13, no. 4 (1971): 18-20.

PANAMA

de Souza, Luis A. Gomez de, and Lucia Ribeiro. Youth Participation in the Development Process: A Case Study in Panama. Paris: UNESCO Press, Experiments and Innovations in Education No. 18, 1976.

PARAGUAY

Gutierrez, Alfredo, et. al. Paraguay: Regional Development in Eastern Paraguay. Washington, DC: The World Bank, 1978.

PERU

Collier, David. Squatters and Oligarchs: Authoritarian Rule and Policy Change in Peru. Baltimore: Johns Hopkins Press, 1976.

Conlin, Sean. "Participation Versus Expertise." International Journal of Comparative Sociology 15 (1974): 15-166.

Hopkins, Jack W. "Comparative Observations on Peruvian Bureaucracy." Journal of Comparative Administration 1 (1960): 301-20.

Keatinge, R.W. "Economic Development and Cultural Resource Management in the Third World; An Example from Peru." Journal of Anthropological Research. 38 (Summer 1982): 211-26.

Long, Norman, and David Winder. "From Peasant Community to Production Co-operatives: An Analysis of Recent Government Policy in Peru." Journal of Development Studies 12 no. 1 (1976): 75-96.

Mangin, William. "Thoughts on Twenty-Four Years of Work in Peru: the Vicos Project and Me." In Long-Term Field Research in Social Anthropology edited by George Foster. New York: Academic Press, 1979.

Stephens, D.B. "Cultural Variation in Leadership Style: A Methodological Experiment in Comparing Managers in the U.S. and Peruvian Textile Industries." Management International Review 21, no. 3 (1981): 47-55.

Weeks, John. Limits to Capitalist Development. The Industrialization of Peru, 1950-1980. Boulder: Westview Press, 1984.

Whyte, William Foote. "Imitation or Innovation: Reflections on the Institutional Development of Peru." Administrative Science Quarterly 13 (1968): 370-385.

PUERTO RICO

Negron, Mario Luis. Public Administration in Puerto Rico: From Model to Crisis. Ann Arbor: University Microfilms International, 1983.

SURINAM

Kalsham, Geert. "Agricultural Extension in Surinam: Communication and the Role of Extension Workers at the Periphery of their Agency" Agricultural Administration 5, no. 3 (1978).

VENEZUELA

Friedman, John. Regional Development Policy: A Case Study of Venezuela, Cambridge: The M.I.T. Press, 1966.

Friedman, John. Venezuela: From Doctrine to Dialogue. New York: Syracuse, 1965.

Getter, D.F. "Introducing a HRD Programme in an Industrializing Society: A Venezuelan Case." Journal of European Training 5, no. 3 (1975): 140-149.

Thiesenhusen, W.C. "A Venezuelan Agrarian Reform Settlement: Problems and Prospects." In Tradition and Dynamics in Small-farm Agriculture. edited by R.D. Stevens. Ames: Economic Studies in Asia, Africa, and Latin America, Iowa State University Press, 1977.

SECTION V

OTHER BIBLIOGRAPHIES AND SOURCEBOOKS

This volume provides only a core for the searching of the rich literature resource available to the professional. There remains a host of publications that touch on related subjects, including the management of specific technical systems such as irrigation, rangeland or integrated rural development. The listing which follows is intended to provide a basis for further enquiry. It should also be emphasized that many citations in this bibliography contain valuable bibliographies, many of which are quite extensive.

Beyond other bibliographies, several helpful sourcebooks are included. These include listings of agencies, institutions, consultants and other information sources for those engaged as professionals in the development of management infrastructures.

African Training and Research Centre. Preliminary Bibliography on Human Resources in Public Administration. Administration for Development. Tangier: CAFRAD, 1972.

Ali, Shaukat, and Garth N. Jones. Planning Development Change. An Annotated Bibliography on Development Administration. Lahore, India: University of Punjab, 1966.

Aminuzzaman, Salahuddin M., and F.R.M. Mortuza Huq. Local Government and Administration in Bangladesh. A Selected Bibliography. Dacca: Center for Administrative Studies, 1981.

Bibliographies in the Public Administration Series: A List of Bibliographies in Print. Monticello: Vance Bibliographies, n.d.

Blair, Patricia, ed. Development in the People's Republic of China: A Selected Bibliography. New York: Overseas Development Council, 1976.

Brode, J. An Annotated Bibliography of the Process of Modernization: Socio-Cultural Aspects of Development. Cambridge: Harvard Univ. Press, 1967.

Caiden, Gerald. American Public Administration, A Bibliogrpahical Guide to the Literature. New York: Garland Pub., 1983.

Carr, Marilyn. (compiled by) Economically Appropriate Technologies for Developing Countries. An Annotated Bibliography. Hudson: Intermediate Technology Development Group of N.A., 1981.

Cohen, John, Gladys Culagovski, Norman Uphoff and Diane Wolf. Participation at the Local Level: A Working Bibliography. Ithaca: Cornell Univ., 1978.

Coldritz, J.M. Educational Planning: A Bibliography with Special Emphasis on Developing Countries. Research Unit for Education System Planning, Univ. of the Orange Free State, 1981.

Commonwealth Secretariat. Training in Public Administration: A Directory of Commonwealth Resources. London: Commonwealth Secretariat, 1978.

Crane, D. "Technological Innovation in Developing Countries: A Review of the Literature." Research Policy 6 (Oct 1977): 374-395.

Departamento de Asuntos Economicos. Bibliografia Selectiva de Administracion Publica en America Latina. Washington, D.C.: Organization of American States, 1968.

De Vries, E. "A Review of Literature on Development Theory, 1957-67." International Development Review 10 (March 1968): 43-51.

Economic Development Institute. Readings for Training Trainers. Washington, D.C.: Economic Development Institute, 1980.

Franklin, Jerome L. Organization Development, An Annotated Bibliography. Ann Arbor: Institute for Social Research, Univ. of Michigan, 1973.

Gellar, Sheldon. Development By and For the People: A Select Annotated Bibliographical Guide to Participatory Development Issues. Paris: Club de Sahel/CILSS, 1982.

Ghosh, Pradip K., ed. Economic Policy and Planning in Third World Development. Westport: Greenwood Press, 1984.

Goehlert, Robert. Policy Studies in Development, A Selected Bibliography. Monticello: Vance Bibliographies, Public Administration Series, 1983.

Gable, Richard W. Development Administration and Assistance--An Annotated Bibliography. Washington, D.C.: Agency for International Development, 1963.

Hart, Donn V. Thailand: An Annotated Bibliography of Bibliographies. De Kalb: Northern Illinois University--rev. JSAS 11 (1977): 227-228.

Hafkin, Nancy J. Women and Development in Africa: An Annotated Bibliography. Addis Ababa: Economic Commission for Africa, 1977.

Hailu, Alem Seged. Rural Development in African Countries: A Selected Bibliography with Special References to Jmali and Kenya. Vance Bibliographies.

Holdcroft, Lane E. The Rise and Fall of Community Development in Developing Countries, 1950-65: A Critical Analysis and an Annotated Bibliography MSO Rural Development Papers, East Lansing: Michigan State Univ., 1977.

Institute of Social Studies. Women in Development: A Bibliography. The Hague: Institute of Social Studies, 1978.

International Committee on the Management of Population Programs. Inventory of Experts and Institutes in Population Programme Management. Kuala Lumpur: ICOMP, 1983.

ILO. Bibliography on Major Aspects of the Humanisation of Work and the Quality of Working Life. Geneva: ILO, 1978.

Joint Bank-Fund Library. The Developing Areas. A Classed Bibliography of the Joint Bank-Fund Library. Boston: G.K. Hall and Co., 1976.

Jones, G.N., S. Ali, R. Barber, and J.F. Chambers. Planning, Development, and Change. A Bibliography on Development Administration. Honolulu: East-West Center Press, 1970.

Joseph, R.M., Jr. Budgeting in Third World Countries: An Annotated Bibliography. Monticello: Vance Bibliographies, Public Admin. Series.

Kocher, James E. and B. Fleischer. A Bibliography on Rural DEvelopment in Tanzania. East Lansing: Dept. of Agricultural Economics, Michigan State Univ., 1979.

Kubr, Milan and Ken Vernon, eds. Management Administration and Productivity. 2nd edition, Geneva: ILO, 1981. An International Directory of Institutes and Information sources.

Kurian, George Thomas. Encylopedia of the Third World. New York: Facts on File, Inc., 1982.

Lambert, Claire M., ed. compiled by Mick Moore; John Connell and Claire M. Lambert. Village Studies Data Analysis and Bibliography (Vol. 2). London: Mansell/IDS, 1978.

Lindfors, G.V. Bibliography: Cases and Other Materials for the Teaching of Business Administration in Developing Countries--South and Southeast Asia. Boston: Graduate School of Business Administration Harvard University, 1968.

Murrell, Kenneth L., and Peter B. Vaill. O.D. Sources and Application. Madison: ASTD, 1975. 1979 updated.

McHenry, Dean E. Ujamaa Villages in Tanzania, A Bibliography. Uppsala: Scandinavian Institute of African Studies, 1981.

Miller, W.E., and R.M. Miller. The Third World: Natural Resources, Economics, Politics and Social Conditions. Vance Bibliographies, 1981.

Norbaard, Ole. Social Science Literature on Developing Countries: An Annotated Guide to Information Sources. Copenhagen: Centre for Development Research.

Niehoff, Arthur H., and Charnel J. Anderson. A Selected Bibliography of Cross-cultural Change Projects. Alexandria, VA: Department of Defense, Human Resources Research Center, 1965.

Peterson, Richard B. Bibliography on Comparative Management. Occassional Paper 21, Office of Faculty Publications, Seattle: Grad. School of Bus. Admin., University of Washington, 1969.

Obern, A. Gaylord, and Richard I. Nunez. Annotated Bibliography on Staff Training and Development in the Public Sector and on Public Finance Management, Accounting and Audit. New York: Unipub, 1983.

Pate, L.E., K.W. Rowland and P.D. Hall. Developing Organisations: A Bibliography and Review. West Yorkshire, England: MCB Publications, n.d.

Powelson, John P. A Select Bibliography on Economic Development: With Annotations. Boulder: Westview Press, 1979.

Rihani, May. Development As If Women Mattered: An Annotated Bibliography. Washington, D.C.: Overseas Development Council, 1978.

Roberts, K.H. International Research Related to Organizational Behavior: An Annotated Bibliography. Stanford: Graduate School of Business, Stanford University, 1972.

Rondinelli, Dennis, and Aspy Palia. Project Planning and Implementation in Developing Countries: A Bibliography on Development Project Management. Honolulu: East-West Center, 1976.

Santora, Joseph C. Organizational Change; A Selected Bibliography of Articles. Monticello: Vance Bibliographies, Public Administration Series, n.d.

Saulniers, Suzanne S., and C. Rakowski. Women in the Development Process: A Select Bibliography on Women in Sub-Saharan Africa and Latin America. Austin: Institute of Latin American Studies, Univ. of Texas, 1977.

Shields, Elisabeth. Social Development Management: An Annotated Bibliography. Washington, DC: NASPAA, 1982.

Siddiqi, A.H. The Muslim World: A Selected Bibliography on Its Socio-Economic Development. Monticello: Vance Bibliographies, Public Admin. Series, 1982.

Siddiqi, A. H. Planning Policies, Strategies and Peformance in the Agricultural Sector of Developing Countries: A Selected Annotated Bibliography. Monticello: Vance Bibliographies, Public Admin. Series, 1982.

Slattery, Alice. *Agricultural and Rural Development in Kenya, A Selected Annotated Bibliography, 1960-81*. Kenya: USAID, 1982.

Spitz, Allan R. *Developmental Change: An Annotated Bibliography*. Lexington: University Press of Kentucky, 1969.

Third World Development, Vol. 1-3. New York: Business Press International, 1985.

United Nations Secretariat. *Monitoring and Evaluation Systems for Assessing Developmental Impact at the Local Level: An Annotated Bibliography*. Washington, DC: United Nations Secretariat, 1976.

United Nations. *Development Perspectives for the 1980's, A Selected Bibliography*. New York: U.N., Asian and Pacific Development, 1981.

UNCRD. *India: An Annotated Bibliography on Regional Development*. New York: UN, 1976.

UNCRD. *Pakistan: An Annotated Bibliography on Local and Regional Development*. New York: UN, 1981.

UNCRD. *Philippines: An Annotated Bibliography on Regional Development*. New York: UN, 1979.

UNCRD. *Sri Lanka: An Annotated Bibliography on Regional Development*. New York: UN, 1981.

USAID. *Administration of Agricultural Development. A Selected List of References for A.I.D. Technicians*. A.I.D. Bibliography Series, Development Administration, Washington, D.C.: USAID, 1971.

Verbic, Nada, ed. *Bibliography on Economic Cooperation Among Developing Countries, 1981-1982: With Annotations*. Boulder: Westview Press, 1984.

Viet, J. *International Co-operation and Programs of Economic and Social Development*. Paris: UNESCO, 1961.

West, H.W., and O. Sawyer. *Land Administration: A Bibliography for Developing Countries*. Cambridge: Dept. of Land Economy, University of Cambridge, nd.

Whitson, Tom, Peter Sanker and Petrine MacDonald. *An Annotated Bibliography on the Relationship Between Technological Change and Educational Development*. Paris: UNESCO, 1980.

APPENDIX I

CONTRIBUTING ORGANIZATIONS

The editors wish to specifically thank the following organizations who contributed to this volume. Each represents a valuable resource for more information concerning their respective countries and areas of expertise.

ADB Quarterly Review
Asian Development Bank
Information Office
P. O. Box 789 Manila, PHILIPPINES

African Administrative Studies
African Training & Research Center
in Administration for Development
Box 310
Tangier, MOROCCO

African Business
International Communications Ltd.
Box 261, Carlton House
69 Ct Queen St.
LONDON, WC2B, 5BZ

Asian Productivity Organization
4-14 Akasaka, 8-chome
Minato-Ku Tokyo 107
JAPAN

Barbados Institute of Management
   and Productivity
Wiley, St. Michael
BARBADOS

Center for Research in Business
   Economics
Department of Organization
   and Management
Erasmus University
ROTTERDAM

IFTDO. Who's Who in International HRD.
Madison: International Federation of
Training and Development Organization, 1984.

Institute of Development Management
P. O. Box 1357
Gaborone
BOTSWANA

Institute of Development
   Studies
University of Sussex
Brighton, SUSSEX BNI9RG

Inter American Development
   Bank

International Committee on
   the Management of
   Population Programs
RS141, Jalan Dahlia
Taman Uda Jaya
PO Am pang
Selangor
MALAYSIA

International Consultants
   Foundation
International Consultants
   Registry
Washington: ICF, 1985

International Development
   Research Center
P. O. Box 8500
Ottawa K1G 349
CANADA

International Institute
   for Organizational and
   Social Development, S.V.
Predikherenberg 55
B - 3200 Leuven (Kessel - LO)
BELGIUM

Journal of Management,
   Business & Economics
University of Dacca
Institute of Business
   Administration
Dacca, 2, BANGLEDESH

Journal of Public Administration
SAIPA
P. O. Box 2752
Pretoria, SOUTH AFRICA

Malaysia Management Review
Malaysian Institute of Management
Fitzpatrick Bldg., 15th Fl. 86
Jalan Raja Chalan
Kuala Lumpur 05-10, MALAYSIA

Management Association of Pakistan
24 - 3rd Floor
Auriga Complex
Gulberg 11
Lahore, PAKISTAN

Management Dan Usahawan Indonesia
University of Indonesia
Institute of Management Studies
Universitas Indonesia, Lembaga Mgt.
Jalan Salema 4
Box 404
Jakarta, INDONESIA

Management Development and Productivity
    Institute
P. O. Box 297
Accra, GHANA

NASPAA
National Association of Schools of
    Public Affairs and Administration
1120 G Street, NW
Suite 520
Washington, DC 20005

OP Search
Operational Research Society of India
75 J.S. SansanwalMarg
New Dehli, INDIA 110016

Organization for Economic Cooperation
    and Development
2 rue Andre- Pascal
5775 Paris Cedex 16, FRANCE

Prashasan
The Nepalese Journal of Public Administration
HMG Ministry of General Administration
Hari har Bhavan
Pulchowk Lalitpur, NEPAL

Rural Development Committee
Center for International
    Studies
170 Uris Hall
Cornell University
Ithaca, NY 14853

Singapore Management Review
S. I. of Management
Thong Teck Bldg.
3rd Fl.
Scotts Road
Singapore 0922, SINGAPORE

Studies in Development
Middle East Technical
    University
Faculty of Administrative
    Sciences
Ismet Inonu Bulvari
Ankara, TURKEY

Tanzania Management Journal
Institute of Development
    Management
Box 5
Mzumbe, Morogoro, TANZANIA

Thailand Management Develop-
    ment and Productivity
    Center
Rana 6 Road
Bangkok, 10400 THAILAND

U.S. Department of
    Agriculture
Office of International
    Cooperation and
    Development
International Training
    Division
Room 4112, Auditors Bldg.
Washington, DC 20250

Vikalpa
Indian Institute of
    Management
Ahmedabad, Vastrapur
Ahmedabad 380015, INDIA

The World Bank
181 H St., N.W.
Washington, DC 20433